Perma/Culture

T0304040

In the face of what seems like a concerted effort to destroy the only planet that can sustain us, critique is an important tool. It is in this vein that most scholars have approached environmental crisis. While there are numerous texts that chronicle contemporary issues in environmental ills, there are relatively few that explore the possibilities and practices which work to avoid collapse and build alternatives.

The keyword of this book's full title, 'Perma/Culture,' alludes to and plays on 'permaculture,' an international movement that can provide a framework for navigating the multiple 'other worlds' within a broader environmental ethic. This edited collection brings together essays from an international team of scholars, activists and artists in order to provide a critical introduction to the ethico-political and cultural elements around the concept of 'Perma/Culture.' These multi-disciplinary essays include a varied landscape of sites and practices, from readings from ecotopian literature to an analysis of the intersection of agricultre and art; from an account of the rewards and difficulties of building community in Transition Towns to a description of the ad hoc infrastructure of a fracking protest camp.

Offering a number of constructive models in response to current global environmental challenges, this book makes a significant contribution to current eco-literature and will be of great interest to students and researchers in Environmental Humanities, Environmental Studies, Sociology and Communication Studies.

Molly Wallace is Associate Professor of English at Queen's University, Canada. She writes about and teaches contemporary literature and ecocultural studies.

David Carruthers is a PhD candidate in English at Queen's University, Canada. His recent work appears in *Mosaic: Journal for the Interdisciplinary Study of Literature*.

The *Routledge Environmental Humanities* series is an original and inspiring venture recognising that today's world agricultural and water crises, ocean pollution and resource depletion, global warming from greenhouse gases, urban sprawl, overpopulation, food insecurity and environmental justice are all *crises of culture*.

The reality of understanding and finding adaptive solutions to our present and future environmental challenges has shifted the epicenter of environmental studies away from an exclusively scientific and technological framework to one that depends on the human-focused disciplines and ideas of the humanities and allied social sciences.

We thus welcome book proposals from all humanities and social sciences disciplines for an inclusive and interdisciplinary series. We favour manuscripts aimed at an international readership and written in a lively and accessible style. The readership comprises scholars and students from the humanities and social sciences and thoughtful readers concerned about the human dimensions of environmental change.

Perma/Culture

Imagining Alternatives in an Age of Crisis

**Edited by Molly Wallace
and David Carruthers**

Routledge
Taylor & Francis Group

LONDON AND NEW YORK

from Routledge

First published 2018 by Routledge

2 Park Square, Milton Park, Abingdon, Oxfordshire OX14 4RN
52 Vanderbilt Avenue, New York, NY 10017

Routledge is an imprint of the Taylor & Francis Group, an informa business

First issued in paperback 2018

British Library Cataloguing-in-Publication Data
A catalogue record for this book is available from the British Library

Library of Congress Cataloging-in-Publication Data
Names: Wallace, Molly, editor. | Carruthers, David V., editor. Title: Perma/
culture : imagining alternatives in an age of crisis / edited by Molly Wallace
and David Carruthers. Other titles: Permaculture Description: Abingdon, Oxon ;
New York, NY : Routledge, 2017. | Series: Routledge environmental humanities |
Includes bibliographical references. Identifiers: LCCN 2017006137 |
ISBN 9781138284845 (hbk) | ISBN 9781138400429 (ebk) Subjects: LCSH:
Permaculture. | Sustainable agriculture--Social aspects. Classification: LCC S494.5.P47
P46 2017 | DDC 631.5/8--dc23LC record available at
https://lccn.loc.gov/2017006137

ISBN: 978-1-138-28484-5 (hbk)
ISBN: 978-0-367-15244-4 (pbk)

Typeset in Bembo
by Fish Books Ltd.

Contents

Contributors

David Carruthers is a PhD candidate in English at Queen's University. His recent work appears in *Mosaic: Journal for the Interdisciplinary Study of Literature*.

Leda Cooks is Professor of Communication at University of Massachusetts, Amherst. In honor of her surname, Cooks is an occasional 'made from scratch' caterer and private chef. She teaches courses on the intersections of food, identity, power, and culture, and has authored numerous chapters and articles on food, identity, and other subjects. Much of her current research and activism focuses on the con/disjunctures between food waste and recovery movements, power and social group identities. She holds campus and community dinners and dialogues on the topics of food waste, social justice and sustainability to help build collaborative efforts toward sustainable communities. In 2012, she co-founded (with E. Polk and L. Herakova) and still sustains the Pioneer Valley Community Breadhouse, a space where community members create, bake and break bread together while telling stories about food and life. She is co-editor (with Jennifer Simpson) of the anthology *Dis/placing Race: Whiteness, Pedagogy, and Performance* (Lexington 2007). Another book, *Food Makes a Family* (with L. Herakova) is currently under contract with Peter Lang.

Dominique Ferraton is a multidisciplinary artist from Montreal with a practice in sound art, photography and drawing. Her work explores personal relationships with place and space, with a particular focus on the few wild spaces created or found in urban areas. She has exhibited in Montreal, Toronto, and Ottawa and created audio work for CKUT, CBC Radio and NAISA. She is a member of the Wild City Mapping art collective.

Nina Gartrell is a writer, reader, permaculturalist, seed-saver and gardener. She is also currently a Doctor of Creative Arts (Creative Writing) candidate at the University of the Sunshine Coast (Australia), where she is affiliated with the Sustainability Research Centre. Her thesis, "Seeds: cultivating permaculture travel memoir through applied permaculture design," marries her lifelong passions for permaculture, travel and writing. Her 'permatravel' memoir, *Seeds* (currently under development), is an autobiographical tale about a journey that led Nina overland from England to Australia via a series of unique, beautiful and abundant home-scale farms and gardens in countries as diverse as Morocco, Italy, Bulgaria, Georgia and Indonesia. Her narrative explores themes of gardening, home, belonging, (im)permanence and ecological sustainability. Read more about Nina's perma-travels on her blog, www.permaculturetraveller.com.

Tiffany Higgins is a poet, writer, and translator. She is the author of *The Apparition at Fort Bragg* (2016), an e-chapbook, and winner of the *Iron Horse Literary Review* e-single contest for a long poem, selected by Camille Dungy. Available free online, the place-based poem set in Northern California explores our interwoven relationships with trees, economy, and creatures. Her book *And Aeneas Stares into Her Helmet* (Carolina Wren Press 2009) was selected by Evie Shockley as winner of the Carolina Wren Poetry Prize. A chapbook of translations from Portuguese of Rio poet Alice Sant'Anna's poetry, *Tail of the Whale*, was published by Toad Press in 2016. Her poems appear in *Broadsided Press*, *The California Journal of Poetics*, *Catamaran Literary Reader*, *From the Fishouse*, *Kenyon Review*, *Massachusetts Review*, *Poetry*, *Prelude*, *Taos Journal of Poetry & Art*, and are forthcoming in *Ghost Fishing*, an anthology of ecojustice poems (University of Georgia). In addition to ecocriticism on Brazilian poetry, she is currently writing on threats to indigenous and traditional communities in Brazil's Amazon. To read more, please visit www.tifhiggins.blogspot.com

Natalie Joelle is writing a transdisciplinary study of gleaning as an agricultural and thinking practice at Birkbeck, University of London, funded by the Arts and Humanities Research Council. She has published on Georges Seurat's drawing 'The Gleaner' and *The Book of Ruth*; her forthcoming book chapters include considerations of gleaning in the works of Peter Larkin and Jim Crace.

Patrick Jones is a writer, researcher, permaculturalist, artist, community food gardener, forager and diverse-economies activist. He is part of the performance collective *Artist as Family*. In 2014 Jones was awarded a doctorate for his thesis *Walking for food: reclaiming permapoesis*. In 2015 he co-authored with Meg Ulman *The Art of Free Travel* (NewSouth), which was shortlisted for an ABIA award in 2016.

Ruth Lapp is a farmer and current PhD student in the Cultural Studies Program at Queen's University. Her doctoral research is on re-indigenizing soil communities as a means to build food sovereignty.

Robert Lovelace is a faculty member in Global Development Studies at Queen's University and a retired Chief of the Ardoch Algonquin First Nation. His writing and activism have tackled problems of human rights and environmental (in)justice, and his work has persistently queried what constitutes the 'commons.' He was very active in struggles over uranium mining in Sharbot Lake, Ontario in 2007, and has since been involved in the organizations On the Commons and the Freedom Flotilla Coalition. His "Notes from Prison: Protecting Algonquin Lands from Uranium Mining" appears in *Speaking for Ourselves: Environmental Justice in Canada* (UBC 2010).

Claire Males is an undergraduate student in History at Cambridge University. The inspiration and material for her piece comes from having spent three months as a protestor at Balcombe.

Andrea Most is Professor of American Literature at the University of Toronto. She is currently at work on *A Pain in the Neck,* an exploration of how climate change, species extinction and the discovery of the human microbiome are transforming the way we think and write about our lives. Professor Most also serves as Creative Director of Bela Farm, a centre for land-based art, scholarship, and activism in Southern Ontario. Before turning to environmental studies, she specialized in American popular culture and Jewish studies. Her first book, *Making Americans: Jews and the Broadway Musical* (Harvard 2004), won the MLA/Kurt Weill Prize for the best book in Music Theater. Her second book, *Theatrical Liberalism: Jews and Popular Entertainment in America* (NYU 2013), was a finalist for a National Jewish Book Award.

Leah Penniman is an educator, farmer, and food justice activist from Soul Fire Farm in Grafton, NY. She is committed to dismantling the oppressive structures that misguide our food system, reconnecting marginalized communities to land, and upholding our responsibility to steward the land the nourishes us. As a core member of the Freedom Food Alliance, Leah cultivates life-giving food for incarcerated people and their loved ones and for families living in food apartheid neighborhoods. She also runs an on-farm restorative justice program that is an alternative-to-incarceration for area teens, and a training program for aspiring Black and Latino activist-farmers. Her work as a farmer and educator has been recognized nationally by the Fulbright Distinguished Awards in Teaching Program, Presidential Award for Science Teaching, *YES! Magazine,* the Teaching Channel, Food First, New Technology Network, College Board, National Science Teachers Association, Edutopia, Center for Whole Communities, and Rethinking Schools.

Emily Polk is a Lecturer in the Program in Writing and Rhetoric and the Writing Specialist for the School of Earth Energy and Environmental Sciences at Stanford University. Prior to getting her doctorate, Dr. Polk worked for nearly ten years around the world as a media professional, helping to produce radio documentaries in Burmese refugee camps, and facilitating a human rights-based newspaper in a Liberian refugee camp. She has also worked as an editor at *Whole Earth Magazine* and at CSRwire, a leading global source of corporate social responsibility news. Her own writing and radio documentaries have appeared in *National Geographic Traveler*, the *Boston Globe*, NPR, and elsewhere. Her first book, based on her research in a transition town, is *Communicating Global to Local Resiliency: A Case Study of the Transition Movement* (Lexington 2015).

George Price listens, learns, contemplates, studies, and teaches at the University of Montana as well as on the permaculture farm on the Flathead Indian Reservation, where he lives with his wife, Barbara, their son, Noah, and grandson, Wakiyan. He is an American of several diverse ethnic and cultural ancestries (including Assonet Wampanoag, Massachusett, Choctaw, African, French, and Scottish) who has explored human identity issues all his life, both personally and professionally, but in the last ten years has prioritized his interests towards environmental activism. Publications include *Past and Present: an Introduction to Native American Studies* (Plymouth, Michigan, Hayden-McNeil 2015) and *To Heal the Scourge of Prejudice: the Life and Writings of Hosea Easton*, edited with James Brewer Stewart (University of Massachusetts Press 1999). His activism was recently featured in a piece in *YES! Magazine*.

Camille Roulière is a PhD candidate at the J. M. Coetzee Centre for Creative Practice (University of Adelaide, Australia) and ERIBIA (University of Caen Basse-Normandie, France). Her research maps and investigates the links between place and art, and particularly music, in Lower Murray Country (South Australia).

Molly Wallace is Associate Professor of English at Queen's University. She writes about and teaches contemporary literature and ecocultural studies. Her recent book is *Risk Criticism: Precautionary Reading in an Age of Environmental Uncertainty* (University of Michigan Press 2016).

Andrew Weigert is Professor of Sociology at the University of Notre Dame. He has authored numerous articles and the last two of nine books are *Self, Interaction, and Natural Environment* (SUNY 1997) and *Religious and Secular Views on Endtime* (Mellen 2005).

Amanda White is a PhD candidate in the Cultural Studies program at Queen's University and a visual artist based in Toronto, Canada. Her current work examines cultural imaginings of nature through interdisciplinary research and art practice.

Stephen Zavetoski is Professor of Sociology at the University of San Francisco. He teaches courses in the area of Environmental Sociology. Dr. Zavetoski's research areas include environmental sociology, social movements, sociology of health and illness, and urban sustainability. He has published more than 40 articles and book chapters and co-edited *Social Movements in Health* (Blackwell 2005) and *Contested Illnesses: Citizens, Science, and Health Social Movements* (UC Press 2012). Dr. Zavetoski's current work explores strategies to address both sustainability and public health through urban and transportation planning. This work has culmin - ated in *Incomplete Streets: Processes, Practices and Possibilities* (Routledge 2014), co-edited with Julian Agyeman. Dr. Zavetoski is co-editor of Routledge's book series, 'Equity, Justice, and the Sustainable City.'

Acknowledgements

This research was supported in part by the Social Sciences and Humanities Research Council of Canada.

Poem

The Seeds of Aleppo

Tiffany Higgins

The bazaar has burned,
The gathering of seeds dispersed

Sent to Morocco and Mexico;
with escort, to Turkey.

Seeds who escape,
Seeds who flee.

And far in the Svalbard archipelago,
Blue light over glacier,

Swirls of snow. Abrupt
triangle, armed guard

into vault.
Vault of seeds.

For asteroid impact,
nuclear glow.

Now, though, first
withdrawal of deposit:

Syria's seeds petition
to return to desert

peas and beans,
packets of light.

Each sample temporary,
a memory to grow.

Each seed repeats,
Of course, if we could return,

Then of course,
We would go.

Introduction

Perma/Culture

Molly Wallace and David Carruthers

> The very ability to conceptualise of something better than what is here—whether it's a political system, a social relationship, the way our food is grown or our cities built—requires us to develop a critical analysis of the present. If this critique is not grounded in a certain optimism, a shred of belief that this imagined better world can exist in some form in this world now, it risks turning into another theoretical model, abstract and cynical or another excuse to wait for the perfect moment—the revolution, the collapse, the last judgement—a sure recipe for hopelessness.
>
> Isabelle Fremeaux (Laboratory of the Insurrectionary Imagination)

> Or maybe we could give up saving the world and start to live savingly in it.
>
> Wendell Berry

Big problems: scale in the anthropocene

Climate change, species extinction, toxic contamination, ocean acidification, habitat loss, pervasive plastics, genetically modified organisms, nuclear meltdowns, tailings ponds visible from space, fracking's temblors and flammable tap water, mountaintop removal, urban smog, suburban and exurban sprawl, e-waste: a litany of ever-proliferating environmental horrors is unfortunately simple to produce. We are surrounded by such events daily, not just in the news, but in our lives. Though environmental destruction is hardly uniform, even the most protected of "backyards" is presently under threat. And even if we do not see crises, we are continuously aware of our complicity in them. The catastrophe of the Albertan tar sands, to take a Canadian example, may not be literally in our backyards here in southern Ontario, but insofar as we drive, fly, run our oil or gas furnaces, use plastic containers, we participate in the devastation of these and other extractive practices, even as we, in our turn, produce carbon emissions and turn plastic products into waste (even if we delay that process by one or two cycles of plastics recycling). In such times, it is fairly easy to despair, to resort to chronicling the planet's demise or our melancholy in the face of it. After all, much as we might acknowledge our participation in the systems that we decry, it is often difficult to imagine doing anything differently—and often feels in any case futile. Divergences in scale—the individual on the one hand and the "climate" on the other—are the primary challenges of what scholars are increasingly calling "the Anthropocene," this epoch in which humankind has taken on the role of a geologic force, producing the "environment" that subsequently confronts us as though from the outside. As Timothy Clark usefully puts it, the Anthropocene is a Leviathan, "paradoxically, a total effect of innumerable human decisions," and yet seemingly "as imperturbably closed to human direction as is a hurricane or the tilt of the planet's orbit" (2015, 16). Even if we individual, earnest environmentalists, don the hair shirt of self-restraint, the scales at which destruction occurs so vastly outreach us, as the world rolls on, whether we walk or drive, huddle under sweaters and blankets or simply (a simplicity that hides, of course, its complexity) turn up the heat.

In the face of what seems like a concerted suicidal—or ecocidal—effort to destroy the only planet that can sustain us, critique is an important tool. And it is in this vein that most scholars in our fields—in our case, literary and cultural studies specifically, and environmental humanities more generally—have approached environmental crisis. In an age of peak oil, food crisis, and a changing and unpredictable climate, cultural critics have drawn on the strategies of critique amply available in the broader cultural studies toolkit. To the oil economy, to the legacies of nuclear, coal, and gas industries, to industrial agriculture, cultural critics have quite rightly said "no," providing richly layered historical diagnoses variously indicting the Enlightenment, capitalism, imperialism, or anthropocentrism. From Rob Nixon's exposé on "slow violence" (Nixon 2011) to Frederick Buell's analysis of apocalypse as "way of life" (Buell 2004); from Stephanie LeMenager's discussion of petro-cultures and "living oil" (2014), to Stacy Alaimo's critique of the treatment of those suffering from multiple chemical sensitivities (2010), to Ursula Heise's new work on extinction (2016), ecocritics and environmental humanists have provided a chronicle of our times, pointing to the extremes of crisis in order to explicate and thereby expose and criticize a dominant cultural (il)logic. Such critique is vital to understanding and addressing global injustice. After all, as Rob Nixon reminds us, "We may all be in the Anthropocene but we are not all in it in the same way" (2014)—some, in other words, are more ecocidal than others; some more vulnerable to ecocidal effects. As scholars interested in environmental justice and injustice, we should most certainly say "no" to Shell and ExxonMobil and Chevron and Suncor. And global grassroots protest movements are absolutely vital to transforming the infrastructural landscape. Demonstrations like that taking place at Standing Rock—to halt the Dakota Access pipeline—are a crucial way to communicate "no" to global petro-culture.

As useful and necessary as this form of critique has been, however, it can remain somewhat vulnerable to the paucity of imagination that characterizes the world more generally. To what, a beleaguered ecocritic might ask, can we say "yes"? Now more than ever, it seems to be easier, as Fredric Jameson (1994) opined some years ago, "to imagine the deterioration of the earth and of nature than the breakdown of late capitalism," a phenomenon partly due to our residual postmodern fear of utopian metanarratives (xii). We thus follow cultural critic and activist Naomi Klein, who argues, in *This Changes Everything*:

> There may have been a time when engaging in resistance against a life-threatening system and building alternatives to that system could be

meaningfully separated, but today we have to do both simultaneously: build and support inspiring alternatives …—and make sure they have a fighting chance of thriving by trying to change an economic model so treacherous that nowhere is safe.

(2014, 405)

We need, in other words, to say "yes" as well as "no," a lesson that we, critics in the environmental humanities, might take to heart, for while we are exceptionally well-trained in critique, we tend to be less skilled in building.

In building these "inspiring alternatives," though, we do not, fortunately, have to begin from scratch. Though there may be no single utopian model for an entirely new world, there are, as many of the contributors in this volume demonstrate, micro-utopian practices among us. Not content to wait for some future revolution, some total transition, our contributors work to seed alternatives in what activist/artist Isabelle Fremeaux has called the "cracks" in the capitalist system (2012, 246). *Perma/Culture: Imagining Alternatives in an Age of Crisis* collects original essays by an international group of scholars (in English, Cultural Studies, Sociology, and Communication), activists, and artists, all of which turn critical and creative attention to extant or emergent alternatives that exist alongside crisis. The essays offer a varied landscape of sites and practices, from rereadings of ecotopian novels to African American back-to-the-land movements; from an account of the rewards and difficulties of building community in Transition Towns to a description of the ad hoc infrastructure of a fracking protest camp; from a scholar's analysis of freegan living to an artist's account of her community-based mapping of Montreal's urban wilds. And our project is unique in bringing together a range of voices, from seasoned scholars to undergraduates, from artists to activists, all of whom offer diverse imaginings of alternatives, rooted in the practices with which they are most familiar, whether that is literary criticism, sociology, artistic endeavor, or agricultural or horticultural practice in the field.

"Small, slow solutions": permaculture

The title of Claire Males's essay in this volume recalls the slogan of the World Social Forum in response to the Thatcherite mantra, "There is no alternative": "Another world is possible!"[1] But while there is often a consensus on the problems of the present, there is seldom consensus on the "other world" that might replace it. How, then, to bridge from this world to that, and how to honor the diversity of views on what "another world" might look like, are open questions. The two directions that seem to be offered by the Anthropocene are to go "forward"—generally cast as an optimistic large-scale techno-fix—or "backward"—a direction seemingly populated by technophobic Luddites and neo-primitives. As Paul Kingsnorth (2012) reminds us, these are in many ways mirror opposites of each other: "'Romanticizing the past' is a familiar accusation, made mostly by people who think it is more grown-up to romanticize the future" (2012). Insofar as activists, academic and otherwise, offer only critique, we do not begin to imagine alternatives to these directions. One might be tempted to follow the Zapatistas who suggested that the "other world" that is possible would be one in which "many worlds fit," but clearly there would need to be some common ecological vision that governed all such worlds, or one would risk destroying the planet for the rest.

Our title's keyword, "Perma/Culture," alludes to and plays on "permaculture," an international movement that we believe provides a framework for navigating the multiple "other worlds" within a broader environmental ethic. Permaculture began (in the back-to-the-land 1970s) simply by offering a protocol for designing agricultural systems that mimic natural ecosystems, but has evolved to reference something much more broadly ethicopolitical and cultural. Introduced in Bill Mollison and David Holmgren's inaugural text, *Permaculture One: A Perennial Agriculture for Human Settlements* (1978), permaculture is a portmanteau word that combines "permanent" and "agriculture" to advocate for a system of food pro-duction in the face of what the authors then perceived to be an unsustainable industrial food system. Taking insights from Indigenous and traditional land practices as well as the sciences of ecology and physics (thermodynamics), Mollison and Holmgren advocated for an agriculture in tune with nature, using practices that follow what the land could itself support (rather than imposing human desires upon it), resulting in an agricultural aesthetic that eschews the geometrical rows and squares of industrial monoculture in favor of diverse spirals and companion planting. Permaculture advocates patience, beginning with careful observation of the land itself (its seasons, vegetation, topography, water courses), and long-term planning, as in the planting of perennial nut forests that might not produce for a number of years, and it is predicated on the conservation of energy at all scales, from the use of renewables like solar or wind to the consideration of the energy stores of the individual permaculturalist on his or her walks to and from different sectors of the farmstead.

The permaculture of *Permaculture One* is in many ways a product of its time (evinced, for example, in references to the "back to the land" movement that was then extant), but the concept itself has gone on to flourish, as, in the intervening years, permaculture has become a truly global movement, inspiring home gardeners and farmers, intentional communities and design courses, and artists and activists, and coming to reflect more broadly on all aspects of culture, and referring as much to an ethics of life and the living as to principles of conscientious and efficient design. Such wide appeal is doubtless due to the affirmative and even utopian nature of permaculture's ethic. In a context in which there is so much environmental bad news, permaculture offers a vision of alternatives—describing not just what *not* to do (burn fossil fuels, apply pesticides or genetic engineering) but also what *to* do—and as such contributes something otherwise rare in contemporary environmental discourse. As Holmgren explains in his more recent *Permaculture: Principles and Pathways Beyond Sustainability* (2002), permaculture offers a model for a "graceful and ethical descent" from what critics have taken to calling the "peak everything" crises of the present.

Permaculture most certainly posits an impending apocalypse. The end (of the energy glut) is nigh, and permaculture practitioners urge us to prepare. But permaculturalists are not waiting for the apocalypse to implement their designs; rather, permaculture practitioners are starting to live as though that future were already here. It may well be that our problem, in the end, is not a shortage of oil, but a surplus—available to anyone willing to render the planet uninhabitable for planetary life. Whether the climate change apocalypse beats out the peak oil apocalypse, though, permaculture imagines a salutary alternative. And in the face of pervasive despair in the Anthropocene, there is a joy in permaculture that is worth celebrating—not the kind of perverse joy that some people seem to take in apocalypse and destruction, but the joy of doing something affirmative, something progressive, of taking matters into our own hands and producing a different future, one that will not only weather the low energy conditions to come, but thrive in them. As Anthony Weston has argued, most schemes for mitigating environmental crisis end up in a kind of depressingly neutral place: "All of that ingenuity and expense to make *less difference*? Not to mention, once again, that we cannot make (so to say) less difference enough" (2012, xi). His alternatives echo those of permaculture: "Why not joyfully reforest the planet, not only more than offsetting carbon emissions but also rebuilding habitat for other creatures and for alternative human cultures?" (2012, 19). Such joyful reforesting echoes the food forests of permaculture, a mode of generating abundance for human and nonhuman creatures alike.

We, in the Anthropocene, are used to contemplating human beings, including perhaps ourselves, as means, not just to *an* end, but to *the* end, the kind of apocalyptic combination of guilt, shame, and despair to which many of us have become almost complacently inured. But we are less accustomed to thinking of ourselves as means to some more fruitful material ends. In this context, we believe, as Mark Hathaway has argued, that permaculture can provide a constructive response to the question: "How can humans assume an appropriate share of the responsibility for the well-being of the Earth community while avoiding the kind of managerial ethos and obsession with control and 'progress' that often characterize the worldviews of the modern technocratic societies that have caused so much ecological destruction?" (2015, 446–7). Permaculture is necessarily concerned with the needs of human beings. Mollison and Holmgren lead off their *Permaculture One* (1978) with this definition: "Permaculture is a word we have coined for an integrated, evolving system of perennial or self-perpetuating plant and animal species useful to man" (1). The permaculture practitioner takes inspiration from extant ecosystems, now selecting and designing such that the system is more productive of food and other useful materials. But even if permaculture might seem to offer its design and ethical principles as means to human ends, the position of the human in permaculture requires, not only that the designer take the "ends" of other species into consideration (in order to be successful in thinking through the interactions of the components in the system), but that the human also be calculated as a part of the system, both manager and participant in the processes—perhaps an apt model for the new Eaarth with two "a"s that Bill McKibben has suggested we now inhabit. Permaculture can thus be seen as a variant of geoengineering, now reconceived as small scale, site-specific, and slow solutions that use those older "technologies" like reforestation, polycultures, composting, and soil building. In this project, culture workers like ourselves can contribute both by representing the micro-utopian models that might shift our thinking and by participating in the kind of hybrid, interdisciplinary practices that might bridge intellectual, activist, and practical divides.

In some ways, permaculture itself "thinks big," for its principles and ethics are meant to apply globally and at all scales. Permaculture is governed by twelve basic principles that are to guide the permaculturalist's design, from "observe and interact," to "catch and store energy," to "produce no waste," to "integrate rather than segregate," to "use edges and value the marginal," and "creatively use and respond to change" (Holmgren 2002). But though there is something of a metanarrative in the principles and ethics, its application is local; permaculture's mandate is to "use small and slow solutions." Indeed, even if permaculture appears to be universalist, the principle to "apply self-regulation and accept feedback" ensures that its approach is dynamic and responsive to local conditions. Holmgren describes it as top-down thinking with bottom-up doing—a slightly different gloss on "think globally act locally." And he at several points situates permaculture squarely in the "postmodern" era, "where all meaning is relative and contingent" (2002, xv). Permaculture draws omnivorously on modern ecological science and traditional ecological knowledges, articulating both into its larger frame. These borrowings are clearly salutary in principle, but they have also, in practice, produced problems for permaculture's reputation in academic and activist circles: permaculture's focus on balance has not kept pace with more recent ecological work on dynamism and resilience, and permaculture's embrace of Indigenous thought can border at times on cooptation— or even, to borrow a term from Robyn Francis, "permacolonialism," especially when it is taught back to local communities (quoted in Birnbaum 2014, 10). Nonetheless, important work on sharpening both forms of collaboration in knowledge production is ongoing, whether in articulating permaculture with agroecology (Ferguson and Lovell 2013) or in the work of the Woodbine Ecology Center, which puts Indigenous traditions at the heart of its mission.

Permaculture is thus interesting for environmental humanists, both as a historical and cultural phenomenon, and as a potential store of tropes and practices, but though permaculture has received some academic attention, it is almost unknown in humanities departments, despite its focus on "culture." In some ways this is not surprising, since permaculture is perhaps more compatible with landscape architecture or planning than it is with history, literary or cultural studies, or philosophy. One recent exception is the work of anthropologists Joshua Lockyear and James Veteto, who, in a co-authored article (2008) and subsequent co-edited book (2013), explore both permaculture sites themselves as cultural phenomena and the possibilities of reading permaculture's ethics and principles alongside agroforestry, ethnoecology, and political ecology. *Perma/Culture* takes these approaches a step further into cultural practices that may not, at first glance, meet the criteria of true permaculture sites— not the "ecovillages," say, that Lockyear and Veteto describe, but the reading of literature, the discussion of global travel, the mapping of Montreal's green spaces, the teaching of a university course. And though not all of our contributors would identify their work with permaculture per se, all essays attend at least implicitly to a three-part set of ethics that has come to be associated with permaculture, often shorthanded as "earth care, people care, fair share."

Gathering these diverse essays under the umbrella of "permaculture" necessarily means changing what permaculture signifies. Our title thus cracks the term into two—Perma/Culture—in order to invoke and mark a distance from those practices.

Permaculture in the field has become a worldwide movement of practitioners, courses, and centers, all interested in the design principles for permanent sustainability for human cultures on the planet. Our book draws from the spirit of these practices to posit something like a "permacultural studies," at once interested in permaculture as a set of cultural beliefs and practices, and also invested in gleaning what we can from permaculture for thinking about work in the environmental humanities. This is a way of moving from critique and toward affirmation, as we highlight the micro-ecotopian possibilities that are extant. And unlike most academic work in our field, the essays we have collected here do not remain at the level of ideas. As Holmgren suggests in *Permaculture: Principles and Pathways Beyond Sustainability*, "unless we get out there, and open our eyes and use our hands and our hearts, all the ideas in the world will not save us" (2011, 24). Our authors, too, model "getting out there," getting hands dirty, as it were, in community projects, interactive arts, and farming and gardening practices.

Perma/Culture: the essays

Our hope in gathering the essays in this volume is that we have begun the observational work of paying attention to the other worlds that are nascent in our present, those that posit abundance rather than lack, community rather than isolation, and ecophilia rather than ecophobia. In the face of big problems, when individuals can feel isolated and ineffectual, we believe that highlighting the actually existing other worlds, growing like tenacious weeds in the cracks of an unsustainable system, is a crucial first step, a micro-utopian start for an ecotopian world in which many worlds fit. As Bill Mollison suggested, "against such universal insanity the only response is to gather together a few friends and commence to build the alternative" (*Permaculture Two* 137). The essays that follow are in many ways diverse—drawn from different disciplines, life experiences, and global locations—and they are framed by two poems—Tiffany Higgins's offering personified seeds, Natalie Joelle's an interventionist gleaning. In a context in which environmental crisis requires thinking across disciplinary divides—and, we believe, across academic, artistic, and "real world" divides—we see *Perma/Culture*'s diversity as a part of its strength. Among permaculture's principles are "use and value diversity" and "use edges and value the marginal" and, of course, "obtain a yield" (Holmgren 2002); our hope here is that drawing on various voices in different contexts, we have created a kind of intellectual and political polyculture that might provide a rich and diverse harvest.

Part I, "Pattern languages," invokes a term borrowed from architect and design theorist Christopher Alexander that is often also echoed by permaculture practitioners. Noting that the "character of what you build will be given to it by the language of patterns you use to generate it," Alexander's *A Pattern Language* (1977) offers a series of patterns as solutions to common problems in design (xxxvii). While Alexander was using "language" metaphorically to describe an architectural vernacular, we are re-literalizing the term in order to describe the practices of our authors, each of whom begins, arguably, with the permacultural imperative to "observe and interact" with extant social and cultural systems in order to discern other languages that might be heard subtly within, against, or alongside the dominant voices, intervening in hegemonic pattern languages to produce new patterns.

Chapters 1 and 2 are rooted in the practices of our own field of literary studies, and each offers a model for discovering new patterns in old literary texts. Andrea Most's chapter is literally grounded in her work at Bela Farm, a center for land-based Judaism, where, for the past four years she has been collaborating with a small design group to research, design and create a hub for scholarly research, multi-faith community education and outreach, and a vibrant farm business. Her focus in the chapter is a new kind of literary subjectivity, which is inspired by George Eliot's *Middlemarch* and characterized by the kind of close observation demanded by permaculture farming practices. Similarly drawing on a literary text, Zavetoski and Weigert's chapter takes inspiration from Ernest Callenbach's 1975 novel, *Ecotopia*, in order to measure its usefulness in contemplating how twenty-first century moderns will transition to a just and sustainable alternative future. Is it possible, they ask, that small-scale practices of voluntary simplicity, commoning, or localization can catalyze a transformation? Here, the authors read Callenbach's promising but flawed utopian text alongside the work of Novella Carpenter, whose micro-utopian practices demonstrate the potential for ad hoc implementation of some of the broader initiatives Callenbach represented. Though they are cognizant of the ways in which food and green gentrification may unintentionally reproduce current social and economic injustices, the authors see promise in more radical experiments in urban agriculture and bicycling for transportation as reinvigorated cultural practices intended to bring forth desired futures.

The final three chapters in this section turn to the languages of management, mismanagement, neglect, and renewal. Chapter 3 offers the provocations of permaculturalist artist/author Patrick Jones, who describes his own struggle to act and communicate with compassion as both a participant of a small community in regional southeast Australia and as a monetized subject of the traumatized global village. Drawing on the discourses of nonviolent communication and permaculture, Jones advocates language performances that might generate acts of reciprocity, care, gifts, and returns. Also situated in the Australian context, Camille Roulière turns to water management conflict in the Murray-Darling Basin. Focusing on two Aboriginal cultural productions, the National Cultural Flows Research Project and *Ringbalin*, Roulière notes the ways in which these cultural texts intervene in the binary core of present water management practices by offering radically different imaginings of water and promoting an eco-sentient understanding of the river. In so doing, these texts answer an ethical call, petitioning not only for the long-overdue recognition of Indigenous water rights in Australia, but also for respectful, yet profitable, use of the waterways. Roulière's chapter argues that the production and reception of these Aboriginal cultural practices could represent a promising model for a shift away from hegemonic Eurocentric practices and the hesitant development of genuinely collaborative water management policies.

Following Roulière's analysis of the mapping of flows, Dominique Ferraton's chapter turns to maps that flow. Sustainable cities include accessible and integrated green spaces. While managed and manicured parks provide some of these, undeveloped lots where vegetation is left to grow spontaneously are increasingly seen as having value. Ferraton explores their cultural, social, and ecological roles through *Wild City Mapping*, a collaborative, community-based project which maps the personal significance of Montreal's wild green spaces. On this ever-evolving, online map, Ferraton and collaborators tag each wild green space with photos and descriptions submitted to the project. These submissions document activism, urban flora, guerrilla gardening, and site-specific art projects, but a greater number of them are simply intimate experiences that citizens have in the green spaces they love. Centered on a selection of these images and written reflections, this chapter considers the ways in which wild green spaces can change our perception of a city even as they create new modes of engagement with it.

Part II, "Transitions in practice," moves, as in one of Holmgren's twelve permaculture principles, from "patterns to details," tracking specific instances of putting new pattern languages into practice. Tackling the fraught question of eco-travel in discursive and material registers, Nina Gartrell's chapter asks: What are we to make of the emergence of "permatravel" as a contemporary travel practice? Does it represent a viable alternative to socially and ecologically unsustainable modalities of travel? Gartrell puts her own experiments with applying permaculture's principles to travel in conversation with an emergent discourse on "permatravel" that she has identified, and the chapter concludes by offering a set of alternative metrics "permatravellers" might use to evaluate their journeys other than measuring and offsetting carbon emissions. Similarly turning attention to her own practices "in the field," Emily Polk addresses the Transition Town movement, which seeks to develop and support community-based projects for greater resiliency, including alternative local economies, sustainable food production and consumption, and more efficient transportation. Reflecting on her own position as a researcher who participated in— and wrote an academic book about—a Transition community, Polk assesses the pitfalls of burnout, explores the potential solutions that have emerged from research focused on longer-lasting Transition initiatives, and reflects upon the ways in which the lessons learned in those academic and activist pursuits continue to inform her practices as a teacher.

Inspired by the idea that "another world is possible," the subsequent two chapters in this section offer glimpses of other actually existing micro-utopian practices. Claire Males's essay turns to the anti-fracking protests in Balcombe, England in 2013, exploring the extent to which the protest camp created an off-grid, ecologically conscious community, which offered, in miniature, a model for a more sustainable future. Though the camp was, by its nature, temporary, Males discusses its potential for activist longevity by tracking the subsequent practices of those whose worldviews were substantially influenced by the camp experience. The subsequent chapter, by permaculturalist and academic George Price, tackles what he calls "the problem of money" by exploring the possibilities in permaculture and organic gardening, "really really free markets," and "time banks."

The final section is titled "Revolution Disguised as Gardening," which is a phrase sometimes used to describe permaculture itself. Here, each of our contributors discusses some aspect of food production. David Carruthers's essay frames the section by examining the inherent relationship, both causal and rhetorical, between industrial agriculture after the Second World War and global militarism today, working to critique popular *invasion-ecology* approaches to the environment (which can echo those militaristic discourses) in favour of the holistic, agroecological practices at the small and local scales promoted by permacultural thinking on methods of sustenance farming and social organization.

Grounded in an analysis of a history of oppression in the United States, Leah Penniman's chapter notes that some of the country's most cherished sustainable farming practices—from organic agriculture to the farm cooperative and the Community Supported Agriculture (CSA)—have roots in African wisdom. Yet, African American farmland ownership has declined to less than one percent, and black communities suffer disproportionately from illnesses related to lack of access to fresh food. Her chapter asks: What is the story of land loss and food injustice? What work is being done to reclaim ancestral rights to belong to the land and have agency in the food system? How are people using food and land as tools to end mass incarceration and institutional racism? In answer to these questions, Penniman highlights examples of returning-generation black farmers, as she describes her own food sovereignty work at Soul Fire Farm, New York, offering examples of those who have revived and reclaimed cooperative economics, regenerative agriculture, and Earth-centered healing in their effort to create a just and sustainable food system.

Also describing work that is literally "in the field," Ruth Lapp and Robert Lovelace's chapter develops an understanding of re-indigenizing agricultural communities through a fusion of analysis and practice. Organized as a back-and-forth conversation between student and instructor, the chapter describes the experiences that both underwent in the course of a project of ecological remediation that took place on Robert Lovelace's property. Describing the outcome of three different test plots, Lapp and Lovelace discuss the complexities of soil: as substance, community, facilitator, and evolutionary matrix. Soil has a life completely independent of humanity yet it is the sustainer of all human life, and it can be read as a barometer of a history of complex relationships that range from Indigenous to colonial. Lapp and Lovelace argue that understanding how this coding can be translated into emerging and extant Indigenous cultural systems will be essential for marginalized and displaced populations.

Addressing the staging of food production and consumption, Amanda White's chapter turns to the ways in which food practices have been taken up by artists. White notes that the current social turn in contemporary art practices has sought to create spaces for participation and collaboration outside of art discourses, and has often involved sharing food or meals to initiate such social engagements. For many artists, eating and making and sharing food also become practices through which to address and discuss more political issues in agriculture such as food security, agro-biodiversity, sustainability and cultural knowledge. White's chapter discusses several examples of such projects by artists and collectives, from the *Fallen Fruit Project*, to Ron Benner's *Corn Roasts*, to Jon Rubin and Dawn Weleski's *Conflict Kitchen* and EcoArtTech's *Edible Ecologies*, noting that each of these projects embodies a utopian imaginary by using the symbolic power of art to make social interventions, exploring alternative ways of living and engaging with each other, the community, and the environment through food practices.

Leda Cooks's piece provides apt closure for the volume by focusing on food waste and reclamation. Freegans, a morphing of the words "free" and "vegan," believe in building sustainable communities while living outside of capitalism. In the past five years as popular interest and press in freeganism has waned, attention to food waste has grown to the point of almost daily news stories of excess. As Cooks notes, we are told we eat too much, waste too much, but remarkably don't consume too much. This chapter provides a brief overview of the freegan movement, its variations, manifestations, and contradictions, and then it discusses the food recovery efforts that have more recently gained press and popular attention. Perhaps because of its more radical message, Cooks argues, freeganism and its provocations have been obscured if not subverted by the Food Loss movement in the U.S. and UK.

The project concludes with a found poem by Natalie Joelle titled "The Gleaner Difference," the material for which was "found" in advertising copy for large-scale agricultural machinery. The afterword, by Molly Wallace, provides a reading of the poem as a jumping-off point for addressing the potential to glean something affirmative from the contemporary environmental context. Reflecting back on the volume itself, the afterword gleans from the essays, and from a reading of Agnès Varda's documentary film on gleaning, a set of questions for a "permacultural studies," critical and material practices that might, together, offer protocols for further politically, ethically, and ecologically engaged work. Gleaning here appears in its material and metaphorical registers, both the practices of gleaning (in food reclamation movements in the field), and the ways in which gleaning has been mobilized as a critical and artistic practice.

Obtaining a yield and sharing the surplus

The yield that we hope readers glean from this book is of course primarily intellectual and ethicopolitical. We have collected these essays in part as a preliminary step in a larger project of moving toward a more affirmative response to environmental crisis. We believe that this shift in orientation might help to make the environmental humanities—like the environmental movements that have inspired many of us—more "sustainable," both by imagining actual practices of sustainability and by offering the kind of hope necessary for us to go on, even in the face of the Leviathan of the Anthropocene. In this work, we are heartened by the contributions of those in our local community who work on a daily basis to bring the ethics of "earth care, people care, and fair share" to life around us. In the spirit of sharing any financial surplus generated from this book, then, we have arranged for all royalties to go to Loving Spoonful, a food justice organization in Kingston, Ontario, whose projects of food reclamation and distribution, cooking education, and community and public school gardening are a constant source of inspiration.

Note

1   That slogan was formulated at the 2001 meeting in Porto Alegre, Brazil. The website for the World Social Forum updates it: "Another world is needed. Together, it is possible!" See https://fsm2016.org/en/sinformer/a-propos-du-forum-social-mondial.

References

Alaimo, Stacy. 2010. *Bodily Natures: Science, Environment, and the Material Self.* Bloomington: Indiana University Press.

Alexander, Christopher et al. 1977. *A Pattern Language.* New York: Oxford University Press.

Berry, Wendell. "On Being Asked for a Narrative for the Future: Revolution Starts Small and Close to Home." *YES! Magazine* (Spring 2015) 45–7.

Birnbaum, Juliana and Louis Fox. 2014. *Sustainable (R)evolution: Permaculture in Ecovillages, Urban Farms, and Communities Worldwide.* Berkeley: North Atlantic Books.

Buell, Frederick. 2004. *From Apocalypse to Way of Life.* New York: Routledge.

Clark, Timothy. 2015. *Ecocriticism on the Edge: The Anthropocene as a Threshold Concept.* Bloomsbury.

Ferguson, Rafter Sass and Sarah Taylor Lovell. "Permaculture for Agroecology: Design, Movement, Practice, and Worldview. A review." *Agronomy for Sustainable Development.* 34.2 (April 2014) 251–274.

Fremeaux, Isabelle (for Laboratory of the Insurrectionary Imagination). 2012. "Geographies of Hope." Amber Hickey (ed.) *Guidebook of Alternative Nows.* E-book: 241–256.

Hathaway, Mark. 2015. "The Practical Wisdom of Permaculture: An Anthropoharmonic Phronesis for Moving toward an Ecological Epoch." *Environmental Ethics* 37: 445–463.

Heise, Ursula. 2016. *Imagining Extinction: The Cultural Meanings of Endangered Species.* Chicago: University of Chicago Press.

Holmgren, David. 2011. *Permaculture: Principles and Pathways Beyond Sustainability.* Hepburn, Victoria: Holmgren Design Services (originally 2002).

Jameson, Fredric. 1994. *Seeds of Time.* New York: Columbia University Press.

Kingsnorth, Paul. 2012. "Dark Ecology." *Orion.* Available online at: https://orionmagazine.org/article/dark-ecology (last accessed 4 May 2017).

Klein, Naomi. 2014. *This Changes Everything: Capitalism Versus the Climate.* Toronto: Knopf Canada.

LeMenager, Stephanie. 2014. *Living Oil: Petroleum Culture in the American Century.* Oxford: Oxford University Press.

McKibben, Bill. 2010. *Earth: Making a Life on a Tough New Planet.* New York: Henry Holt and Company.

Mollison, Bill. 2010. *Permaculture Two: Practical Design for Town and Country in Permanent Agriculture.* Sisters Creek TAS: Tagari Publications, (originally 1979).

Mollison, Bill and David Holmgren. 1990. *Permaculture One: A Perennial Agriculture for Human Settlements.* Sisters Creek TAS: Tagari Publications (originally published 1978).

Nixon, Rob. 2011. *Slow Violence and the Environmentalism of the Poor.* Cambridge: Harvard University Press.

Nixon, Rob. "The Anthropocene: The Promise and Pitfalls of an Epochal Idea." *Edge Effects* (6 November 2014). Available online at: http://edgeeffects.net/anthropocene-promise-and-pitfalls (last accessed 4 May 2017).

Veteto, James and Joshua Lockyer. 2008. "Environmental Anthropology Engaging Permaculture: Moving Theory and Practice Toward Sustainability." *Culture and Agriculture* 30.1&2: 47–58.

Veteto, James and Joshua Lockyer (eds). 2013. *Environmental Anthropology Engaging Ecotopia: Bioregionalism, Permaculture, and Ecovillages.* New York: Berghahn.

Weston, Anthony. 2012. *Mobilizing the Green Imagination: An Exuberant Manifesto.* Gabriola Island: New Society Publishers.

Part I
Pattern languages

1 A pain in the neck and permacultural subjectivity

Andrea Most

A few years ago, I emerged from routine abdominal surgery with a mysterious neck injury, and when traditional medical approaches failed to heal it, I set out to explore alternative options, soon finding myself confronting jarring questions about the integrity of my body. Simultaneously, my growing interest in food, agriculture and environmental activism had led me to join an all-women design team working to create Bela Farm, a centre for land-based art, scholarship, activism and spiritual practice in southern Ontario. As part of that project, I spent many months studying the history, language and process of permaculture.[1] The confluence of these two experiences served as the impetus for my current work-in-progress, a set of narrative non-fiction essays entitled A Pain in the Neck, *which is about what happens to life-writing when individual human bodies – shaped by a long-standing cultural mythology that separates mind, body and earth – are suddenly reconnected to the body of the world.*

In the introduction, I describe how, for decades, well-intentioned feminists have been trying to solve the seemingly intractable problem faced by a generation of women exhausted by the competing demands of home and work. At the same time, in another sphere, equally thoughtful writers and activists have been attempting, with limited success, to create and implement urgently needed solutions to our environmental crises. The first part of A Pain in the Neck *shows how the core problems in these two apparently distinct spheres can be understood as a part of the same narrative roadblock. Whether depleting our bodies or draining our aquifers, we are following the plotline of a story that tells us that we are invulnerable to and in control of nature, but avoids the unspeakable reality that we are nature.[2]*

After defining the narrative problem, I set out on a circuitous quest (one which I am still pursuing) to unearth possible solutions, gradually recognizing the key importance of the permacultural design principles I'd been practicing on the farm to the development of both a new literary method and a new relationship between land, mind, and body. Much of the second part of the book centers on how to express this new subjectivity in writing. What kind of voice, what literary forms might emerge to articulate this permacultural subjectivity? What narrative structures, characters, voices and life experiences might comprise a genre that can express the experiences of our biological bodies as effectively as those of our minds? And more specifically, what relationship might this voice and form have with the history of life-writing about the body (especially the modern tradition of women's writing) and how might this kind of writing open up new avenues for understanding the self as nature, and hence a more productive understanding of the human body in a post-human culture? The book itself aims to be both an explanation and an example of permacultural subjectivity and literary form.

In the manuscript, I refer to a number of the permaculture principles outlined by David Holmgren in his book, Permaculture: Principles and Pathways Beyond Sustainability *(2002). I discuss Principle #2, "Catch and Store Energy," for example, in terms of feminist arguments about so-called work/life balance while Principle #8, "Integrate Rather than Segregate," becomes the jumping off point for a philosophical discussion on the relationship between mind and body in light of discoveries about the microbiome.*

I include here an excerpt from the manuscript that first introduces permaculture Principle #1, "Observe and Interact." It opens with an epigraph from Michael Pollan. As the excerpt begins, the insomnia caused by my aching neck has led to a whole host of unpleasant symptoms: digestive disorders, hormonal disarray, anxiety, depression, and migrating aches and pains. A sympathetic naturopath keeps telling me to "listen to my body," but as an academic living in a Cartesian culture in which minds speak and bodies don't, I am mystified. Slowly, however, through close reading of texts, one kind of listening leads to another.

> Gazing across the meadow of sagebrush, I found it difficult to imagine the invisible chemical chatter, including the calls of distress, going on all around—or that these motionless plants were engaged in any kind of "behavior" at all.
>
> Michael Pollan, "The Intelligent Plant"

People kept telling me to "listen to my body," but I couldn't for the life of me figure out what language my body spoke and how to hear it. I could read four languages but my body communicated in a dialect in which, for most of my life, I had had little or no interest. I could generally be relied upon to mishear or disregard even those common elementary phrases that we are all basically born knowing—"I'm tired, maybe I should go to sleep" or "my foot hurts, maybe I should change shoes"—the sort of nagging truths that the world in which I lived fully supported me in ignoring. I was richly rewarded for my deafness with professional accolades, a personal sense of achievement, and increasingly serious health troubles.

In fact, I had spent most of the last two decades, maybe even my whole life, trying to get my body to shut up. And in comparing myself with many of the women I'd known since college—the vomiters, the who-needs-maternity-leavers, the marathoners, the botoxers—I was a rank amateur. I remember the time when, as an untenured junior professor, I was attending a conference in New York soon after my second child was born. Perpetually sleep-deprived, I was nearly nodding off in a session about representations of race in the short stories of Grace Paley when Irina, an old friend from graduate school, slid into the seat next to me, visibly pregnant. I hadn't seen her in years so I shook myself awake, leaned over to kiss her on the cheek, congratulated her and asked her when she was due.

> "About five weeks from now," she whispered, adding, with a wry smile, "and I just found out!"

> "Found out what?" I asked, assuming she meant the due date, or sex of the baby, or, with a slight frisson of anticipated intrigue, maybe the identity of the father.

"That I was pregnant," Irina hissed into my ear. I stared back at her, utterly dumbfounded.

"You didn't know you were *eight months pregnant*?" I blurted out in astonishment, eliciting affronted shushing from the audience members nearby. Irina was a large woman, but still, was this actually possible? She leaned back in her seat.

"I'm an academic," she quietly replied with a guilty shrug. "I have a long-distance relationship with my body."

And although I certainly knew well before eight months each time I was pregnant, I too had experienced the perils of this sort of long-distance relationship. I figured I would need a whole new degree to learn to hear the language of my body. Maybe my naturopath had a textbook on her shelf to teach me how to corral the loud clatter in my mind, to create the quiet space necessary to *hear* those long-suppressed signals and fainter frequencies on which my body seemed to express itself. And once I figured out how to listen, what would I do with what I heard? I would still need an advanced seminar in data interpretation, with a weekly lab for learning how to properly assess the evidence and respond to the findings.

I'm an English professor. So to solve a crisis of language I turned instead to the methods with which I am most comfortable. I wandered into the room at the front of our house, which features rows and rows of bookshelves and which, with the exception of the particular books and photos on the shelves, has been largely unchanged since the house was inhabited, nearly a hundred years ago, by another English professor and his family. This was the room that convinced me, the moment I stepped foot in it, that we had to find a way to live here. I stood for a few minutes staring out the windows at the massive beech tree which held court in our little patch of earth out front. I heard a scuffle, a rustling of leaves, and then saw two skinny black squirrels chasing each other up and down the tree in a mad spring mating dance. We had just taken down the storms and put up screens and the window was cracked open a bit to let in the still-cool spring air. The squirrels were so diverted by their games that they didn't notice me, and I ventured perilously close to the window, and the branches beyond, so close that I could almost fancy I heard them breathing as they paused for a moment to contemplate one another. One squirrel turned, stared straight at me, and we both started back in surprise.

I clambered up on the window seat between two piles of already-read novels that I'd been meaning to shelve for months. The fiction section was a mess, but since I hadn't touched Eliot in years, those volumes were still neatly shelved just above my left shoulder under "E." I was searching for *Middlemarch*, wondering if I might find in the familiar words of a trusted old friend the direction I sought. I glanced over the row of hefty volumes, which ranged from stately hand-tooled leather editions purchased during a brief fling with the Folio Society, to falling-apart paperbacks gleaned from the used book stores which formed my favorite shopping destinations during my years in New York, pages grown brittle from years in damp grad school apartments, and in perpetual danger of falling from their bindings and scattering on the floor like autumn leaves.

Ever since high school I had loved *Middlemarch,* and especially its central character, Dorothea Brooke, a young lady with too much passion and enthusiasm in a world which simply had no viable outlet for such immoderate drive housed in a woman's body. Even as a teenager, I knew Dorothea's passions not only made her a fascinating character, they also got her in trouble – that disastrous marriage to the much older and duller Casaubon, her too-high principles which kept her apart from Ladislaw for so long, her naïveté and her often misplaced faith. As an eager and terribly earnest young woman myself, I certainly didn't see these as problems. After all, Dorothea did get Ladislaw in the end, and was always beautiful and good even when she was mistaken. And so, I blithely assumed, was I.

But now, with my adolescence safely consigned to memory, swaddled instead in the stable comforts of my own late-Victorian home, secure in a tenured position at an important university, and only barely hanging on to the fluttering wisps of a once-fierce romantic passion to *do right* and *be right,* I was looking to Eliot for a different purpose.

I finally located the weighty tome and was immediately drawn to a passage in the Preface in which Eliot tells the reader, in no uncertain terms, that she does *not* intend to center her tale on an epic character like Saint Theresa, a martyr who was memorialized and celebrated because her passions fit into a grand story that the Catholic world wanted to tell. Eliot figured that Saint Theresa had received enough attention already. Rather, her interest was in the women whose passion and brilliance were lost in the "meanness of opportunity," who found no grand historical stage for their deeds and therefore sank "unwept into oblivion" (Eliot 1985, 25). Eliot's task, as she explained in the first few pages of the novel, was to serve as the poet of these unsung women, who dreamt grand dreams while stuck in a limited provincial life. With a shock of recognition, I realized that only a woman in middle age, a woman who had dreamt many dreams for herself, and suffered the disappointments of a full life in which sometimes some dreams simply don't turn out as planned, could write such a story. Hope flared that this novel, which had long ago been consigned to the dustbin of my past, could speak to me once again, could offer me hints about how to hear the faint whispers of my now middle-aged body and figure out how to heal it. And so I moved to the couch and settled in for the long haul (the novel is, after all, nearly 1000 pages) eagerly, even desperately, searching for wisdom, as I neared the age at which Eliot wrote her masterpiece.

I lugged that book around with me everywhere that summer, drawn in once again by Eliot's learned, careful prose, challenging and comforting in equal measure. I read it on subways and airplanes, in bed and on the beach, in New York, in Toronto, on the way to a conference in Paris, and finally finished it in the back garden of a cottage in a small village in Oxfordshire, immersed in the landscape and architecture of the very provincial British towns which Eliot had described in such loving and particular detail. I groaned anew at Dorothea's bad choices while remembering how I too strode through my youth similarly proud and self-righteous. I still disliked Rosamond but now I saw that she was not entirely to blame for Lydgate's troubles. I noted, with a little shudder, that in my own scholarly obsessions I might actually resemble Casaubon – the dried-up forty-something pedant obsessed with finding the Key to All Mythologies – more than I would care to admit. And I questioned this time whether or not Dorothea's long-awaited marriage to Ladislaw was, indeed, the perfect happy ending.

But it wasn't until page 900 or so that I began to worry that perhaps Eliot didn't have an answer to the questions that kept me awake at night. *Middlemarch,* like so many other stories of the time, is a novel about women with extremely limited options, forced into the same unpleasant compromise over and over again, the expectations of society taking precedence over the calling of their souls, the limited range of motion allowed to their bodies curtailing the sharp activity of their minds. Eliot changed English literature by resisting that compromise herself, at great personal cost (of her real name – Mary Ann Evans – and identity, to mention only two of many sacrifices), and then writing from her own lived experience about the narrowness of Dorothea's palette of choices and the impact of that restriction on her interior life, whose contours were still recognizable to me centuries later, even if my range of options was considerably broader.

Nonetheless, I was disappointed: a reaction which I knew was unreasonable. Eliot was, for all of her brilliance, a creature of her time and place, a woman publishing under a male pseudonym and living with a man she could not marry. A woman writing at the beginning of the modern industrial age, and in the early days of liberal society, could hardly be expected to offer solutions to a confused middle-aged woman at the other end of that history, after more than a hundred and fifty years of the kind of political and environmental and industrial change that served as the backdrop for her novel. How could I expect her to solve my twenty-first century problems for me? And yet, I had found wisdom and solace in *Middlemarch* before and so I persisted. I flipped back to one particular passage, somewhere in the first part, that I had always found inexplicably moving and which I suspected offered more than I had yet understood. I had marked it each time I read it so that by now the words were nearly obscured by the multiple generations of stars (1985), exclamation points (1990), and underlining (2012) which adorned the passage. The page had been folded down so many times that the book practically fell open to that spot.

Dorothea has been married six weeks, she is beginning to recognize that Casaubon is not what she thought and married life is proving a disappointment. She is in Rome, surrounded by the most exquisite art and architecture, and she is sobbing bitterly. No one, the narrator interjects, would consider this tragic. It is a commonplace that a young romantic girl will be disappointed when she is forced to confront the quotidian reality of married life. We are not, the narrator reminds us, generally moved to grand passions by such ordinary disillusionment. The kind of tragedy that emerges from everyday disappointments has thankfully "not yet wrought itself into the coarse emotions of mankind" (*Middlemarch*, 226). After all, the narrator wonders, if we were to feel the disappointments of everyday life with the same intensity with which we experience the tragedy of unusual events, how much of that could we bear before we fell apart under the strain? "If we had a keen vision and feeling of all ordinary human life," she continues, "it would be like hearing the grass grow and the squirrel's heart beat, and we should die of that roar which lies on the other side of silence. As it is, the quickest of us walk about well wadded with stupidity" (ibid.).

Does Eliot really mean that we should shield ourselves from keen feeling? That we should wad our ears and hearts with stupidity rather than feel Dorothea's pain as profoundly as she does? After plowing through over two hundred pages of detailed descriptions of Dorothea's hopes and fears, passions and disappointments, I had spent long hours with her already and cared about her deeply. And so, when I encountered this poignant description of her tears, I felt her disappointment within my own being. I was moved by her tears precisely because they were commonplace, because I too had experienced similar disillusionments and had similar reactions yet had never seen them represented in just this way, given such prominence in a novel considered among the best in the English language. And that reaction, I suspect, was Eliot's goal. If I did not consider Dorothea's everyday passions to be worthy of my attention, as worthy as those of more lofty and celebrated tragic heroes, why would I continue reading? At the same time, by simultaneously pointing out how commonplace Dorothea's disillusionment was, and insuring that I would be moved by it, Eliot played a clever trick on me. She demanded that I notice not only Dorothea's tears, but my own; she drew my attention to the fact that I was actually being moved in a way that was not customary, by a character (an ordinary provincial woman) and a situation (disillusion in love) which I really ought to dismiss as trivial. To notice that I was – willingly or not – getting a taste of what "a keen vision and feeling of all ordinary human life" might feel like was to experience, for a moment, what might happen if I were to open my mind, and my ears, to different frequencies, to "hear(ing) the grass grow and the squirrel's heart beat." I was impressed by Eliot's audacity in attending so closely to the ebbs and flows of the emotional life of a woman who was neither queen nor warrior nor martyr, who was only noteworthy in that the author had decided to notice her and write a story about her. To listen to the texture of an ordinary woman's life so closely (rather than "walk[ing] about well wadded with stupidity") is, (and was, especially in the mid-nineteenth century), rare, and dangerous. Hardly anyone in English letters before Eliot had attempted it. The effect of this kind of listening on her readers was uncertain, and remains surprisingly risky a hundred and fifty years later. I thought of my shelves laden with the fiction of nearly two centuries of women writers. So many who had paid close attention, after all, had indeed "die[d] of that roar which lies on the other side of silence." On the other hand, I had just heard it and survived.

As I returned to the passage, I noticed that Eliot had structured this part of the story so that, if you wanted to read *Middlemarch* (and I did!), you had to make a choice. You had to enter into the precarious zone of heightened listening. After the narrator's digression, the next paragraph blithely returned me to Dorothea exactly where I'd left her: "However, Dorothea was crying..." (ibid.). There was no way for me to escape Dorothea's tears; I needed to read through and beyond them to get to the next part of the story. And Eliot didn't stop there. She took me by the hand and led me into Dorothea's own mind, where I encountered yet another quandary. "And if she had been required to state the cause, she could only have done so in some such general words as I have already used." Who can know, Eliot seems to ask, why a woman is crying? If the woman herself can find no language to articulate the contours of her own sadness, how can I, the reader, be expected to understand the murky details of her emotional landscape? But the narrator did not leave me there either, safely "wadded with stupidity." She continued:

> To have been driven to be more particular would have been like trying to give a history of the lights and shadows; for that new real future which was replacing the imaginary drew its material from the endless minutiae by which her view of Mr. Casaubon and her wifely relation, now that she was married to him, was gradually changing with the secret motion of a watch-hand from what it had been in her maiden dream.
>
> (ibid.)

Now Eliot rose from the page, looked me, her reader, in the face, middle-aged woman to middle-aged woman, and smiled in the calm assurance that I would surely understand the stark difference between the young Dorotheas we once were and the older women we had become, who either narrated Dorothea's life or read about it. This elder narrator not only dared to listen closely to a woman's thoughts, to describe with startling acuity the emotional shifts a young woman might experience in the months after the conclusion of an (unsatisfactory) marriage plot, but also explained, with the wisdom of age and experience, the subtle and elusive ways in which feelings – and lives – change in response to the tiniest shifts in perspective. Eliot had little interest in the heightened melodrama of love at first sight, the lightning strike which throws everything into sharp relief. Instead, she focused on a "history of the lights and shadows." She chose to tell a story for which the English language is inadequate; how do you represent in words the ever-changing play of light and shadow on a wall, the impossibly faint sound of grass growing, the often unremarked alterations in feeling which characterize the most intimate of human relationships?

Instead of the exciting rush of high drama, Eliot chose patient observation, a kind of contemplative attention that was, although she couldn't have known this, already being rendered obsolete by the onslaught of industrialization which formed the backdrop for her novel. A quality of attention whose near-extinction in my own world was indeed the result of the very march toward modernity that Eliot's writing signalled and celebrated. Eliot was asking me to make a remarkably counter-cultural choice, to accompany her on a quiet journey of observation, something I had never before had the time to do, and to make use of skills, which, despite my fancy education and advanced degrees, I had never been taught. Over the course of hundreds of pages, Eliot showed me how to notice the ways in which little things that happen during a day, every little offhand comment, gesture, or choice in clothing, food, or amusement, every twinge or exertion or insult to our bodies has a slow but steady impact on our emotional lives, just as the hand of a watch tick-tocks away the seconds, the minutes, the hours, with maddening regularity. Finally, I felt that I was getting somewhere. If I could muster the courage to attend closely to the details of my own sensory reactions, to hear the sounds of the world around me and inside me, as Eliot suggested, maybe I would discover a whole universe that had been previously unheard, a world which would at first be terrifying but, given time and attention, might also delight me, teach me, reveal me to myself. Maybe I could even learn to listen to my body. The roar on the other side of *that* silence was already nearly deafening me at times.

There is one more thing I noticed reading the passage this time around that hadn't occurred to me before. Something which Eliot herself may or may not have intended but which struck me with peculiar force now, as I switched back and forth between the pages of the novel and the coverage of Hurricane Sandy on CNN. In between chapters, I watched in mute horror as the storm crashed into the world of my childhood, eradicating forever the New Jersey beaches where I spent summer weekends jumping the waves and licking the residue of pink cotton candy from my sticky fingers and playing Skee-Ball with sketchy adolescent boys. Those images had long ago disappeared – as this beach was now disappearing – from my memory and were only dredged up as I watched in stunned silence as the boardwalks were broken like twigs by the furious winds of an overheated planet. I averted my eyes in order to continue reading, only to find the reality of that hurricane seeping unbidden into my communion with Eliot. To make her point about observation, Eliot chose examples of things we *never* listen to – the grass growing, the squirrel's heart beating – because we all know that to hear such things with human ears is impossible. But, Eliot reminded me, it was, for her, equally impossible to imagine plumbing the depths of a woman's emotional life. In Eliot's time, a woman's interior emotional terrain was assumed to be as impenetrable as the everyday, non-human landscape which surrounds us and which we also take for granted.

I remembered a childhood fantasy that the flowers could talk and the trees could feel. Imagine, my friends and I would whisper to one another in our sleeping bags after the lights were turned out, what it might sound like when the lawn is being mowed, if we could hear the screams of every blade of grass as it was cut! How horrible! But if Eliot could place Dorothea's everyday emotions at the center of her novel, and I could hear and feel them with her, and I emerged from the experience transformed but alive, then maybe, just maybe, I might also want to try listening to the grass and squirrels. I got up from the couch, stared out into the yard, the storm windows now installed against the coming winter cold shutting out most of the sounds from the yard and the street, and watched a single fat squirrel, with a discarded bit of bagel gleaned from a trashcan down the street protruding from its bulging cheeks, lumber up the branches to some unseen nest, where it too was preparing for the oncoming snow, burrowing its way under and behind our eavestrough and into our roof. Why was one kind of listening possible and the other necessarily impossible?

It was time for me to clear away the noise. I needed to listen more closely, to learn to hear impossible sounds.

It wasn't until spending many days on Bela Farm, however, studying and practicing permaculture, that I began to fully understand the challenges inherent to this kind of listening. David Holmgren, its founder, describes permaculture ("permanent culture") as human landscapes (farms, towns, buildings, parks) consciously designed to mimic the patterns and relationships of nature, building on his basic assumption that, although we may be unusual in the natural world, human beings are, nonetheless, subject to the same scientific laws that govern the material universe. There are many different ways in which permaculture shapes the design and work process on a farm, but I was stuck for months on Principle #1 – observe and interact. "Good design," Holmgren writes, "depends on a free and harmonious relationship between nature and people, in which careful observation and thoughtful interaction provide the design inspiration, repertoire, and patterns. It is not something generated in isolation," he cautions, "but through continuous and reciprocal interaction with the subject" (2002, 13).

"Observe the land" sounded right, but was, in practice, as opaque and disconcerting a maxim for me as "listen to your body." Before we had learned about permaculture, my farm design group had made mistakes borne of speed and inattention, moving too quickly to plant, not realizing until a couple of years later that, after much fanfare and investment of time and energy, we had probably chosen the wrong location – too windy, too exposed – for our first small fruit orchard. As we began to immerse ourselves in permaculture principles, however, our process underwent a noticeable shift in pace and intensity. I strove to develop senses I didn't think I had and a patience I knew I lacked. I was, to be honest, most at home sitting with the group – as we often did – at a table in a conference room on the top floor of a university building in the heart of the city, poring over texts and images. But in order to lay down the roots we dreamed of, we needed another kind of knowledge.

And so we headed out of town for a few days each month and began to walk the land, trying to engage our surroundings with multiple senses on the alert. We went out to the farm in every season. We mapped hills and gullies, water flow, insects and animal life. We watched wind patterns and noticed what grew where, attending to what thrived and what withered and why. It sounds romantic and contemplative, but was – and still is – actually incredibly difficult work for an English professor. Despite (or because of) my extensive reading in literary representations of nature, political approaches to the environment, historical and religious attitudes toward land use, my observational faculties were woefully inadequate to the task at hand. I almost always felt exhausted by the end of those days, not because of the physical demands, which weren't particularly excessive, but because of the emotional and intellectual effort required to simply *pay attention.*

I needed to learn to recognize different plant species, to notice things that had never occurred to me as important before – the angle of the sun, the relationship of a stand of trees to a neighboring field, the closest source of water, the sound of the wind over a hill. Often after only a few minutes out walking, trying hard to keep focussed on the botanist's discovery of new wildflowers, or the wind patterns from a neighboring field laced with pesticides that our beekeeper feared would harm the bees, or the arc of a particular hill which the painter in the group found so arresting, or the heft, moisture content, color, and smell of the shovelful of soil that our neighboring farmer had just dug up for us to inspect, I found my mind wandering, back to my desk, to my books. I had spent my entire childhood in rural New York, but I had always escaped into books, never considering that I might need to pay attention to anything but words. I lacked the filters necessary to discern patterns in the complex weave of sounds, smells, tastes and sensations, the vast numbers of plant, animal, insect species present in each square foot of every acre, the intricate interactions and reactions, the light, temperature, humidity, weight, of the air and water and soil, which changed from moment to moment, from season to season.

Walking the land I felt strangely unbounded, spilling out of myself into the vastness of endless pastures and windy hilltops and alien languages I could barely hear, much less speak. I felt like a baby, learning all over again how to name and understand the world around me. It was terrifying. And humiliating. While the others often seemed invigorated by our walks, I usually ended up feeling guiltily enervated, my consciousness quickly overloaded by sensory stimulation. I strolled through fields and woods with my colleagues, feigning attentiveness as I struggled to contain and temper the roar on the other side of silence which entered my consciousness unbidden and threatened to deafen me with its powerful cacophony. I veered wildly between wonder at the immense complexity which had opened up before me and shame at my disgraceful ignorance.

Environmental theorist Christopher Manes offers an explanation for why this task of listening to the land is so challenging, especially for people like myself, immersed in the texts and worldview of western culture. He writes that "nature is silent in our culture (and in literate societies generally) in the sense that the status of being a speaking subject is jealously guarded as an exclusively human prerogative" (1996, 15). He worries that we have "compressed the entire buzzing, howling, gurgling biosphere into the narrow vocabulary of epistemology" (ibid.). Why is this a problem? Because we only give moral consideration to those we deem "speakers" and historically we have only taken seriously those who are "privileged speakers" ("priests and kings, authors, intellectuals and celebrities"). For centuries, this left out most women – as George Eliot so adeptly demonstrated in *Middlemarch* – and still omits non-human nature. I considered what happened when our western culture – prompted by authors like Eliot, as well as activists, revolutionaries, and many others – began to listen to those formerly deemed incapable of serious speech. After much political struggle, the power structures of liberal societies slowly created space (albeit often still inadequate) for non-whites, non-Christians, former slaves, poor people, women, and homosexuals, as speaking subjects, with rights and privileges and voices. Manes asks what would happen if we went a step further and assumed nature had a voice too, and if we found ways to listen more carefully, or differently, in order to hear it. We might very well "die of the roar that lies on the other side of silence," just as old patriarchal and autocratic societies were often upended by the roar of newly speaking subjects.[3]

Or at least the myth we hold about who we are as human beings in relation to the rest of the Earth might crumble. The more I learned about the farm and the land and the Earth, the more the myths that I had long clung to also began to fray at the edges. Many days, in order to meet my obligations and live the life I had carefully crafted, I spent every bit of energy I had sewing patches onto the increasingly tattered remnants of a mythology that told me that my mind was more important than my body, that my personal resources – and the Earth's resources – were limitless, that individual human freedom trumped all other imperatives. Other days, I wearily let my personal story slip, and, stripped of narrative, succumbed to vertigo. To the kind of disorientation that a character in Martin Amis's novel, *The Information,* called "The History of Increasing Humiliation", the sense of being dethroned, of recognizing that we are not, after all, at the center of the universe.[4]

But some days, months, and even years after my first walk on that land, faint murmurs on other frequencies would catch me by surprise, speaking around the edges and even from within the core of my own mythology. At those times, I could just barely discern the outlines of new stories about human bodies and the world, emerging from the cacophony, sometimes whispered sometimes shouted, in a language I was just beginning to comprehend.

Notes

1   For five years I served as the consulting scholar for the farm, helping the more agricul-turally adept members of the team conceptualize and realize our educational mission. This past year I have become the Creative Director for Bela Farm, and the land has become my research laboratory. I am currently exploring ways to combine my scholarly and pedagogical work as a professor and cultural historian with the land-based, experi-ential and embodied realities of planting, growing and harvesting. My first experiment explores the value of permaculture principles in reimagining life writing. My research team will learn about permaculture, practice it, and then write about their own lives in light of this experience.

2   In this work I am much indebted to the many scholars of ecofeminism who have, since the early 1980s, explored the important role of feminist thought in understanding environmental issues. At the same time, I devote more attention to exploring the signif-icance of environmental narratives for political feminism rather than the reverse – a connection much less discussed in the scholarly literature. To do this, I enter into the politically charged conversation in twenty-first century North American feminism about the fate of the overwhelmed working mother, but instead of focussing on the problem of lingering inequality and the specific policy solutions that might close those gaps, I investigate links between these so-called women's lifestyle issues and broad environ-mental and medical concerns. The depleted women I interview in this book are "canaries in the coal mine" not only for feminist but also for environmentalist reasons; their exhaustion serves as a wake-up call for a culture – and a species – desperately in need of new narrative models for a sustainable life.

3   Finding ways to hear and represent the voices of non-human nature is an oft-debated topic among ecocritics. Among the most interesting recent contributions to this conver-sation is Robin Wall Kimmerer's essay "Learning the Grammar of Animacy," which compares the First Nations Potawatomi language to English and demonstrates the key role that language and grammar play in determining what we can and cannot "hear" and how we ascribe meaning to it (Kimmerer, *Braiding Sweetgrass,* Minneapolis: Milkweed Editions, 2013, pp. 48–61).

4   My attention was drawn to Amis's novel by Michael Pollan's article, "The Intelligent Plant" (2013).

References

Eliot, George. 1985. *Middlemarch.* New York: Penguin Classics (originally published 1872).
Holmgren, David. 2002. *Permaculture: Principles & Pathways Beyond Sustainability.* Victoria, AU: Holmgren Design Services.
Manes, Christopher. 1996. "Nature and Silence." In Cheryll Glotfelty and Harold Fromm (eds) *The Ecocriticism Reader.* Athens: University of Georgia Press.
Pollan, Michael. "The Intelligent Plant." *The New Yorker* (23 December 2013). Available online at: http://michaelpollan.com/articles-archive/the-intelligent-plant (last accessed 4 May 2017).

2 Bringing forth an ecotopian future

The production of imagined futures through contemporary cultural practices

Stephen Zavestoski and Andrew Weigert

> Turning and turning in the widening gyre
> The falcon cannot hear the falconer;
> Things fall apart; the centre cannot hold ...
>
> From William Butler Yeats, "The Second Coming"

Whether named the Age of Crisis, the Anthropocene, or something else, the times in which we live are unprecedented: from the terrorist attacks of 9/11, to the near-collapse of the global financial system under the weight of risky mortgages that had been magically turned into low-risk securities, to the protests and revolutions of the Arab Spring, to an onslaught of extreme weather events causing massive destruction and loss of life from Russia to the Philippines to New York City, to what may be the first stages of the unraveling of the world's "deepest and broadest free trading zone" (HM Government, 2016) with the exit of Great Britain from the European Union, to the repeated and seemingly unprovoked killings of young American black men by police. Yeats might say about these times, "Things fall apart; the centre cannot hold."

What, exactly, is falling apart? What has become destabilized? At the time of Yeats's writing of "The Second Coming" in 1919, according to Tabor, the "widening gyre" was pulling apart more than just political and social order. What appears to be destabilized in these moments of crisis are not only the institutions entrusted with maintaining political and social order, but also the very sense of self, formed and shaped within a relatively stable perception of the present. These destabilizations, in turn, disrupt the pragmatic practice of discerning preferable (and possible) futures. Given the growing sense of a center that is losing control, what evidence might we find around us of efforts to stake out stable ground around which new futures can be negotiated?

We turn to Ernest Callenbach's now quite dated 1975 novel *Ecotopia* to explore a possible answer in the form of what we call "micro-utopian practices." In an attempt to move beyond all-too-common critiques of utopian fiction, we acknowledge the shortcomings of Callenbach's original vision while nevertheless pointing to the seeds of micro-utopian practices found within it. We do so through an amalgamation of the reactions of our students to Callenbach's novel; an exchange between Callenbach and the urban farming pioneer and author, Novella Carpenter; and informal sociological observations of emerging cultural impulses in early twenty-first century urban America. By re-engaging with Callenbach's *Ecotopia* from this new perspective, we argue that micro-utopian practices present the possibility of a realistic and incremental movement toward a desired, if not utopian, future. This pragmatic possibility sidesteps the often disempowering and sometimes morally problematic politics of revolution and transformation typically envisioned as part of the transition to utopia. Rather than a blueprint for revolutionary transformation, we interpret Callenbach's vision of Ecotopia in terms of the contemporary prolif- eration of everyday ecotopian practices – from urban farming and the sharing economy to co-ops, bicycling and tiny houses – all undertaken in the quintessen- tially ecotopian DIY spirit of small-scale experimentation, tinkering, hacking and making.

We begin the chapter by briefly arguing that recent trends in dystopian literature stunt our ability to discern preferable and possible futures. Next we draw on social psychologist George Herbert Mead's understanding of moral reasoning to suggest that newly emerging cultural "impulses" can be interpreted as micro-utopian practices to bring forth visions of anticipated and preferred futures. Drawing on Callenbach's interview with Novella Carpenter and reactions from our students' readings, we reinterpret *Ecotopia* as a description of everyday practices for living within the Earth system rather than a blueprint for revolutionary transformation. But before arriving at the possibility of an ecotopian future, we must begin with dystopia.

Salvaging utopia from a dystopic anthropocene

It is no surprise that dystopian visions abound during the approach to, and at the start of, an age of crisis. Yet, as is also the case with most utopian visions, dystopian visions confine the imagination of what's possible with their linear views of history. As Giorgos Kallis and Hug March explain in their examination of degrowth as a utopian alternative to capitalism's pursuit of endless growth, "under enlightenment, modernism, and in deterministic versions of Marxism, the new world to come is a sequential outcome of the old one" (2015, 362). To break from this linear model, Kallis and March point to Ursula Le Guin's approach to utopia in her science fiction novel *The Dispossessed* (1974/2015). For Le Guin, they explain, there is no causal link between past and future. Rather, a variety of futures emerge from human action in the present. As a result, the future is always latent in the past (2015, 362).

If the future is always latent in the past, then the future depends on these latencies becoming manifest through present possibilities. "The task," according to David Harvey, "is to pull together a spatiotemporal utopianism – a dialectical utopianism – that is rooted in our present possibilities at the same time as it points towards different trajectories for human uneven geographical developments" (2000, 196). For Harvey, dialectical utopianism must be grounded in contingent matrices of existing and already achieved social relations that include political-economic processes while also acknowledging its embeddedness in a physical and ecological world that is always changing (Harvey 2000, 231).

The impulse towards Harvey's dialectical utopianism in which human action in the present brings forth a variety of possible futures appears to be diminishing the impulse towards dystopianism that peaked with best-selling trilogies like Suzanne

Collins' *The Hunger Games* (2008, 2009, 2010) and Veronica Roth's *Divergent* (2011, 2012, 2013). Writer and cultural critic Adam Sternbergh reports that a prominent book agent told *Publishers Weekly* in 2013 that, "thanks to a market glut, it's now almost impossible to sell any young-adult novel that has 'even the whiff of dystopia about it'" (Sternbergh 2014). One hypothesis for the end of the decade of dystopia is the inability to imagine a "future world that's worse than what's happening right now" (ibid.). "If the current moment feels dystopian," asks Sternbergh, "why bother imagining a fictive dystopia of tomorrow?" (2016). Frederic Jameson offers one possible reason in pointing to dystopian science fiction's ability to "defamiliarize and restructure our own present" (2005, 286). The job of the futurist then "is no longer speculating about what might come," writes Sternbergh, but rather "to comprehend what's already here" (2016).

Which brings us back to the Anthropocene, a moment of crisis that paradoxically forecloses promised futures while opening up opportunities for alternative futures. Catastrophic climate change and the Anthropocene evoke, for some, claims of the end of our species (Hamilton 2011) and for others, the end of our civilization (Scranton 2015). For Gerry Canavan, apocalyptic critique opens up a utopian potentiality and is therefore a "necessary critical move to rescue us from a diagnosis of the world situation that would otherwise appear utterly hopeless" (2014, 16). Ecocritique, according to Canavan, can collapse utopia and apocalypse into one another, each a "disguised version of a single imaginative leap into futurity." The 200-year old tradition of science fiction that Canavan calls "our culture's vast, shared, polyvocal archive of the possible; from techno-utopias to apocalypses to ecotopian *fortunate falls*, can help us collectively 'think' this leap into futurity in the context of the epochal mass-extinction event called the Anthropocene" (2014, 16).

Beyond ecological utopia: micro-utopian practice in ecotopia

We turn now to an interpretation of *Ecotopia* – one informed partially by our own experiences using the text in undergraduate classes for the last 20 years – not as an imagined ecological utopia but rather as a demonstration of the kinds of everyday practices that might open possible pathways to the pragmatic dialectical utopianism for which Harvey calls. Callenbach, in fact, never used the word 'utopia' in the novel and over the years reminded audiences that Ecotopia, the place, is "not a perfect world, it's not a utopia in the ordinary sense" (Gund Institute 2011). Ecotopia is not a utopia in another sense – against utopia's translation from the Greek as "not place," Ecotopia is imagined as a geographically real and bounded place. *Ecotopia*'s epigraph explicitly defines 'ecotopia' with reference to the Greek 'oikos' (household or home) and topos (place).

However, our interpretation of *Ecotopia* as the location of pragmatic micro-utopian practices – where, in accordance with Le Guin's interpretation of utopia, a variety of futures might emerge from human action in the present – depends less on Callenbach's definition of ecotopia and more on the contemporary historical context. Before unpacking the significance of this historical reorienting in reading *Ecotopia*, a brief introduction to the novel is necessary.

First published in 1975 by the full title *Ecotopia: The Notebooks and Reports of William Weston*, Ecotopia takes place in 1999 as New York journalist Will Weston makes the first officially arranged visit to Ecotopia since its secession from the United States 20 years earlier. Through a combination of diary entries and dispatches to the *Times-Post*, the reader comes to learn about the ways in which everyday life in Ecotopia – from politics, technology and work to gender relations, transportation, education, recreation, race, and communication – has been adapted according to Ecotopia's principle of a stable-state society.

What we learn is that Ecotopia did not arise out of a grand utopian vision. Many people were already living, in various ways and to varying degrees, according to the post-secession ecotopian cultural practices. The secession represented a break with the American past and a diversion from the future towards which its current trajectory carried it. Callenbach offers limited details of the so-called helicopter wars through which Ecotopia gained its independence, and armed resistance to the secession was supposedly thwarted by the threat of nuclear bombs rumored to have been placed under several major American cities. Otherwise the story focuses on Weston's discoveries about Ecotopia, both through his dispatches and through his more private diary entries; together, these chronicle Weston's slow transformation of self as he first resists then gradually embraces ecotopian customs and practices.

Prior to the turn of the millennium, a typical student engagement with *Ecotopia* might begin by pondering whether the events of the novel could actually unfold – could Callenbach's "predictions" come true? From 2000 onward, when the novel's imagined future exists in the reader's past, the complicated question about whether *Ecotopia* might predict our own path to the future is less relevant.

This shift in historical perspective also reorients new millennium readers to what were previously moral sticking points around race and gender. For example, in Callenbach's Ecotopia black separatist parties demanded that major cities' black areas become officially designated as city-states within Ecotopia, so-called "Soul Cities" whose primary contributions to mainstream ecotopia are cultural commodities like music. And though Callenbach portrays Ecotopia as a society of gender equality governed by a female-dominated political party and female president, there are also disappointing inconsistencies. The main character's sex life and his observations of sexual relations portray Ecotopia's culture as suspiciously similar to the stereotypical male heterosexual fantasy of unencumbered sex. Equally incompatible with Ecotopia's supposed gender equality is the exclusion of women from the culture's ritual war games in order to focus their competitiveness on "rivalry over men to father their children" (96).

The novel's problematic handling of race and gender complicate the underlying impulse in pre-millennium readings of *Ecotopia* to dream about the possibility of Ecotopia's desirable characteristics actually existing. Our contention is that the impossibility of Callenbach's Ecotopia in the present millennium – a simple temporal foreclosure occurring once a reader's present moment exists later in time than the point at which the supposed future Ecotopia would have come into existence – allows for a more detached reading in which racial and gender sticking points, not to mention threats of nuclear bombs, can be read more easily as vestiges of the author's historical moment rather than as essential components of a utopian blueprint that must be accepted whole cloth. Consequently, closer attention can be paid to the small-scale, decentralized and DIY-driven innovations in Callenbach's Ecotopia that inspire comparisons to actual everyday ecotopian practices occurring in our present moment.

Such a reading is consistent with the notion that the future is always latent in the past (and emergent in the present). In other words, letting go of the problematic identity politics and the question of whether Ecotopia might actually predict our future, readers instead focus on innovations in the organization of labor, housing design, agriculture, timber harvesting, education, and so on. To the extent that Ecotopia's innovations around everyday livelihood and lifestyle practices are seen as already existing in a reader's present moment, the notion of a variety of futures emerging from human action in the present begins to resonate. Callenbach even provides an underlying "stable-state" philosophy, out of which the "multiple futures" perspective emerges, illustrated in a conversation between Weston and an Ecotopian journalist. Weston wonders how progress and change are possible in a stable-state society after learning of Ecotopia's fundamental premise that assumes that humans "were meant to take their modest place in a seamless, stable-state web of living organisms, disturbing that web as little as possible ... [and that] people were to be happy not to the extent they dominated their fellow creatures on earth, but to the extent they lived in balance with them" (43–44).

Weston and his Ecotopian comrade Bert debate the dynamism of a stable-state:

> Thought I'd do some probing. "Doesn't this stable-state business get awfully static? I'd think it would drive you crazy after a certain point!"
>
> Bert looked at me with amusement, and batted the ball back. "Well, don't forget that we don't have to be stable. The system provides the stability, and we can be erratic within it. I mean we don't try to be perfect, we just try to be okay on the average—which means adding up a bunch of ups and downs." "But it means giving up any notions of progress. You just want to get to that stable point and stay there, like a lump."
>
> "It may sound that way, but in practice there's no stable point. We're always striving to approximate it."
>
> (33)

What the notion of variation within a stable-state system allows, however, is the possibility of an infinite range of small experiments in micro-utopian practices, each with the potential to bring forth a unique ecotopian future.

Our twenty-first century interpretation of *Ecotopia* identifies an underlying tension between what we call micro-utopian practices and what others might describe as experiments in pragmatic survival and reflects a tension that exists within *Ecotopia* as well. Just as Ecotopians debate whether they can isolate themselves within their own ecological utopia or must work towards transformation of the rest of the world to a stable-state society, contemporary practitioners of micro-utopian practices question whether they have any capacity or obligation to contribute to a broader utopian project. This tension is particularly relevant in an interview with Callenbach and Novella Carpenter, author of *Farm City: The Education of an Urban Farmer* (2009).

Having been raised in a rural hippie household, Carpenter describes herself as disillusioned with the Ecotopian-style ideals that shaped the lives and dreams of her parents, instead "preferring to focus on concrete, hands-on, small-scale projects like the urban farm she started in Oakland, California in 2000" (Smith 2010a).

In the course of the interview, the interviewer points out that the San Francisco Bay Area has "a million projects like Novella's farm, where people are trying to create the world they want to exist in, in these little bubbles" and asks Callenbach if he thinks these kinds of projects have influenced the wider culture. Callenbach responds with an ecological metaphor:

> I try to look at everything biologically, including what human beings do. And you could apply the concept of succession to what's going on now. The industrial era has laid waste, visibly or invisibly, to huge parts of our society. And in nature what happens when you disturb something, … first you get really quick-growing little plants that produce a lot of seeds and don't last very long but they take up the ground; during that time, none of the bigger plants can come in. Then finally you get to the point where the land is hospitable again. So I think all these little start-ups and stuff … you could say in a way that they're demonstration projects and they're very important.
>
> (Smith 2010a)

"They're experiments," adds Carpenter. To which Callenbach replies,

> Very important experiments. But they're also the equivalent of what we often call weeds. They're coming up in battered areas where the regular society doesn't know what to do anymore and little by little people learn what works and what doesn't.

In a continuation of the interview, Carpenter is asked, "Do you see Ecotopia as a vision that you're working towards on your farm?" "No," she answers:

> The thing is, I'm not part of that. Because that was like my parents' deal. They were utopians. They were gonna go and live back to the land and all this stuff and I think that's kind of bullshit. My tendency is to react against that, is to not ever think there's going to be Utopia. It's sort of a pessimistic optimism, is what I call it. So, you're like, "I want to do this thing but everything's fucked up."
>
> (Smith 2010b)

Carpenter follows up her answer by making a comparison between her "make do" survival mode and what she sees as a privileged utopian mode:

> [I]n my world, the apocalypse has arrived … There's abandoned buildings, there's broken glass, it's fucked up … I just react against that kind of utopian thinking because I don't think it's sustainable … So I'm just doing what I can right now … but I have no sort of delusions that this can continue, because I'm squatting on this land and I'm just getting what I can out of it while I can. It's

a survival mode. And that's totally different from the utopian mode, which is written from a place of great comfort and privilege, to just be like, "Oh, cool, I am going to go live back to the land," and all this stuff and you have these ideals. Mine is just like, do what you can with what you have right now. End of story. Don't even think of the future because there is no future.

(Smith 2010b)

We see a similar orientation in our students who read *Ecotopia*. Born after the publication of Bill McKibben's *The End of Nature* (1989) and in the Anthropocene epoch, most of our students have grown up in a world where the bifurcation of human and nature is meaningless. Whereas previous environmentalists worked within the intellectual traditions separating humans from nature, Millennials have grown up in a world where nature has always been hybrid. The apocalypse, as Carpenter describes, is here. Rather than struggling with utopian visions that reconcile a human-nature split they have never experienced, young people seek to get on with the business of survival. Such pragmatic action ought to be seen as every bit as much an attempt to bring forth a desired future as the grand visions of utopian literature like *Ecotopia*. Both in their own way offer hope.

Later in the interview, for example, Callenbach described his book as an attempt to run a flag up the flagpole to see if anyone will salute:

It gave people a symbol of alternativeness, and whether we think this alternative would ever happen in anything like the way I portray, or not, is in a certain way not the whole question – the question is whether it makes sense to think beyond where we are.

(Smith 2010b)

When asked if her urban farm is having any impact in Oakland, Carpenter gave a surprisingly similar answer:

I think there's an impact. I think it's … a positive thing that people can see, and say, "Hey, it could be like this." You know, there's an empty lot on every street corner. Every block has an empty lot. And it's not—by no means do I feed everybody here, but people do come by and harvest food. And I feel like it just gives people a different option. It gives people a sense of hope or maybe this idea of the impossible being possible.

(Smith 2010b)

The gap in understanding is not between a twentieth-century environmentalist's dreamy notion of an ecological utopia where humans are at spiritual oneness with nature and a hardscrabble existence of constantly hustling young people living in dystopia. The gap in understanding rather is the difference between a fully developed vision of ecological utopia and a pragmatic attempt at redefining our present predicament, as Carpenter does through a largely forgotten and abandoned corner of her city. Grand utopian visions and micro-utopian practices are both attempts to offer hope for the future.

Both Ecotopians and actual twenty-first century urban homesteaders, people like Novella Carpenter, are engaged in a form of permaculture. While permaculture usually refers to a system of agricultural and social design principles derived from the patterns and features observed in natural ecosystems, the implications of a permaculture practice can have deeper social, political, and moral implications including "a politico-ethical imperative not only that there should be a future but that the people in it deserve a decent world in which to live" (Canavan 2012, 236). Permaculture is also full of learning and adapting through experimentation, observation, and even playfulness, all of which are essential to life in Ecotopia as well as contemporary micro-utopian practices to bring forth desirable futures.

Science fiction author Kim Stanley Robinson goes so far as to propose taking "the political and aesthetic baggage out of the term utopia by replacing it with permaculture. I've been working all my career," explains Robinson, "to try to redefine utopia in more positive terms. People tend to think of utopia as a perfect end stage, which is, by definition, impossible and maybe even bad for us." Robinson concludes that "maybe it's better to use a word like permaculture ... Permaculture suggests a certain kind of obvious human goal, which is that future generations will have at least as good a place to live as what we have now" (quoted in Canavan 2012, 240). Whether utopia or permaculture, the essential practice is one of bringing forth desired futures. It is towards a sociological unpacking of this "worldmaking" that we now turn.

A pragmatic utopianism through everyday 'worldmaking'

The notion of humans as "worldmakers" has at least three different meanings. First, in the Anthropocene epoch humans as geological force have made the world we now inhabit. Second, historians might refer to the modernist project to "comprehend the world, to organize and capture its variety in a single, harmonious frame" (Ramachandran 2015, 4) as a practice of worldmaking. Third, in a literary sense, and especially for science fiction concerned with terraforming (Dozois 2001), worldmaking is a figurative practice.

A sociological perspective offers a fourth interpretation of humans as worldmakers. Through everyday social practices humans produce social worlds that always exist within, and thus give shape to and are shaped by, our given physical world. For social psychologist George Herbert Mead, social actions generate emergent events. These novel events, collectively, produce our social worlds. According to Mead, "the novel is constantly happening and the recognition of this gets its expression in ... the concept of emergence [and] brings in something that was not there before" (1934/2015, 198). Mead goes on to describe this in terms of water, which was not there before, appearing through the combination of oxygen and hydrogen.

As worldmaking social actors, at least in terms of the near horizon, we are inherently future-oriented. In social interaction, according to Mead, we learn from other social actors' reactions to our actions how to anticipate responses in future social situations. Meaning arises not out of the initial action but in the response to it. As such, the meaning of our actions, and subsequently the meaning of self as subject, is always emergent.

Pragmatically speaking, socialization, and in turn moral development, depend on our ability to predict future responses to our actions by placing ourselves in the future and looking back at the self as an object to which others respond. Morality, when defined in terms of the principles that distinguish between behavior that is right or good and behavior that is wrong or bad, exists not only to ensure an agreed upon social order but also to extend that order into the future. Ethical actions arise within interactive and cognitive efforts to attain shared descriptions and interpretive analyses to inform coordinated responses towards production of desired futures. When routine actions no longer produce desired futures or when following socially prescribed paths produces undesirable futures, moral challenges ensue. When desired futures are no longer agreed upon, determining right action becomes problematic and space for negotiating new core values opens. Because they ultimately point to an alternative future, newly negotiated core values require the construction of moral narratives around collective goals in order to reason together how to attain the axiomatic grounding value (Milbrath 1989). In this manner, morality is the mechanism through which imagined and desired futures are enacted. Whether an individual holds an explicit vision of a desired future or not, an intended future is implicit in her choice of moral actions.

Herein lies the relevance of Mead's social psychology as moral discipline to our discussion of dystopia/utopia. When "the centre cannot hold" and institutions and meanings are destabilized, routine action no longer produces desired futures; or, more profoundly, the desired futures that social life processes aim to produce are deemed unobtainable or problematic. In such circumstances, new futures may be envisioned. New moralities, defining new right actions, will emerge whether social actors are experimenting with bringing newly envisioned futures into existence or simply operating in Carpenter's "survival mode."

If we are indeed worldmakers, and if new moralities arise in the process of worldmaking, it might be useful to identify emerging practices that appear to be alternatives either to routine actions that no longer produce desired futures, or to the morally normative paths that produce undesirable futures. Toward this end, we propose examining the trends of urban agriculture as a local alternative to the global industrial food system and bicycling for transportation as an alternative to automobile dependence. Whether they are goal-directed pursuits aimed at producing alternative futures, or simple acts of adaptation (i.e. "survival") in an unpredictable economic environment, urban agriculture and bicycling can be viewed as micro-utopian practices with pragmatic possibilities for producing alternative futures.

Our concern is with the two previously elaborated scenarios: routine actions failing to produce desired futures and socially prescribed paths producing undesirable futures. Especially for younger generations, such as the readers of *Ecotopia* in our classes over the past 15 years, historical and structural contexts have blocked them from carrying out certain scripts written into social life processes such as completing college degrees, embarking on a stable work life, marrying, and buying a home.

Furthermore, the social life processes into which these generations were born generally require access to at least modest economic resources for purchasing material goods around which social meaning, status, and values revolve. Blocked from engaging in such processes, one report (Pew Research Center 2014) tells us how Millennials, for example, are forging a "distinctive path into adulthood" (i.e. rejecting routine actions that fail to produce the promised or desired future) that includes living with their parents through their 20s and marrying later. Additionally, material goods are far less important with 30 percent of surveyed Millennials indicating no intent to buy a car in the near future and another 25 percent expressing indifference toward automobile ownership (Goldman Sachs 2015).

Goldman Sachs' analysis concludes that "the must-haves for previous generations aren't as important for Millennials. They're putting off major purchases—or avoiding them entirely … Instead, they're turning to a new set of services that provide access to products without the burdens of ownership" (Goldman Sachs 2015). Such analyses can be contrasted with an equal number of studies reporting Millennials to be more self-absorbed, wasteful and greedy ("Millennials See Themselves as Greedy, Self-absorbed and Wasteful, Study Finds" 2015). These seemingly contradictory understandings of Millennials can be explained by returning to the two types of scenario that trigger moral reflection. In other words, perhaps greedy and self-absorbed Millennials are simply doubling down on the routines they were raised to believe would produce the desired future of success and happiness as defined by wealth and possessions. Meanwhile, other Millennials perceive themselves blocked from, and therefore choose to reject or at least question, such a future and the routines believed to produce it. Our aim of understanding how imagined futures might be brought into existence through contemporary cultural practices requires that we focus on newly emergent practices rather than old routines.

By examining urban agriculture and bicycle transportation as cultural impulses, we hope to illustrate how new desired futures are being constructed out of micro-utopian practices. Growth since the start of the millennium in the practices of urban agriculture and bicycling for transportation practically illustrate contemporary efforts to forge new identities with new meanings through enactment of new cultural forms. While both practices are embraced by many different generations, Millennials engage in these practices at higher rates. For example, with respect to declines in the use of automobiles, Noreen McDonald finds that "lifestyle-related demographic shifts between Millennials and Generation X (those born in the late 1960s to the late 1970s) account for 10 percent to 25 percent of the observed decrease in automobility, while Millennial-specific factors such as differing attitudes to mobility account for 35 percent to 50 percent of the observed decrease in auto use" (2015, 1–2). According to McDonald, another 40 percent can be attributed to declines in auto usage across all demographic groups during the late 2000s. These findings provide counter evidence to the lifespan arguments claiming that Millennial characteristics are not unique to the generation but rather to a period in the lifespan that all generations pass through. We are not unique in our optimism that these cultural impulses might be reflecting deeper social change.

Early manifestations of both urban agriculture and bicycling as transportation show signs of being reactions against the failed institutions of the industrial food and mobility systems, urban planning, and municipal governments. On the urban agriculture front, we see guerrilla gardeners spray medians, curb strips and other urban dead spaces with "seed bombs"; community-minded individuals occupy vacant lots with vegetable beds; impassioned food activists launch farm stands and farmers markets; all of which inspire innovations such as rooftop farms, mobile gardens and vertical farming. More importantly, these practices are leading to transformations of institutions and systems. For example, years of advocacy in Los Angeles by community groups like L.A. Green Rounds recently resulted in a code change that now allows Angelenos to plant fruits and vegetables in city-owned curb strips. As one commenter on an article about the new policy explained, "Edible parkways are not strictly about fresh food access. They are also about beautification, connection and communion" (Fox 2013), all of which are identified by studies of Millennials as key generational values (Goldman Sachs 2015; Pew Research Center 2014).

For some, like Novella Carpenter, an alternative food system might be a survival strategy in the face of an industrial food system that ravages the health of the planet and the health of the individual. For others, like author and essayist Rebecca Solnit, everyday alternative food system practices are nothing less than micro-utopian practices and revolutionary acts of hope. "We are in an era when gardens are front and center for hopes and dreams of a better world," writes Solnit, who sees gardening as a moral act:

> [I]magine the whole world as a garden, in which case you might want to weed out corporations, compost old divides, and plant hope, subversion, and fierce commitments among the heirloom tomatoes and the chard. The main questions will always be: What are your principal crops? And who do they feed?
>
> (Solnit 2012)

Across the U.S., urban policies ranging from health and building codes to parking and land use laws are being transformed by urban agriculturalists engaged in practices from backyard animal husbandry to home-based preparation of commercial foodstuffs.

Similarly, on the transportation front, in cities around the world guerrilla bike activists paint bike lanes to address the failure of transportation planners to design safe streets for bicyclists; "bike parties" are supplanting the contentious and political Critical Mass rides that arose in the 1990s; on-street parking for cars converted to "bicycle corrals" that hold up to 20 bicycles in the space previously reserved for a single car; car-free streets events are now a global phenomenon thanks to the influence of Bogotá's 40-year tradition of Ciclovía that closes certain streets to cars each Sunday; and relatively new events like Park(ing) Day, an annual celebration originating in San Francisco during which the public spaces of street parking are taken over and turned into "parks," have also spread globally. Lusi Morhayim contends that "[t]hese events have not only been effective in promoting bicycle culture, but they have also resulted in a reimagining of the potential for public engagement in the quality of urban streets" (2015, 227). In short, structures of civic engagement, as well as civic codes themselves, are being transformed. Incrementally, through micro-utopian practices, new futures are being constructed.

The practices of urban agriculture and bicycling as transportation represent emergent routines of action intended to address a specific human or social need in alternative ways to the dominant cultural norm. While they may harken back to countercultural practices of the 1960s, neither reflects strategies of the old dominant social life processes such as working within institutions or seeking culturally identified goals as means to producing future desired outcomes. In both cases, Millennials as well as urban dwellers across a wide range of race, class and generational categories are envisioning the future of their cities and, frustrated with the inability of standard social life processes to produce the desired future, experimenting with alternatives. To the extent that their experiments are inclusive, meliorative, and aimed at the public good, they can be seen in Meadian terms as moral actions resulting from the exercise of choices arising from empirical methods for discerning preferable futures and pursuing cooperative social action to achieve them.

To conclude, we would like to bring our discussion back around to Callenbach. In particular, we would like to imagine how Callenbach might have interpreted Yeats. When the gyre widens and the centre cannot hold, what would Callenbach imagine might be a rational response? When institutions and even self-concepts are destabilized how do we find hope? How do we move forward?

In "Epistle to the Ecotopians" (Callenbach 2012), a document found on Callenbach's computer after his death, we have a possible answer. "When old institutions and habits break down or consume themselves," wrote Callenbach, "new experimental shoots begin to appear, and people explore and test and share new and better ways to survive together." Callenbach continued:

> It is never easy or simple. But already we see, under the crumbling surface of the conventional world, promising developments: new ways of organizing economic activity (cooperatives, worker-owned companies, nonprofits, trusts)... new ways of building compact, congenial cities that are low (or even self-sufficient) in energy use ... A vision of sustainability that sometimes shockingly resembles Ecotopia is tremulously coming into existence at the hands of people who never heard of the book.

If the future is emergent in social interaction, then we propose interpreting the "experimental shoots" to which Callenbach alludes as micro-utopian practices aimed at building "pragmatic utopias." Essential to these pragmatic utopias is their grounding of both existential hope and utopian thinking. As Patrick Shade explains, the "social dimension of hoping thus becomes especially clear" when we view "our ability to foster connection between our own ends and abilities and those of others" as a vital resource (2001, 90).

More than four decades removed from its publication, and in the context of contemporary cultural impulses and "experimental shoots," Callenbach's *Ecotopia* takes on new meaning. Rather than serving merely as an "either-or" contrast to a hypothetical dystopia, Ecotopia becomes a way of pointing to the pragmatic possibilities of "both-and." We *both* occupy the potentially dystopian Anthropocene, *and* engage hopefully in micro-utopian practices and "experimental shoots" with the intention of bringing forth an Ecotopian future. Returning once again to Le Guin's understanding of futures always being latent in the past, we find compelling a twenty-first century interpretation of *Ecotopia*, not as prescription for utopian future, but as a lens for reading cultural impulses emerging at the start of the twenty-first century as micro-utopian practices through which new moralities are negotiated and alternative futures generated.

The only questions that remain are how enduring these cultural impulses and "experimental shoots" will be and how widespread they will become? While the falcons among us do the daily work of building alternative futures by undertaking small experiments in permaculture or practicing the cultural impulses we describe, the falconers tempt them with the degenerate utopias of Hollywood's entertainment and Silicon Valley's social media streams. But at least some of the falcons cannot hear the falconers. Meanwhile, a vast majority continues to embrace the future that we have described here as destabilized. As their tenuous grip on such an uncertain future slips, they too will begin the collective work of envisioning new futures, constructing new moralities, and defining new right actions. And these futures, assuming they are built around core values such as the desire to sustain ecosystems supportive of human life (a large but necessary assumption), will in the end finally produce permacultures with all their dynamism and erraticism, yet always within the evolving limits of a stable system.

References

Callenbach, Ernest. 1975. *Ecotopia: The Notebooks and Reports of William Weston*. Berkeley, CA: Bantam Tree Books.

Callenbach, Ernest. "Tomgram: Ernest Callenbach, Last Words to an America in Decline." *TomDispatch*. (6 May 2012). Available online at: www.tomdispatch.com/post/175538/tomgram (last accessed 4 May 2017).

Canavan, Gerry. 2012. "Theories of Everything: Science Fiction, Totality, and Empire in the Twentieth Century." PhD dissertation, Duke University.

Canavan, Gerry. 2014. "Introduction: If This Goes On." In Gerry Canavan and Kim Stanley Robinson (eds) *Green Planets: Ecology and Science Fiction*, 1–21. Middletown, CT: Wesleyan University Press.

Carpenter, Novella. 2009. *Farm City: The Education of an Urban Farmer*. New York: Penguin.

Collins, Suzanne. 2008. *The Hunger Games*. New York: Scholastic.

Collins, Suzanne. 2010. *Mockingjay*. New York: Scholastic.

Collins, Suzanne and Elizabeth B. Parisi. 2009. *Catching Fire*. New York: Scholastic.

Dozois, Gardner (ed.). 2001. *Worldmakers: SF Adventures in Terraforming*. New York: St. Martin's Griffin.

Fox, Hayley. 2013. "The push to grow fruits, vegetables on the land between streets and sidewalks in Los Angeles," *KPCC radio*. Available online at: www.scpr.org/news/2013/09/09/39061/the-push-to-grow-fruits-vegetables-on-the-land-bet (last accessed 28 October 2016).

Goldman Sachs. 2015. "Millennials: Coming of Age." Available online at: www.goldman-sachs.com/our-thinking/outlook/millennials (last accessed 28 October 2016).

Gund Institute. "Life in a Desirable Future." (YouTube, June 8, 2011). Available online at: https://youtu.be/W7nSASQy0ys (last accessed 23 October 2016).

Hamilton, Clive. 2010. *Requiem for a Species: Why We Resist the Truth about Climate Change*. New York: Earthscan.

Harvey, David. 2000. *Spaces of Hope*. Berkeley, CA: University of California Press.

HM Government. (n.d.) "What is the EU?" Available online at: www.eureferendum.gov.uk/what-is-the-eu/# (last accessed 28 October 2016).

Jameson, Frederic. 2005. *Archaeologies of the Future: The Desire Called Utopia and Other Science Fictions*. New York: Verso.

Kallis, Giorgos and Hug March. 2015. "Imaginaries of Hope: The Utopianism of Degrowth." *Annals of the Association of American Geographers* 105(2): 360–368.

LeGuin, Ursula K. 2015. *The Dispossessed*. Hachette UK.

McDonald, Noreen C. "Are Millennials Really the "Go-Nowhere" Generation?." *Journal of the American Planning Association* 81, no. 2 (2015): 90–103.

McKibben, Bill. 1989. *The End of Nature*. New York: Random House Incorporated.

Mead, George Herbert. (1934/2015). *Mind, Self and Society* (The Definitive Edition). Chicago, IL: The University of Chicago Press.

Milbrath, Lester W. 1989. *Envisioning a Sustainable Society*. Albany, NY: SUNY Press.

"Millennials See Themselves as Greedy, Self-absorbed and Wasteful, Study Finds." *The Guardian*, September 3, 2015. Available online at: www.theguardian.com/society/2015/sep/04/millennials-see-themselves-as-greedy-self-absorbed-and-wasteful-study-finds (last accessed 28 October 2016).

Morhayim, Lusi. 2015. "Fixing the City in the Context of Neoliberalism: Institutionalized DIY." In *Incomplete Streets: Processes, Practices and Possibilities*, edited by Stephen Zavestoski and Julian Agyeman, 225–244. New York: Routledge.

Pew Research Center. 2014. "Millennials in Adulthood: Detached from Institutions, Networked with Friends." Available online at: www.pewsocialtrends.org/files/2014/03/2014-03-07_generations-report-version-for-web.pdf (last accessed 28 October 2016).

Ramachandran, Ayesha. 2015. *The Worldmakers: Global Imagining in Early Modern Europe*. Chicago, IL: University of Chicago Press.

Roth, Veronica. 2011. *Divergent*. New York: Katherine Tegen Books.

Roth, Veronica. 2012. *Insurgent*. New York: Katherine Tegen Books.

Roth, Veronica. 2013. *Allegiant*. New York: Katherine Tegen Books.

Scranton, Roy. 2015. *Learning to Die in the Anthropocene: Reflections on the End of a Civilization*. San Francisco, CA: City Lights Publishers.

Shade, Patrick. 2001. *Habits of Hope: A Pragmatic Theory*. Nashville, TN: Vanderbilt University Press.

Smith, Jeremy Adam. 2010a, 20 July. "The Weeds of Ecotopia." *Shareable*. Available online at: www.shareable.net/blog/the-weeds-of-ecotopia (last accessed 28 October 2016).

Smith, Jeremy Adam. 2010b, 20 July. "The Weeds of Ecotopia, Part Two." *Shareable*. Available online at: www.shareable.net/blog/ernest-callenbach-novella-carpenter-ecotopia-part-two (last accessed 28 October 2016).

Solnit, R. 2012. "Revolutionary Plots." *Orion Magazine*. Available online at: https://orionmagazine.org/article/revolutionary-plots (last accessed 28 October 2016).

Sternbergh, Adam. 2014, Aug 22. "We've Reached Peak Dystopia, But Is It Possible to Imagine Utopia Anymore?" *Vulture*. Available online at: www.vulture.com/2014/08/why-cant-anybody-write-a-utopian-novel-anymore.html (last accessed 28 October 2016).

Sternbergh, Adam. 2016, July 27. "Is the Present Worse Than Any Fictional, Futuristic Dystopia?" *Vulture*. Available online at: www.vulture.com/2016/07/the-present-worse-than-fictional-dystopias.html (last accessed 28 October 2016).

Tabor, Nick. 2015, 7 April. "No Slouch." *The Paris Review*. Available online at: www.theparisreview.org/blog/2015/04/07/no-slouch (last accessed 28 October 2016).

3 Reclaiming accountability from hypertechnocivility, to grow again the flowering Earth

Patrick Jones

A predicament

At a time when neoliberalism is still widely considered the steady ship in a rocky harbour—a safe vessel in which sits the possibility of transport for our dreams, comfort and desires—where does accountability reside? Have we obfuscated personal, household, community and locasphere[1] responsibilities by the way in which we perform our unarguably anthropocentric lifeways? By the way in which we farm out our resource gathering to unknowable, faraway, vested interests? By how these interests extract with a linear, even violent hatred of what Martín Prechtel (1999) calls "the Flowering Earth," because taking from another isn't the same thing as taking from one's own?

With western-constructed demands, specifically neoliberalism's insistence on maintaining an entertaining dominance over all subjects and things, what has happened to our sense of collective purpose that Deborah Bird Rose identifies as "[a]n ethical response to the call of others?" (2011, 18). It appears that a significant limit of the so-called "global village" is a somewhat flippant disregard for the intimacy and sovereignty of a walked and loved homeplace—diverse and animist and not governed exclusively by people. Is it the case today that we are too energetically capable to be intimate with such a place and its many communities? Must we car, bus, train and fly to further fields because we are bored by a now limited sense of what constitutes *local* as we've come to experience "the other" from far away? We might still walk out from the hearth of our dwelling place, and sense a neighbourly warmth with it, but what immediate knowledges of, or relationships with, a flowering locasphere do we possess as we approach our local shopping centre selling originless food, inebriates and other mined and packaged consumables we've come to pay money for?

Only imperialist cultures place technology and industry ahead of the communities of the living that give agency to the flowerings of the earth[2] that make more life possible. In foregrounding technology we have backgrounded our understanding of how our locaspheres function. We have left this work to specialists, to ecologists who sit at desks computing figures and statistics, and after brief "field" trips make general claims about the operations of intimate life from university offices far away. Can we name our neighbouring species, the ones that live in our guts, on our skin, in our mouths and around our homes that contribute to making more life possible? Do we know their functions? Do we sense the gifts that are being made to us each day by the more-than-human communities of the living?

The ringtail possum has recently made the newcomer hawthorn its desired habitat tree, a tree whose dense thorny branches protect it from foxes, dogs and powerful owls. In return, the possum drops waste nutrients for the tree to take up, or the tree's mycelium to convert into food. The mycelium draws up and distributes minerals to the tree through its roots so it can grow upright and head towards the giving sun, and then in exchange the tree returns sugars to the mycelium, provides habitat for critters and releases oxygen into the atmosphere so all can breathe and sing more life forth. And while there is much more going on than this simple narrative of interspecies relationships, ecologists from faraway universities haven't ascribed any ecological status to the hawthorn in my intimate locasphere, despite its emplacing relationships of reciprocity with such others. According to official science, the hawthorn doesn't appear on a list of "correct" species; rather, it appears on an "invasive" list, and therefore is subject to poisons, burnings and bulldozing.

The marking of things with specific labels enables them to be either accepted or rejected in extreme terms. Labels such as "intruder" or "invader," are what Alphonso Lingis (1994) recognizes as value-terms, and "for every value-term," he writes, "there is its opposite: good-bad, just-unjust, virtuous-vicious, beautiful-ugly, and useful-useless. These terms," he continues, "seem to be constructed as specifications of the most extreme kind of opposition, that of positive and negative … the meaning of the one can be the simple negation of the other" (47). For each species categorized in Australia, ecologists will group them as either indigenous or non-indigenous. A hierarchy exists that establishes "indigenous" as legitimate and "non-indigenous" as not, even if the species has come from another part of the nation-state continent, or has been included as part of the food economy of Indigenous people in Australia after colonization. This creates an oppositional line falling either side of the year 1788, the point at which Australia was invaded by imperialist science, technology and industry and ascribed such things as numbers according to a Christian calendar. Scientists themselves, however, are not confined to categorization because there exists a Promethean belief in the godlikeness of western agency. In other words, we consider ourselves immortal due to our technical apparatuses, despite the fact we are animals that must die. Agricultural and garden plants, which are bought and sold, belong to a uniquely different classification than indigenous or non-indigenous. While they remain encased within fences and in a marketplace they retain a privileged status or classification not really ascribed to ecology. Our own lives, lived behind walls, screens and fences, place us in this same class. Like monetized agricultural plants and animals, we are domesticated, and, in our complementary domestication with fossil energies, we have produced a powerful force against life, which I call *hypertechnocivility*.

Hypertechnocivility can be understood as the foregrounding of cities and technology contiguous with the imperatives of one of the west's creator-masters, Prometheus, at the expense of our ecological wits, or memory, as played out in our double creator, Prometheus's twin, Epimetheus, whom Bernard Stiegler calls the God of the Fault of Forgetting. The west's creation story is an endless doubling of total mastery and totalizing amnesia and, therefore, true to this story, Prometheus is a household name and Epimetheus is barely known. While Epimetheus can be considered a metaphor for implementing the precautionary principle, he is rarely, if at all, called upon to do this. Stiegler (1998) suggests that "permanent innovation" involves permanent "techno-scientific war." A restless innovation anxiety fanned by industry is part of the condition of our eternal unsettlement and unrest.

How we class ourselves and others by ascribing value-terms might be considered a trigger point for the violent hatred we commit to the non-domesticated flowering earth, which we rationalise or justify to claim our comforts and rights of possession. Lingis doesn't consider value-terms as conceptual or mental constructions, but rather contagions, infecting "the language…picked up like a virus" (1994, 61). In creating the word hypertechnocivility to describe extreme Prometheanism and what Deborah Bird Rose calls "man-made mass death" (2011, 82), I am very deliberately positioning hypertechnocivility's opposition to flowering earth itself. In this case, this is not a mutual opposition because the flowering earth does not require hyper-technocivility. My intention in creating the term is to produce its redundancy as a set of values and as a force or interruption against life.

Hypertechnocivilians represent an extreme oppositional force in the way in which we gather and process the materials we require to make life, which in turn constructs an essentially go-it-alone speciesism that has established life as a global destructive monoculture, absorbing diverse cultures to construct one large mediated "blob," to cite Thomas de Zengotita (2005). An almost indescribable blob whose main organizing force is the global pool of money, or rather IOUs.

What is it that we now do for trees, mycelium, possums? While industry art and science are central to Promethean cosmology, where do our "earth others," to reference Val Plumwood (2002), reside within the west's most archetypal and influential creation myth, second only to Judeo-Christianity's expulsion from the garden? As mammals, perhaps the very least we could do is return our body's waste to the humus of the earth that makes more life possible. But where has all the humus gone? And where have the water-absorbing perennial grasslands and desert ecologies (not made by humans) gone? Ecologies that could also take in our micturates and excreta and turn them back into more life. Instead of performing returns (death, decay and waste), we are encouraged to rationalize our interruptions and destruc-tiveness, and focus only on new life, youth and consumption. Under such a seemingly linear but actually viral conception of life we chop down more forests every year, and advance aggregating plant monocultures to feed originless food to mostly human-only populations, throwing out a third of it annually.[3] Those who fall under the intoxicating spells of western idolatry, rationalize the destruction of the other as the foremost imperative of Promethean domination by ascribing value-terms such as "invasive." It is never one who obeys the imperatives of western idolatry who is considered the "invader" or "destroyer".

Waste production, via complicated, globalized, energy-intensive distribution systems, is not only a byproduct of affluent consumption, but a byproduct of the imperative of western values, which must place demands upon, or simply destroy, the other. We are so many things—machines, gods, mortals, mammals. And in this cacophony we grow up fending for ourselves, making relationships with those who will support our desire to make our lives comfortable at whatever cost is necessary. But is this all we are?

Two responses

I want to examine now the possibilities of two complementary movements that present a challenge to modern imperialism (now shrewdly rebranded as global development), and whose ethics call for, and set forward, principles that attempt to reclaim personal accountability for one's communications, resources and actions.

The two movements are nonviolent communication (NVC) and permaculture, which can be considered more broadly as empathic listening (or compassionate communication) and regenerative bioregional accountability (or regenerative relocalization), respectively. Both are language modes, and both have been conceived as responses to the imperatives of demand and destruction that the west's dominion-ideology has established. Both share similar origin points, both are movements based on principles whose moral compasses were set in the global peace movement of the late 1960s, early 1970s. Both are responses to the predicament of systemic violence. And both call upon personal accountability, taking responsibility for one's actions.

Nonviolent communication is a language mode that orientates the mind towards "reclaiming the evidence of the heart," to call on Anthony Steinbock (2014), in order to listen deeply to the needs of others and the needs of oneself. Permaculture is a biophysical language that applies or mimics ecological processes to perform life in which waste, death and decay share equal value with birth, growth and consumption, so that regeneration is made possible.

Such responses to the predicament of our time cannot be thought of in absolute terms. All movements present problems and there cannot be one simple fix to the multifarious challenges of our age. Both NVC and permaculture offer promising, not exclusive, principles and ideas for our multifarious transitions towards peace and ecological functioning.

I first want to examine NVC.

Marshall Rosenberg—who developed and gave form to NVC, taking on the empathic work of Carl Rodgers, Mahatma Gandhi's nonviolent philosophy, and eastern thought more generally such as Mahayana Buddhist action theory that states all violence begins in the mind—developed the idea that violent action and communication stem from unmet needs. Rosenberg's work particularly addresses communication that blocks compassion:

> We all pay dearly when people respond to our values and needs not out of a desire to give from the heart, but out of fear, guilt, or shame. Sooner or later, we will experience the consequences of diminished goodwill on the part of those who comply with our values out of a sense of either external or internal coercion. They too, pay emotionally, for they are likely to feel resentment and decreased self-esteem when they respond to us out of fear, guilt, or shame. Furthermore, each time others associate us in their minds with any of these

feelings, the likelihood of their responding compassionately to our needs and values in the future decreases.

(2003a, 17)

For forty years until his death in 2015, Rosenberg worked with couples, families, communities, feuding gangs and with opposing groups in war zones, developing the theory and practice of NVC. A man of Jewish ancestry, he once famously role-played a conversation with Adolf Hitler (2003b) where he empathically queried him and listened to his responses to ascertain what his needs were and why they weren't being met. For Rosenberg there is no monster. A monster is formed in the mind and becomes a self-fulfilling prophecy among a community of people who don't respond to that suffering person with attention and tenderness.

In a number of YouTube presentations, Rosenberg speaks about the origins of NVC as deriving from traditional peoples. Peoples who raised their children without scoldings, scorn or punishment. Sven Lindquist writes on the contact wars in Australia, referring to the diaries of white explorers and early settlers:

> What a provocation, the Aborigines' whole lifestyle, particularly their inter-action with their children, must have been to the British! A childhood without shame, without guilt, without punishment! Surely a great sense of loss must have welled up inside them, a sense of missing all these things they were now condemning as neglect, defective hygiene, lack of manners and discipline.
>
> (2012, 69)

Rosenberg (2000) asserts that before imperialism we all spoke "Giraffe", which is his (albeit global blob) metaphor for "big-hearted." Prechtel gives an example of what this looked like for his beloved Mayan village before anthropocentric forces— Marxists, fascists and Catholicism—smashed it apart in the 1980s. He writes:

> In those days of chiefs, initiations, and feasts, true Tzutujil elders like Ma Maxit were called Echo People, not because they had a lot of knowledge but because their vision and creativity caused a lot of knowledge to be learnt. An Echo Person never enforced eloquence with slaps, violence, or scolding but by simply ignoring everything that wasn't eloquent or heartfelt. The effects of this kind of inspiration echoed on the Earth long after his or her tired old heart gave out, and for this they were never forgotten. Their echoing sound merged like a memory spoken with the sounds the Gods made as they perpetually sang the world alive.
>
> (1999, 270)

Making the world more alive through compassionate speech, song and empathic listening is Rosenberg's ambition for NVC.

The opposing language to Giraffe is what Rosenberg termed "Jackal," which can be understood as a language of invasion, retaliation, coercion and propaganda, which is, in short, playing the game of right and wrong. Rosenberg (2000) wrote that we are born Giraffe but are quickly schooled or scolded to learn Jackal, to perform reactionary thought and behaviour, opportunistic violence, governed by a pack mentality.

It's perhaps ironic, if not a limit of NVC, that a method of training people to move beyond polarizing evaluations of others sets up such an overt dichotomy using two animals with markedly opposing characteristics as a metaphor. Another limit to consider for the development of NVC is Rosenberg's use of the word shame. "Shame is a form of self-hatred," he writes, "and actions taken in reaction to shame are not free and joyful acts"; he goes so far to as write that shame and guilt are "destructive energies" (2003a, 131). Steinbock has a somewhat broader understanding of the word. He writes that "[t]he creative personal dimension of shame as self-revelatory enables shame to have a critical dimension; it can modify how I understand myself and how I am to be" (Steinbock 2014, 76). While Steinbock acknowledges the coercive, often violent tendencies of shame (onto oneself) and shaming (onto others) that Rosenberg addresses, there is more to the word than just this narrative. "Shame calls me into question," Steinbock writes, "it is not something that I will; and is in fact an experience I wish to avoid" (76). Rosenberg writes of such avoidance that

> [t]here may be some tasks we choose to do to avoid shame. We know that if we don't do them, we'll end up suffering severe self-judgement, hearing our own voice telling us there is something wrong or stupid about us. If we do something stimulated solely by the urge to avoid shame, we will generally end up detesting it.
>
> (2003a, 131)

Both Rosenberg and Steinbock are seeking ways in which to re-engage the heart and be clearer about the emotions that sit behind us as we speak to ourselves or to others. Steinbock writes,

> [shame] holds me in check precisely in my sovereignty over others as self-salience and resistance to others. But just because this aspect of my freedom is called into question as insistence/resistance, it does not mean that shame is not "creative" or that it does not occur within the sphere of the person.
>
> (Steinbock 2014, 76)

So shame can be both destructive and creative, and most likely a mix of the two, depending on what stands behind the shame and the language constructed for and around its arrival. The same goes for guilt, risk, duty, obligation, and indebtedness, which are predetermined by organized frameworks that belong to our personal histories, as Krishnamurti articulates:

> Observe for yourself how the brain operates. It is the storehouse of memory, of the past. This memory is responding all the time, as like and dislike, justifying, condemning and so on; it is responding according to its conditioning, according to the culture, religion, education, which it has stored.
>
> (1972, 75)

Binaries are hidden in the conceits of our prejudices. Critique is by nature always grappling with binaries, and regardless of our scholarliness or intuitive wisdom it is impossible to experience, observe and form logic, values or meaning without setting up oppositions. Krishnamurti writes that dualism resides in experience, as the experiencer and the thing experienced are at once in duality. Dualism is intrinsic to human life; it is unavoidable to experience. But it need not be reduced to "the sticky addictive web of simplistic polarized Eurocentric thinking," which Prechtel observed in the annihilation of the indigenous community that had so graciously adopted him and he so willingly loved, admired and communed with, for the overriding project of making the earth flower again and again, generation after generation.

This same polarizing thought governs our institutions that legalize western political imperatives of incarcerating and leaving in limbo those fleeing the wars the west has initiated or fanned under the banner of development.

NVC requires a critical identification that there is indeed something wrong with the way in which human beings are communicating, and this results in the extent of destructive violence apparent in the world. That our communications are not always eloquent or heartfelt and wholly purposed to enable the earth to flower again is evident in the way in which we make deserts and poison the land for agriculture, detonate it for minerals, drill for fuels that enable even more destruction, and construct mass poverty through resource wars, displacement, superiority, and cultural meddling and shaming.

Nonviolent communication begins with awareness, before one speaks or writes. *What am I feeling? What will I express now I know what I'm feeling? Am I thinking in superior terms? Am I meeting my needs?* Then after I am aware of what stands behind me before I speak, *what is my intention? Do I need to connect with another, or do I need to punish, manipulate or control?* By understanding the intention, we can turn the lens back onto *who we are*, rather than fixate on *we are not that*. So rather than, *You said that cruelly*, which is an evaluation where the person speaking assumes a righteous position to judge what is "cruel," the language shifts to, *I felt wounded when I heard that spoken*. It is a seemingly subtle shift, but the social implications are significant. Rather than retaliation, which can be considered the violence of minorities or those that feel disempowered, a conversation is instead enabled because the person in pain doesn't hit back, but rather seeks to connect by expressing what is being felt. This takes courage.

Those who, due to historical, educative or economic privilege, incite a violence of dominance must recognize that we are beneficiaries of the comforts, products and entertainments neoliberalism creates that coopt and make us so indebted to its cause. While compassion is central to NVC it should not become a language mode that apologizes on behalf of those who implement and endorse destructive forms of life making and economy. How NVC can aid a peaceful transition from the permanent war economy of neoliberalism to permanent flowering accountable bioregional economies is not by obfuscating critique but rather enabling a way for language to be used that becomes postwar, compassionate and productive.

Words make wars well before guns and bombs, armies and drones are brought in. While I wish for neoliberalism to be composted, I do not wish to see retribution, killings and more bloody revolution in its overhaul. I want to see diverse, walked-for, non-monetized, fully relocalized, organic gardening economies flourish so all people have nourishing food, and all peoples can make connections and form relationships with the communities of life that are much more than human. But these bioregional worlds cannot be constructed by force. They have to aggregate with love, care, and ecological knowledge that become everyone's imperative regardless of what else people do in their lives. The flowering earth, not man-made mass death, has to become a universal framework to support relocalization of diverse cultures, lifeways, economies.

While the language modes in my life and writing still skip between Giraffe and Jackal, I'm starting to sense what can be achieved in transitioning to more conscious communications, and as a critical thinker I ask how compassion for those with other values can better be heard and understood, and how people's needs, including my own, can be better expressed and met.

Permaculture is the portmanteau for permanent culture. The concept, developed by Bill Mollison and David Holmgren, was inspired by the moment of *The Limits to Growth* report (1972), which identified a serious structural problem with an endless-growth hegemony imposed on a finite planet. Permaculture may be of little interest to those who believe in inexhaustible human development, or at the very least accept it and believe nothing is broken. Permaculture will not interest those who think there is no industrial culture problem; who think pollution is just a word created by people and therefore has no real biophysicality; who believe the Anthropocene and anthropogenic climate change are not happening, or that bioregionalism is just romantic nostalgia for "premodern ('mythic') societies."[4] But for those who do believe there is in fact a problem, the principles of permaculture are more likely to appeal and therefore may be studied and applied. It is the pragmatism and ecological knowledge of premodern societies, especially in their capacity to work in ecological relationship and within material limits to ensure permanent regeneration, that permaculture regards so very useful to its sciences and arts.

The co-originators of permaculture, Holmgren and Mollison, devised design strategies for human settlements that drew on the collective intelligence of perennial ecologies and the indigenous-agrarian peoples of place who live/lived closely with and imbibed this intelligence.

Permaculture acts as a framework for life beyond pollution, beyond destructive affluence and acute anthropocentrism. It demonstrates how to regain low-tech, low-tooled, low-carbon and low-mediated, lean ways of living where imported resources are increasingly limited and more-than-human patterns of existence can be better understood and applied where people are foremost (before governments, bureaucracies or corporations), accountable for their actions. Permaculture attempts to prepare people for an inevitable energy descent and climate-uncertain future while re-engaging in life as accountable mammals of place.

Vested interests from far away can never hold such intimacy, care and intelligence for a loved locasphere. In a recorded conversation I had with David Holmgren in 2012, I asked him what the models for permaculture have been:

> ...cultures of place that have persisted over long periods. These are primarily indigenous and long established agrarian societies that have worked within those

limits, at least for very long periods of time without a constant growth necessity, and therefore without catastrophic collapses.

It was in learning, then applying Holmgren's principles of permaculture—creatively use and respond to change, produce no waste, use and value diversity, integrate rather than segregate, apply self-regulation and accept feedback, use edges and value the marginal, and so on—that I began to realise how low-mediated, low-tooled foraging, hunting, gardening cultures could be reclaimed that enable people to be increasingly accountable for their actions and lifeways. I sense that a long time ago my ancestors lived in accordance to such limits on sacred land and to have done this they must have had exceptional knowledges—about plants and geology, water and soils, cooking and preparing food, about weather patterns and earth others. Knowledges that are all but lost today, replaced or disappeared by an unprecedented reliance upon technology, mastery and money.

While crude oil has arguably created tremendous levels of Promethean complexity (which to some is considered intelligence), it has also produced twinned or countering amounts of Epimethean amnesia. Such Titan-like hypertechnocivility is eternally robbing Peter to pay Paul; masterfulness falling eternally into forget-fulness. This mastery-amnesia doubling also robs from the spirit to share the world with our earth others. Gifts do not flow with the imperatives of mastery. Perma-culture's redress of the relationship we have to food and energy offers the potential for the redress of relationships we may have with our earth others. An ethical response to the call of earth others is at the heart of this redress.

Flowering, again

While the limits and violence of historical privilege have affected and can further affect the efficacy of NVC and permaculture, there is much to take from both movements.

Prechtel describes his village as being gender-distributed where the hierarchy is forever changing form so that no one person or group dominates. The hierarchy is in service to the collective wellness of the village and to life itself; it is not a vested interest strategizing dominance over the people and the land. The positions are sacred and the elders suffer economically and emotionally because of the great amount of unpaid in-service work they're required to do, particularly in initiating the young people to carry on the work of making the village well and singing the land into abundance and health. Prechtel alerts us to our fate when this work does not occur:

> When there are no true initiations and the people lose their land, entire country, or purpose, their relationship with the Earth evaporates. One of the most common ways groups of destroyed people try to reinvent themselves is by pointing to some others and saying "We are not that" instead of being able to say "We are this."

> (Prechtel 1999, 361)

This essentially is a language shift from peace (*we are this*) to war (*we are not that*), which begins in the mind and tribalizes out into sport, religion, business, institutions and political parties. Tribalism grows out of a fear that *we are not that; that is not good*. As value-terms become more extreme, so too is how the opposition is perceived. Prechtel is describing the exploits of mediated modern imperialism when he writes

> [t]here are tribalist fundamentalist movements in every nation of the world now, peoples who had their original relationship with their stories, music, ancestral histories, and customs destroyed or trivialized by the heavy tread of some other traumatized people...
>
> (1999, 362)

This legacy of aggregating trauma, which stems (if a starting point is indeed possible to determine) from grain bag and horseback imperialism, is what Deborah Bird Rose (2011) identifies through her Aboriginal teachers as an interruption to life. Aboriginal poet, Samuel Wagan Watson, represents such interruption as western "scientific justification":

> ... the shapeshifters skulk around the dingo lounge
> haunted by the screaming engines of the machines of
> consequence
> longevity just a whisper in the wind
> as their numbers dwindle
> and the dark hours are stolen by the monsters of new:
> drug addicts, paedophiles and killers
> the spirits have almost lost their foothold
> the children of the rainbow serpent have no use for demons
> scientific justification has rationalised their roles with prozac
> and institutionalisation...
>
> (2004, 52)

Imperialist science's role in development is implicit. The primary imperative is to drive profits and convert all people to a totalizing dependence on the monetary economy. And it's an unfolding story. But not all science is industry-directed and curtailed. Permaculture offers science reacquaintance with the sacred and with the communities of the living, despite the loathing of the "spiritual" and of "community" that Mollison was subject to spouting.[5] In its repulsion of religion and the sacred, science has emulated a new force of polarizing hatred. Science doesn't like in itself what it sees in religion, because science and religion share developmental history. How the religiosity of the Enlightenment still entangles western-derived science; how yoga, which calls itself a science, appears as religion. Perhaps if religion and science accepted that they were part of the arts and thus bound by subjective experience (or multiple objectivities), and the arts then worked towards a post-anthropocentric frame,[6] such polarizing forces that lead people to mental and physical warring might be greatly reduced.

How did we communicate when our people were foremost involved in making the world flower again and again, when cynicism didn't rule the minds of our elders? When mothership, the ultimate form of regeneration and flowering, was worshipped by all and more expansive than human-centricity? How did we speak to each other when there was no dominant patriarchy but a pantheon of male, female and animal deities who distributed gender and qualities, who understood the man in the woman and the woman in man, and the maleness, femaleness and at times asexualness or other-sexualness of the world's worlds?

My own ancestry begins as indigene then pagan peasant of Europe before becoming Christianized, land dispossessed, working class, boat person, land dispossessing alien, then (via crude oil-induced wealth) middle class in the past two generations. While I recognize the privileges and comforts of my parents' and my own generation, and what this privilege stands upon, I feel closer to the lifeways of my indigenous and peasant ancestors, and the lifeways of the Dja Dja Wurrung, whose country I now call home. And I've felt this since as early as I can remember. So if under examination I'm not represented as: *Displaced indig-peasant emplacing on traumatized yet renewing Dja Dja Wurrung spoken-for country, actively making connections with a new homeplace, attempting to keep my ancestors' deities (whom I only barely sense but wish to open further to) nourished on the stewarded fruits made in community on old sacred Aboriginal country, acknowledging the old deities of this Jaara land, especially Bunjil the eagle and Waa the crow (the creators who taught Jaara people how to perform life as beings much more than human), wanting and aiding the earth to concurrently flower like my own old people*, then I am probably being framed violently.

In a time-impoverished culture of dominance-retaliation, "white-middle-class-male" gets you there faster.

Speed is certainly part of the story of communicative violence and disabling the earth to flower concurrently. An essay such as this, despite the patriarchal form and historical privilege it is welded to, is a chance to go slow, or at least slower, and attend to the sort of negative evaluations that roll from the mind and onto the tongue so quickly. As a writer I sit on privileged stiles, which gives me some access to observe privatized and shocked land, but as a forester, gardener, father and hunter, I know this shock beyond words and fences. As a writer I hold a privileged arena to write beyond retaliation. Yet, as I have discussed in another work (Jones 2014), I note ecological cultures of place that have come before us are oral cultures, and although writing gives political agency, important for the transitions of now, we must also question its validity as we move towards creating new forms of ecological regard and intelligence.

Of course, permaculture, like NVC, is a product of globalism, yet provides the possibility of relocalization, of a return to bioregional accountability and the locaspheric heart. While the practice of both will have to continue alongside violent imperialisms, fanaticisms, and ideologies for a while longer, especially while humans have access to powerful fuels essential for the production of hypertechnocivility, both permaculture and NVC offer people and their communities scope to jump the big neoliberal ship and learn to swim in the rock pools of less certain but regenerative economic models that attempt to commit little harm to the world's worlds, and indeed perform life as ecological participants.

If left unchecked, hypertechnocivility will lead to a total loss of ecological intelligence, species diversity, and leave our own species evermore vulnerable to disasters of our own making, for "[t]echnofix solutions make no attempt," writes Plumwood, "to rethink human culture, dominant lifestyles and demands on nature, indeed they tend to assume that these are unchangeable"(2002, 8).

We can work politically to transform the global imperative from war to blossoming; we can model new, or remodel traditional, economies that are low-harm, regenerative and inclusive; we can learn and relearn to speak with compassion and listen empathically; we can begin or continue this work without being hungry, thirsty, cold, expiring under the sun or alone; and we can do this work without waiting for governments, institutions, businesses or saviours to join the universal project that the entire force of more-than-human life is already involved with— enabling the earth to flower again, generation after generation, life cycle into life cycle, compost upon compost.

Notes

1   Locasphere is a term I have developed to describe the intimate and creaturely homeplace of a loved and walked-for *local* bioregion.
2   I intentionally use lowercase 'e' when using *earth*, to broaden its confining one-world identity as a proper noun, and give it a place of common substance and form with the intimate sensibilities of creatures and within the bioregions of the world's worlds.
3   See Nadia El-Hage Scialabba, ed. 2013. *Food Wastage Footprint: Impact on Natural Resources Summary Report*, Food and Agriculture Organization (FAO). www.fao.org/docrep/018/i3347e/i3347e.pdf (accessed 1 October 2016).
4   For more on this, see Biro (2005) *Denaturalizing Ecological Politics: Alienation from Nature from Rousseau to the Frankfurt School and Beyond*, University of Toronto Press.
5   ABC sound archive replayed in the podcast: *Farewell to the father of the global permaculture movement*, ABC Radio National, Oct 1, 2016 www.abc.net.au/radionational/programs/blueprintforliving/vale-bill-mollison/7887872 (accessed 12 October 2016).
6   See the writings of Val Plumwood, Rosi Braidotti, Martín Prechtel, Deborah Bird Rose, Freya Matthews, Maya Ward, and others.

References

Biro, Andrew. 2005. *Denaturalizing Ecological Politics: Alienation from Nature from Rousseau to the Frankfurt School and Beyond*. Toronto: University of Toronto Press.
Bradiotti, Rosi. 2013. *The Posthuman*. Cambridge: Polity.
de Zengotita, Thomas. 2005. *Mediated: How the Media Shape the World Around You*. London: Bloomsbury.
Holmgren, David. 2012. Conversation with Patrick Jones at Melliodora, Hepburn Springs, Victoria.
Jones, Patrick. 2014. "Literary Stiles and Symbolic Culture: Returning to the Problem of Writing" *Axon* (7) Available online at: www.axonjournal.com.au/issue-7/literary-stiles-and-symbolic-culture (last accessed 5 September 2016).
Krishnamurti, J. 1972. *The Impossible Question*. London: Victor Gollancz Ltd.
Lindquist, Sven. 2012. *Terra Nullius: A Journey Through No Man's Land* (trans. by Sarah Death). London: Granta.

Lingis, Alphonso. 1994. *The Community of Those Who Have Nothing in Common*. Bloomington and Indianapolis: Indiana University Press.

Meadows, Donella H., D.L. Meadows, J. Randers and W.W. Behrens III. 1972. *The Limits to Growth*, Funded by the Volkswagen Foundation and commissioned by the Club of Rome. New York: Universe Books.

Plumwood, Val. 2002. *Environmental Culture: The Ecological Crisis of Reason*. London and New York: Routledge.

Prechtel, Martín. 1999. *Long Life, Honey in the Heart: A Story of Initiation and Eloquence from the Shores of a Mayan Lake*. New York: Penguin Putnam.

Rose, Deborah Bird. 2011. *Wild Dog Dreaming: Love and Extinction*. Charlottesville and London: University of Virginia Press.

Rosenberg, Marshall B. 2003a. *Nonviolent Communication: A Language of Life*. Encinitas, CA: PuddleDancer Press.

Rosenberg, Marshall. 2003b. *Creating A Life Serving System Within Oneself* (CD). The Centre For Nonviolent Communication, Albuquerque, NM.

Rosenberg, Marshall. 2000. *The Basics of Nonviolent Communication with Marshall Rosenberg*, CNVCMedia, San Francisco workshop. Available online at: www.youtube.com/watch?v=YwXH4hNfgPg 12:22–12:32 minutes (last accessed 4 July 2016).

Steinbock, Anthony J. 2014. *Moral Emotions: Reclaiming the Evidence of the Heart*. Evanston, IL: Northwestern University Press.

Stiegler, Bernard. 1998. *Technics and Time, 1: The Fault of Epimetheus*. Stanford, CA: Stanford University Press.

Watson, Samuel Wagan. 2004. *Smoke Encrypted Whispers*. St Lucia: University of Queensland Press.

4 Murray River Country

Challenging water management practices to (re)invent place

Camille Roulière

Hostile nature, obstinate and fundamentally rebellious, is in fact represented in the colonies by the bush, by mosquitoes, natives and fever, and colonisation is a success when all this undocile nature has finally been tamed. Railways across the bush, the draining of swamps and a native population which is non-existent politically and economically are in fact one and the same thing.

So writes psychiatrist Frantz Fanon about the devastating impact of colonisation on his Caribbean homeland (1963, 201). The impact of this particular colonial encounter is easily transposable to most—if not all—settler countries. While of course different in the detail, each act of colonisation tailors the same overall outcome onto what or who it colonises. The common denominator is loss stemming from the fact that colonisation imposes the mythologies of the coloniser upon the colonised, and these impositions rarely generate enriching transformations for their supposedly passive human and non-human objects. As Fanon hints: the colonial encounter aims to force what it touches, what is different and does not bend to its mythopoetic rules, into non-existence.

Murray River Country in Australia is no exception. Since the European "discovery" of the region in the 1820s, a lush, fertile and densely-populated homeland has been transformed into a fragmented geographical space facing such an environmental crisis that the issue has been deemed a national priority (Weir 2009, 40). Loss in Murray River Country is profound and severe. It is everywhere: there is a loss of biodiversity, of emplaced knowledges and relationships, of language, of connectivity, of plurality. And this overarching loss reveals the mythopoetic dimension behind the unsustainable imagining, and subsequent management, of the region.

By definition, myths are omnipresent: they form a language which tinges and influences all aspects of a people's socio-cultural perception and construction of the world (Barthes 1991, 10, 107–8; Harari 2015, 144–65). Cultural geographer John Rennie Short characterises the myths mobilised to build and maintain a Nation as "national environmental ideologies" (1991, xiii, xxii, 55). In Murray River Country, the promoted national environmental ideology is that of the settlers. It stems from their mythologies, and has been imported from the relatively regular rhythms of Northern European ecologies to provide a structure through which to read and append authoritative meaning onto seemingly empty and malleable "antipodean" spaces (Short 1991, 55; Carter 1987).Yet, such a historical and geographical reality is obliterated, and this ideology is presented as atemporal and universal. Literary theorist Roland Barthes argues that lack of anchoring is essential to such myths: their imaginary eternal quality makes them seem justified as they appear to form a factual system rather than the system of values—with its motives and explanations— that they are (Barthes 1991, 120, 142–3, 152–5). Myths are thus the manifestation of a cultural perspective that is presented as though it is the objective and true condition of the world (Barthes 1991, 130; Short 1991, xxii).

Loss in Murray River Country highlights the contemporary repercussions and limits of the settler mythologies when imposed on the pulsative[1] water ecologies of the Australian continent.This loss quietly bears witness to the undeniable failure of these mythologies to move beyond an initial "deplete, destroy, depart" colonising impulse (Grinde and Johansen 1995), and consequently their inappropriateness to promote a sustainable perspective from which to imagine ourselves in place. Such a loss of sustainable mythologies means that water in Murray River Country is mismanaged, and in the end, lacking. As historian Michael Cathcart writes, this represents "White Australia's greatest folly" (2009, 7).Water is the source of all life, and this loss of sustainable mythologies to guide its governance is the loss that determines all other losses in the region.

In the face of ongoing environmental destruction, this chapter focuses on the socio-cultural construction of water in order to reveal how this entity and its management bear the mark of contentious social relations, and to explore how, from a position of loss, there are pathways to sustainably (re)make and relate to place. Throughout, my position is that of the mythologist, showing "at once an understanding of reality and a complicity with it" (Barthes 1991, 157). As a white researcher, I am located and speak from within the framework of settler mythologies: I am critically, and not practically, aware of its presence and impact. As a settler "insider," I draw on Aboriginal mythologies, not to speak about these alternatives,[2] but to subjectively disengage from settler mythologies.Through this disengagement, my objective is to discuss the decolonising potentialities currently arising from the deconstruction of this settler legacy. Barthes writes: "Myth hides nothing and flaunts nothing: it distorts; myth is neither a lie nor a confession: it is an inflexion" (1991, 128). By looking at the points of intersection of conflicting "inflexions," I aim to unveil how settler-induced loss in Murray River Country provides a transgressive outlet to mythopoetically (re)invent our relationships with and to place—that is, to (re)develop alternative mythologies to relate to place and approach place-making in the margin of dominant colonial myths—and this particularly under the impulsion and guidance of the Aboriginal Nations of the Riverland. Loss in Murray River Country is thus not merely an empty void of sterile absence and missed encounters. Instead, this loss can be transformed and act as a soundboard through which we can (re)learn how to listen to past silence; it is a space where collaboration hesitantly oozes through the cracks of colonial "dry thinking";[3] it is a space "full of volatile potentiality and future militancies" (Eng and Kazanjian 2003, 5); it is a space open to the (re)emergence of alternative mythologies and place-making practices. By focusing on the shifts occurring within and in-between mythologies, this essay is consistent with Barthes' argument that "there is no fixity in mythical concepts: they can come into being, alter, disintegrate, disappear completely. And it is precisely because they are historical that history can very easily suppress them" (1991, 119).

My focus here[4] is on two Aboriginal practices—namely the National Cultural Flows Research Project (henceforth NCFRP) and *Ringbalin*—which have emerged as responses to the loss triggered by environmental degradation in Murray River Country. Both campaign for the partial reinstatement of Aboriginal managerial practices to attempt to counterbalance this degradation. I have chosen these two practices because of their local and global connective aspects. They involve Aboriginal Nations from the whole region as they unite around a common cause: achieving an environmentally healthy Country; and they are strengthened by globalised Indigenous networks and the growing interest for Indigenous knowledges worldwide (Weir 2009, 120–3).

This essay consists of three parts. First, I unveil the mythopoetic imaginings of Murray River Country expressed in *Ringbalin* and the NCFRP, discussing the relationships with place these imaginings offer. Here, the extent—both social and environmental—of loss in Murray River Country can be grasped. Then, I look at the means used by these two responses to engage with and disrupt settler forms, structures and legacies. And, finally, I explore how the slow inclusion of these disruptions within mainstream discourses favours plurality in place-making practices and shapes a decolonising pathway away from restoration and into creative (re)inventions.

Beyond silencing

The NCFRP is a research program launched in 2012. It works to embed Indigenous water allocations within governmental water planning and management regimes so that spiritual, cultural, environmental, economic and social Aboriginal practices and interests are sustained perennially. A recent revival of an ancestral travelling ceremony, *Ringbalin* is a performance project initiated by Ngarrindjeri Elder Major "Uncle Muggi" Sumner in 2010. The aim of this yearly ceremony is to regenerate the spirits of Murray River Country's waters and peoples through traditional songs and dances.

The NCFRP's background work was to undertake an in-depth survey of the consistent stories compiled in literature or expressed among Aboriginal Nations of the Riverland to determine how and where water is most needed according to Aboriginal needs and practices. These collected stories are buttressed by situated life rhythms. They are the expression of local technical knowledges acquired, transmitted and adapted to environmental and historical changes through observation and tradition for thousands of years. Similarly, *Ringbalin* articulates an understanding of environmental design that originates in stories. Dancers and musicians journey from the Country's spring to its estuary and perform these stories along the way, singing and dancing the spirit back into the land, river, and people. These performed stories are site- and time-specific: they call on the inner powers of places and ancestors to unleash and heal damaged entities. The released powers belong to there and then. As such, place is not simply an inanimate background to the performance. It is simultaneously its most essential component and its primary intended recipient.

Human practices are tailored to and centred on place. This translates into mimetic relationships between the human and non-human worlds. The unicity of each performance mirrors that of each site and natural element, and the ceremony as a whole mimics water flows and ecological processes.

Ringbalin and the NCFRP can therefore be characterised as telluric projects, i.e. arising from, sustained by, and rooted in their place on Earth. They share a profoundly emplaced understanding of environmental design that is based on the existence and knowledge of complex local environmental, cultural and spiritual webs of relationships. Such is the entanglement between stories—whether collected as part of the NCFRP or performed as part of *Ringbalin*—and their surroundings that these stories can even be interpreted as narrating the environment into being. They often relate its mythopoetic construction, unveiling the meaning and purpose of its constituents, along with what is required for their preservation. As such, stories and environment simply do not exist without one another: stories are environmental and the environment is storied. Nature and Culture are thus strongly interconnected and inter-nurturing. Culture enables Aboriginal peoples to (re)connect with and talk to Country. For instance, the revival of the *Ringbalin* ceremony marked the end of the Millennium Drought.[5] As dancers stomped the ground and musicians made the air vibrate, much-needed rain fell.

This strong dialectics between place and creative impulse attests to how water is imagined as part of *Ringbalin* and the NCFRP. Waters are read as material records, as multifaceted and sentient archives onto which creativity can be articulated and flourish. When discussing water, both practices assimilate it to blood. It is the connective life-force of a larger polyphonic network, and is essential to revitalising ecological and spiritual webs of connectivity. If water does not flow, there is no life: it is like a clot around the heart. These anthropomorphic metaphors represent the manifestation of an eco-sentient understanding of non-human entities, which is consolidated by interspecies kinships. This eco-sentient understanding means that *Ringbalin* and the NCFRP apprehend place as a whole: all ecological constituents, both human and non-human, and all relationships—whether natural, cultural or social—within this environment are taken into equal consideration. If an entity is lost or damaged, the loss or damage is understood as global: it has repercussions which affect the entire Country. Consequently, both practices present good health as reciprocal, and intimately connect environmental loss with social and physical loss. As Aboriginal peoples form a part of Country, their identity and well-being is tied to it.

The articulation of this dynamic interdependency is particularly significant in regards to how the NCFRP and *Ringbalin* approach the agency power of humans: they consider it a responsibility—a strong spiritual obligation—rather than a right to ownership. As such, they promote a holistic and custodianship-based approach to environmental management which recognises and respectfully uses the resilience and agency power of Nature to sustain a "cultural economy" (Weir 2009, 119–29). By opposition, settler environmental ideology relies on engineering resilience. Constantly improved technological arrangements profoundly disrupt flows. Waters are muted; their textuality is denied and erased.[6] Such an approach impedes natural resilience, and supports capitalistic place-making myths of aggregate-growth which obliterate the complexity of ecosystems by removing the unknown and/or incomprehensible. Understood as finite and fragmented, ecological entities are rendered legible (Rose 2000, 69–70). Water flows become passive and pliable amounts to be stored or released at specific times and distributed according to agricultural needs for economic profit. By discarding and rendering invisible emplaced Aboriginal environmental ideologies to impose their own mythologies onto Country, settler management thus generated a man-made disorder of Nature's order (Byrne and Nugent 2004; Gibson 2002; Weir 2009, 45). Ironically, it is supposedly to bring order that settler environmental ideology disrupted and flattened a textured space. This confirms what anthropologist Deborah Bird Rose argues: "[t]o create order is to promote loss" (2000, 60). In a degraded environment, knowledge can no longer be transmitted in an embodied form as places succumb to water stress and disappear (Weir 2009, 136–48). Fragmentation leads to a loss of both ecological and intergenerational connectivity, along with a loss of our capacity to connect and engage with place (Potter et al. 2007, 8–20).

Through disrupting

This ecological fragmentation mirrors that of Aboriginal mythologies, which are often submitted to a "reductionist treatment" (Hawke 2012, 237–8) so that they fit within settler environmental ideology. This reduction is enacted through selective inclusions, which are conditioned by Western frameworks and interests. Indigenous inputs therefore remain subordinated to and shaped by processes and approaches outside of Indigenous control. For instance, the NCFRP's scope, especially in terms of governance issues, is regularly questioned. In 2015, this resulted in a temporary halt to the project for governmental auditing. Additionally, the collected knowledges are not defined as science, so that the superior authority granted to Western science is not undermined. Never apprehended in their entirety, these knowledges are pervasively "dis-membered,"[7] thus seeming to justify their relegation to a complementary position at best. They act as supplemental and punctual pieces of information to fill gaps in settler narratives. This illustrates the "cannibalistic" propensities of settler logic which "readily constructs other cultural possibilities as resources for Western needs and actions" (Haraway 1989, 247).

Ringbalin and the NCFRP act to counter these cannibalistic propensities. They challenge binary settler mythologies in their own logic by engaging with Western forms and structures to articulate dynamic Nature/Culture relationships. This multifaceted engagement is located within the site of settler power, and is primarily enacted through the appropriation of jargons and technological or artistic tools. For instance, the NCFRP draws on academic, scientific and legal English to transform the compiled stories into a rigorous and defendable input which aims to influence water distribution at the governmental level. Its concept of cultural flows offers a good example of this rerouting.[8] Appropriated by Indigenous Nations worldwide, such language offers a scientifically quantifiable system through which to express a socio-cultural understanding of water, and integrate socio-cultural requirements and preferences within Western modes of water needs assessment and allocation (Weir 2009, 81). Combining a systematic, trial-and-error scientific model with cultural knowledges, the NCFRP develops a methodology in continuity with Aboriginal mythologies within a Western framework. This diverted concept of cultural flows becomes a tool of resistance which confronts the politic. It provides Aboriginal Nations with a Western scientific and legal base to defend the validity and importance of the project in front of government agencies. As for *Ringbalin*, it draws on media such as cinematography and cartography. The filmed ceremony became a documentary which travelled from festival to festival. A didactic application was developed based on an interactive map of the region: clicking on a geographical location brings up videos of the ceremony's participants welcoming viewers to Country, explaining their close link to the land and waters, and the purpose of the ceremony. *Ringbalin*'s participants argue that this showcasing of their culture is important to remind themselves of its values, while favouring youth learning, self-esteem, and pride.

This represents a significant shift in practice: rather than being an object of study or side-informants, Aboriginal peoples are the instigators of their own projects and create a self-empowering space where they can speak for themselves. The NCFRP in particular is adamant on its aim to develop, through training and communication, the capacity of Aboriginal Nations to be actively involved in water management.

These creative appropriations of what used to be colonial tools[9] contribute to translating Aboriginal mythologies into a settler framework. These translations are a means for Aboriginal Nations of the Riverland to audibly share and spread their mythologies and values. They also shift the role and place of the settler language in Australia. If English used to be solely the bearer of uprooted and ecologically inappropriate myths (Glissant 1981; Tjukonia 2003), here it is transformed into a (re)empowering tool to voice the "counter-histories" encapsulated in alternative environmental ideologies. These counter-histories disrupt the "monumental histories" contained in settler environmental ideology (Foucault 1977), thus resulting in the deformation—and to some extent, in the "Indigenisation"—of settler forms, structures and languages (Johnson 2014, 324).

As such, these translations fissure colonial monologues: the voices of Aboriginal Nations shine through as they petition for respectful, yet profitable,[10] use of the waterways, and for the long-overdue recognition of Indigenous water rights in Australia.[11] *Ringbalin* and the NCFRP indeed present a healthy Country as the primary requirement for improving Aboriginal health and economic perspectives, and meeting their right to self-determination. Environmental justice becomes both an essential ethical positioning in the epoch of the Anthropocene and a prerequisite for Indigenous justice. The recognition of Indigenous water rights, and consequently the NCFRP, are met with fierce opposition from parties dependent on water allocations, such as irrigators who request the protection (or enhancement) of "water property rights" and consider, in a stereotypical and sadly common Aboriginalist fashion, that Indigenous and environmental needs are—and should be—aligned ("Position Statement" 2016). *Ringbalin* and the NCFRP provide an outlet from which Aboriginal peoples can denounce such a mentality and underline how settler mythologies foster the conditions for symbolic and systemic forms of colonisation, oppression and exploitation to occur. The extent of settler-induced loss is made visible: "shadow" places[12] are created and a "practical reconciliation" agenda— presenting "the final colonial act (normalising the outcome of oppression)" as justice—is implemented (Potter et al. 2007, 113, 117).

The existence of *Ringbalin* and the NCFRP within and through settler forms and structures questions the power balance between settler and Indigenous peoples in practical settings. Both practices use scientific data on generous agricultural water allocations to denounce the comparative lack of water entitlements granted to meet Aboriginal needs. Such interventions make inequitable power relationships obvious and push the government to examine and potentially absorb the wide power-gap between Aboriginal and settler environmental ideologies (Muir et al. 2010). As such, *Ringbalin* and the NCFRP encourage and symbolise an increased recognition of Indigenous knowledges' value (Weir 2009, 69) and of the "broad and direct impacts" of environmental management on Indigenous peoples (Hemming et al. 2010, 95). These recognitions point at the importance of including Aboriginal Nations in environmental management. These inclusions give us the opportunity to shift the way we approach water management, and (re)invent our relationships to and with place.

Into (re)inventing

Doing—whether it is storytelling as part of the NCFRP or performing as part of *Ringbalin*—connects people to their surrounding on a very deep level: a "muscular consciousness" develops (Bachelard 1958). Doing is knowing. It is knowing what is around us, and being able to account for what used to be, but no longer is, there. As such, doing stands against historical and environmental elisions, enabling Aboriginal peoples to reclaim the loss of (de)colonised landscapes and cultures, and representing resistance in the face of ongoing colonisation and assimilation policies. This re-membering is perceived as a duty, not only toward people (and particularly future generations), but also toward the environment. NCFRP and *Ringbalin* acknowledge and bear witness to loss, especially in terms of ecocide and genocide. Participants have seen the degradation happen in their lifetime; they are watching their Country slowly die. These projects thus represent a form of mourning (Derrida 2006), the catalytic stage required to transform a site of loss into a site of creation, "a world of remains" into "a world of new representations and alternative meanings" (Eng and Kazanjian 2003, 5, 20). As such, mourning dissociates place-making from nostalgic practices and opens a pathway for (re)invention[13] over restoration.

Thus these projects avoid the two primary drawbacks of basing place-making and managing practices on nostalgia. Firstly, nostalgia goes against mourning: something that is wanted back is not mourned (Eng and Kazanjian 2003, 22). As such, the extent of loss remains unacknowledged, and both genocide and ecocide are diminished, sometimes even denied. From this position, there is no way forward: if nothing went very wrong, there is no need for dramatic changes. Secondly, nostalgia favours "green orientalism" (Lohmann 1993), that is, an ecological discourse associated, aesthetically and materially, with green perspectives and imaginings. Focusing on man-made destruction and presenting it as a source of despair, this sterile discourse fetishises a hypothetic pre-human-contact natural world; it longs for a lost "wilderness." As such, it separates us from our environment by reproducing, and even encouraging, the maintenance of the divide—the "destructive breach" (Potter et al. 2007, 252)—between Nature and Culture. Yet, this nostalgia also positions us as the centre of our environment (ibid. 247–8), depriving it of agency power. As we retain it all, a restorative approach to environmental degradation is presented as the solution: engineered action becomes the only possible recourse (Weir 2009, 86–87). Permanence becomes tantamount to immutability, and this restorative approach translates into the perpetuation of unbalanced and exploitative relationships. Place-making and managing practices governed by nostalgia are equivalent to an ongoing—albeit mutated—form of colonisation.

Ringbalin and the NCFRP offer, by contrast, an antithetical understanding of permanence. Permanence is characterised by evolution: what is considered permanent regenerates through exchanges and contacts. Ecocide and genocide form a part of this permanence, along with what has emerged in the wake of these destructions. Permanence therefore implies mutability, hybridity, multiplicity and transformation; it means positively adapting to changed circumstances and renewing; it means being resilient. By drawing on a rich oral history, the NCFRP and *Ringbalin* demonstrate the strength of the Aboriginal peoples' ongoing connection to Country, and how these connections have evolved in reaction to environmental and historical changes.

As they juxtapose Aboriginal imaginings of Murray River Country against and next to settler imaginings, *Ringbalin* and the NCFRP highlight the continuous activities of Aboriginal peoples in Murray River Country, rendering obvious the ongoing historical and geographical presence of co-existing water literacies, each with its evolving specificities. Such an intercultural vision destabilises hegemonic Eurocentric practices, and refutes the settler myth of exclusivity and uniformity achieved through annihilating conquest (Carter 1996, 366–8). It counterpoints the construed silence of the colonised land: the "blank" slate—the *Terra Nullius*—is doubly filled, as both the supposedly-erased and the imposed are re-membered. This reveals the presence of meshed and shared landscapes, of multiple and mingling continuities. These continuities, highlighting co-occupancy, are crucial: they embed us into our environment and generate sustainable place-making practices: stories sediment as layers to form, shape and sustain places, and this cultural plurality has positive repercussions for ecologies.[14]

Ringbalin and the NCFRP go even further into the advocacy for emplaced plurality. Because their ongoing existence depends on efficient communication and marketing, these practices must build and develop productive and constructive intercultural interactions to receive funding and diffusion. As such, they campaign for give-and-take reciprocity and mutual respect. They ask for the revalorisation of their input through respect for the "situatedness of knowledges"[15] (Haraway 1988, 581–93). They also present water flows as the most essential thing, thus placing ethical water management above personal, tribal or governmental interests. Such a positioning favours managerial practices which are not centred on human partic-ipants, but on Country. A shared commitment to environmental justice becomes the key to finding common ground and compromise. By drawing on their excellent track record as century-long custodians to ask for managerial partnerships, the NCFRP and *Ringbalin* envision a place where people work side by side, using the power of their combined mythologies for the better; a place where new and hybrid governance approaches to water management are developed. The presence of

Ringbalin and the NCFRP within a settler State does indeed epitomise this slow emergence of more inclusive and composite forms of management which take into consideration, albeit in a limited way,[16] the mythologies encapsulated in these two projects.

Loss in Murray River Country thus fosters confluence and cross-pollination and, in the end, the emergence of alternative eco-cultural literacies. These alternative literacies act as an "agent of connection that builds trading zones for multiple forms of knowledge" (Kincheloe 2008, 193; see also Hemming and Rigney 2008). They draw a path for a reconciliation impetus, toward both Indigenous Nations and Country, as they promote the advent of a cross-cultural and inclusive "new ethos" at the margin of settler environmental ideology, the manifestation of a "border zone in which Indigenous ecological knowledge, Western scientific knowledge and Western philosophical and poetic inquiry converge" (Potter et al. 2007, 8–9; see also Carter 2005).

The practical failure of the settler State to prevent and now attend to environmental loss weakens the position of settler mythologies and places the government under increasing pressure to diversify and consider alternative mythologies and associated modes of place-making. This offers an unprecedented opportunity for Indigenous Nations to disrupt, and potentially subvert, the unsustainable colonial activities and hegemonic strategies of settler mythologies. In Australia, environmental loss can even be interpreted as a necessary stage so that the colonial monologue can fissure and be surpassed. It is within this breach that *Ringbalin* and the NCFRP act. They both call for a decolonisation of Australian place-making practices and foster creative mythopoetic (re)inventions of place and our relationship with it, rather than restorations: a shift away from monocultural imaginings and into emplaced plurality.

As we now threaten the last remnants of our planetary ecosystem, it is urgent that we learn other modes of place-making. While often construed as negative, the loss engendered by environmental degradation therefore has a creative potential. It is both a challenge and an opportunity: a site of (cultural and ecological) crisis and creation, a site of rebellion and decolonisation, a site of relation. It becomes, perhaps counter-intuitively, a site of positive transformation from which many different and yet-unknown futures can be imagined (Eng and Kazanjian 2003, 6–7). Loss reminds us that we only draw on a minuscule fraction of our "horizon of possibilities."[17] It also reminds us of the richness and plurality of Australian mythologies. Through the gaps it creates, we can read beyond the seemingly incontestable settler environmental ideology which gives the impression that there is, and can only be, one Australia. Both the NCFRP and *Ringbalin* sustain mythopoetic (re)inventions which relate us to place, ground us, and promote our engagement to place beyond and above exploitation. They call for place to be met with "head (thinking) heart (feeling) and hand (doing)" (Hawke 2012, 240). They call for love to govern the way we write about, and ultimately make, place (Rose 2000, 74). As such, they call for the (re)invention of eco-literacy in Australia, a country where water is yet to be perceived as existing beyond the economic dimension (Barlow 2009). *Ringbalin* and the NCFRP offer us, non-Indigenous people, the transformative opportunity to discover Murray River Country through Aboriginal eyes as they invite us to accompany them on their journey through Country. Guided throughout richly storied landscapes, we are immersed in strong and living Aboriginal mythologies and given a chance to experience place differently. If waters are "preced[ing] every form and sustain[ing] every creation" (Eliade 1991, 151), *Ringbalin* and the NCFRP offer manners to learn how to listen to these life-sustaining entities, and to flow with them, rather than against them.

Notes

1   The phrase "pulse ecology" was coined to describe Australian ecological rhythms, characterised by long and irregular cycles of scarcity and plenty (Robin et al. 2009).
2   This would be tantamount to celebratory appropriation, and thus amount to a form of colonisation.
3   Coined by philosopher and artist Paul Carter, "dry thinking" represents the opposition to uncertainty, instability and non-linearity which shaped Australian place-making practices. Dry thinking has enabled the settler State to gain and retain control of Australian spaces (2004, 107–9).
4   This analysis is based on my understanding of the material released by the participants of the two practices under scrutiny (see references), and is limited by my complicit position, to reuse Barthes' terminology, in regards to settler environmental ideology.
5   This was a fifteen-year drought which pushed the region's ecosystems to the brink of collapse.
6   This overwriting process summarises the history of Australia from colonisation onward: two environmental ideologies—both resting on radically different modes of perception and resource evaluation—competed, and "one achieved dominance at the expense of the other" (Short 1991, 126).
7   This implies that memory is a material process which consists of putting back scattered pieces together. These different pieces are dis-membered, until memory re-members them (Carter 2004, 10–1).
8   The concept of cultural flows is often used to describe movements across cultures, generally to the disadvantage of minorities whose cultures partially or totally succumbed to western acculturation. The notion then provides a discursive structure to appropriate and distort the cultural experiences of the "Other" through analysis in a Eurocentric frame.
9   Legal English and mapping were used to appropriate Australian landscapes and legitimise claims (Carter 1987). Films, photographs and academic English were used to "other" Aboriginal people and study what was thought to be a "doomed race" (Rose 2004).
10   Through both projects, participants are defending their right to self-determination, which is dependent on their right to access the Riverland for sustenance and trading, as used to be the case. Restrictions such as limited access for conservation/preservation purposes and fishing licences/quotas further impede this right to self-determination, which has already been severely compromised by ongoing ecological degradation and assimilationist agendas.
11   Governments of other settler countries, such as Canada, New Zealand and the USA, are comparatively generous in their treatment of Indigenous water rights.
12   Shadow places designate the sites sacrificed by settler practices in the name of (global) improvements and gains (Plumwood 2008). Illustrating how settler environmental ideology negates connectivity, these shadow places are the "traumatic legacies of colonialism" which are lying "silent in or addressing us through the continent's ground" (Rose 2004, 49; see also Gibson 2002).

13 Re-membering in itself can be seen as a creative act of local invention (Carter 2004, 195).
14 Relying on a vast array of cohabiting and interacting cultures indeed sustains healthy ecologies and accrues resilience (Pretty et al. 2009). By opposition, a monocultural frame implements an anti-resilience paradigm (Muir et al. 2010, 262).
15 Knowledge does not transcend cultural diversity, and believing otherwise devaluates non-Western cultures.
16 The government has a very positive and supportive rhetoric regarding collaborations and inclusions, yet its support and action remain mitigated. Nonetheless, *Ringbalin* and the NCFRP are part of a burgeoning of tentative collaborations between governmental agencies and Indigenous peoples.
17 This phrase is used by historian Yuval Noah Harari to encompass "the entire spectrum of beliefs, practices and experiences open to each society depending on its ecological, technical and cultural limits" (2015, 61).

References

Bachelard, Gaston. 1958. *La Poétique de l'Espace*. Paris: Presses Universitaires de France.
Barlow, Maude. 2009. *Blue Covenant: The Global Water Crisis and the Coming Battle for the Right to Water*. New York: New Press.
Barthes, Roland. 1991. *Mythologies*. Trans. Annette Lavers. New York: The Noonday Press.
Byrne, Denis and Maria Nugent. 2004. *Mapping Attachment: A spatial approach to Aboriginal post-contact heritage*. Hurstville NSW: Dept. of Environment and Conservation.
Carter, Paul. 1987. *The Road to Botany Bay: an Essay in Spatial History*. London and Boston: Faber and Faber.
Carter, Paul. 1996. *The Lie of the Land*. London and Boston: Faber and Faber.
Carter, Paul. 2004. *Material Thinking: The Theory and Practice of Creative Research*. Carlton: Melbourne University Publishing.
Carter, Paul. 2005. *Mythform: the making of Nearamnew*. Carlton: Melbourne University Publishing.
Cathcart, Michael. 2009. *The Water Dreamers: How Water and Silence Shaped Australia*. Melbourne: Text.
Derrida, Jacques. 2006. *Specters of Marx: The State of the Debt, the Work of Mourning and the New International*. Trans. Peggy Kamuf. New York: Routledge Classics.
Eliade, Mircea. 1991. *Images and Symbols: Studies in religious symbolism*. Trans. Philip Mairet. Princeton, NJ: Princeton University Press.
Eng, David and David Kazanjian, eds. 2003. *Loss: The Politics of Mourning*. Berkeley, LA and London: University of California Press.
Fanon, Frantz. 1963. *The Wretched of the Earth*. Trans. Richard Philcox. New York: Grove Press.
Foucault, Michel. 1977. "Nietzsche, Genealogy, History." In *Language, Counter-Memory, Practice: Selected Essays and Interviews*, edited by Donald Bouchard, 139–64. Ithaca, NY: Cornell University Press.
Gibson, Ross. 2002. *Seven Versions of an Australian Badland*. Saint Lucia: University of Queensland Press.
Glissant, Édouard. 1981. *Le Discours Antillais*. Paris: Seuil.
Grinde, Donald and Bruce Johansen. 1995. *Ecocide of Native America: environmental destruction of Indian lands and peoples*. Santa Fe: Clear Light Publishers.
Harari, Yuval Noah. 2015. *Sapiens: une brève histoire de l'humanité*. Trans. Pierre-Emmanuel Dauzat. Paris: Albin Michel.

Haraway, Donna. "Situated Knowledges: The Science Question in Feminism and the Privilege of Partial Perspectives." *Feminist Studies* 14.3 (Autumn 1988): 575–99.

Haraway, Donna. 1989. *Primate Vision: Gender, Race, and Nature in the World of Modern Science.* New York, London: Routledge.

Hawke, Shé Mackenzie. "Water Literacy: An 'other wise', active and cross-cultural approach to pedagogy, sustainability and human rights." *Continuum* 26.2 (2012): 235–47.

Hemming, Steve and Daryle Rigney. "Unsettling sustainability: Ngarrindjeri political literacies, strategies of engagement and transformation." *Continuum* 22.6 (2008): 757–75.

Hemming, Steve, Daryle Rigney and Shaun Berg. "Researching on Ngarrindjeri Ruwe/Ruwar: Methodologies for positive transformation." *Australian Aboriginal Studies* 2 (2010): 92–106.

Johnson, Miranda. "Writing Indigenous Histories Now." *Australian Historical Studies* 45.3 (2014): 317–30.

Kincheloe, Joe. 2008. *Knowledge and Critical Pedagogy: an introduction.* New York: Springer.

Lohmann, Larry. "Green Orientalism." *The Ecologist* 23.6 (1993): 202–4.

Muir, Cameron, Deborah Bird Rose and Phillip Sullivan. "From the Other Side of the Knowledge Frontier: Indigenous Knowledge, Social-Ecological Relationships and New Perspectives." *The Rangeland Journal* 32 (2010): 259–65.

Plumwood, Val. "Shadow Places and the Politics of Dwelling." *Australian Humanities Review* 44 (March 2008).

"Position Statement: Cultural Flows." National Irrigators' Council. March 2015. Available online at: www.irrigators.org.au/assets/uploads/Position%20Statements/Position%20Statement_Cultural%20Flows_March%202015_FINAL.pdf (last accessed 15 June 2016).

Potter, Emily, Alison Mackinnon, Stephen McKenzie and Jennifer McKay (eds). 2007. *Fresh Water: New Perspectives on Water in Australia.* Carlton: Melbourne University Press.

Pretty, Jules, Bill Adams, Fikret Berkes, Simone Ferreira de Athayde, Nigel Dudley, Eugene Hunn, Luisa Maffi, Kay Milton, David Rapport, Paul Robbins, Eleanor Sterling, Sue Stolton, Anna Tsing, Erin Vintinner and Sarah Pilgrim. "The Intersections of Biological Diversity and Cultural Diversity: Towards Integration." *Conservation and Society* 7.2 (2009): 100–12.

Ringbalin–Breaking the Drought. Dir. Ben Pederick. Perf. Major Sumner, Cheryl Buchannan, Kooma/Gwamu Ngyiaampa and Ngarrindjeri: tribal dancers and performers, Ellen Trevorrow, Paul Gordon, Herb Wharton, Beryl Carmichael, Doreen Micthell, Barney Lindsay. 2013. Goodmorningbeautiful films in association with JDR Screen, 2013.

Ringbalin, River Stories. 2013. Application. The Project Factory AU. Web. Last accessed April 19, 2016.

Robin, Libby, Robert Heinsohn and Leo Joseph (eds). 2009. *Boom and Bust: Bird Stories for a Dry Country.* Canberra: CSIRO Publishing.

Rose, Deborah Bird. 2004. *Reports from a Wild Country: ethics for decolonisation.* Sydney: University of New South Wales Press.

Rose, Deborah Bird. 2000. "Tropical Hundreds: Monoculturalism and Colonisation." In John Docker and Gerhard Fischer (eds) *Race, Colour and Identity in Australia and New Zealand* Sydney: University of New South Wales Press, pp. 59–78.

Rose, Deborah Bird. 2000. "Writing Place." In Ann Curthoys and Ann McGrath (eds) *Writing Histories: Imagination and Narrative.* Melbourne: Monash Publications in History, pp. 64–74.

Short, John Rennie. 1991. *Imagined Country: Environment, Culture, and Society.* New York: Syracuse University Press.

The National Cultural Flows Research Project. 2012. National Native Title Council as trustee for the National Cultural Flows Planning and Research Committee. Available online at: http://culturalflows.com.au (last accessed 4 January 2016).

Tjukonia, Vesper. "The Language of the Land." *Canadian Women Studies/Les Cahiers de la Femme* 23.1 (2003): 69–76.

Weir, Jessica. 2009. *Murray River Country: An ecological dialogue with traditional owners.* Canberra: Aboriginal Studies Press.

5 Wild urban green spaces as seen through Montreal's "Wild City Mapping" project

Dominique Ferraton

Two facts are often repeated: first, that the world is becoming more and more urbanized, and second, that spending time in nature is good for us. It makes sense that initiatives to make cities greener abound. Studies show that green spaces are good for our brains, are calming (Foglia 2005), and are essential to children's development (Louv 2008). Ecologically speaking, we need green spaces to combat heat islands and to create green corridors that allow plants, insects and animals to move through the city and beyond. Montreal has encouraged many such initiatives, and is lucky enough to have several large parks, often with significant "wild" areas in them.

On a map, these can easily be seen as large green blocks. At a glance, the blocks that stand out on maps of Montreal are the Parc du Mont-Royal, the Jardin Botanique, and a few of the many Parcs-nature. Zooming in, many small squares of green indicate neighbourhood parks. However, many of the city's wild green spaces cannot be found on a map. These are the under-developed, perhaps abandoned lots where vegetation has been allowed to grow spontaneously. As urban sites whose uses are not predetermined or controlled, they are also used by citizens in a variety of ways: walking paths and community gardens are formed, fire pits and ephemeral artwork appear. Although they are often ignored or unrecognized, the unique ways in which these spaces develop mean that they play important cultural, social and ecological roles, placing them at the forefront of discussions on social inclusion, the commons, community management and urban ecology.

In 2014, Maia Iotzova founded the Wild City Mapping collective. It was born out of a desire to tell the stories that give life to urban green spaces and to assert their place within the urban fabric of Montreal. The centrepiece of the project is an online map, which documents the personal significance of the wild green spaces in Montreal. Created by Maia and her co-founders (Marilène Gaudet, Maya Richman and Igor Rončević), it is now maintained by the collective's active members (Maia and myself). On this ever-evolving map, each wild green space is tagged with photographs and descriptions that are submitted by citizens who frequent them or encounter them. In this way, physical and geographic features are intertwined with personal interpretations of the space. It also keeps a record of the way these green spaces have changed over time, from 2008 to the present. By their very nature, they are temporary, ever-changing spaces. Each addition is colour-coded by year, with some spaces having submissions from several years. Artistic interventions and community initiatives are also identified, as are spaces that no longer exist.

Figure 5.1 Rue Island, August 2015
Photo by Dominique Ferraton

Année de la documentation / Year of documentation

| 2008 | 2009 | 2010 | 2011 | 2012 | 2013 | 2014 | 2015 | 2016 |

| Terrain disparu ou à risque / Disappeared or at-risk space | Intervention communautaire ou futur terrain sauvage imaginé / Community action or wish for future wild space | Visite ou randonnée / Exploratory walk | Lien vers une initiative citoyenne / Link to community engagement | Intervention artistique: portraits et réflexions / Artistic intervention: portraits and reflections | Intervention artistique: tricot-graffiti / Artistic intervention: yarnbombing |

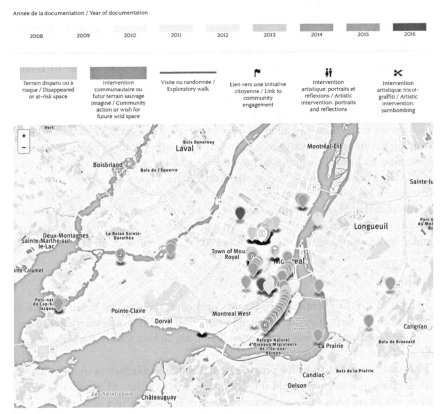

Figure 5.2 Screenshot of the main map from July 2016

Figure 5.3 I like to go here when I'm stressed out, and watch the endless stream of cars pass by. It's got a great view, and is especially fun to go to in the rain because it has an amazing amount of snails and worms all over.

Photo and text by Tom Baird, May 2016

Other names for these wild urban spaces include "empty" or "vacant" lots and "wastelands." These names automatically assign negative connotations to them, assuming they are spaces where nothing of any interest can be seen, temporary spaces that will only become something of value when they are developed. Wild City Mapping provides an alternative view by doing the opposite. By literally "putting them on the map," these marginal areas are given space and value. We use subjective mapping to offer an alternative to standard maps that simply place points on a map. Subverting traditional mapping techniques, we provide space for personal experiences, allowing for a more emotional and poetic view and a more intuitive, exploratory browsing experience.

The included photographs are taken from submissions received and from documentation of activities that Wild City Mapping led or participated in, including guided walks, mapping activities and flora and fauna inventories (or "bioblitzes").

Ecology

On most of the map's entries, what comes through is the need for green space as a refuge from the busy city and its concrete surfaces. There is also a clear desire to get to know and spend time among plants and animals, and we take this where we can get it.

Naturalist Roger Latour has provided a meaningful contribution to the study of urban ecology, notably by publishing a guidebook to urban plants (2009). Wild urban spaces are unique landscapes, allowing us to observe on a smaller scale the steps of growth and succession. An abandoned space that used to be a parking lot

Figure 5.4 Between two industrial parks that run along Highway 30 in St-Hubert, there is a small greenbelt along Boulevard Kimber and the streets running off it. At the end of Rue Noble is a path that is mostly used by snowmobiles during the winter but provides nice scenery as well with a dense forested area of mostly Yellow Birch trees and many shrubs and tall grasses, even with the faint sound of a busy highway in the distance.

Photo and text by Nicolis Bonnema, October 2015

or an office building often has soil that is dry, compacted and poor, and the first plants to colonize it are those that thrive in such conditions. These are often the invasive plants that we know as weeds. The question of "weeds" is a complicated one, placing a subjective selection of plants in the "undesirable" category. Some of the species that take over our yards are indeed aggressive, non-native plants, but a high percentage of all of our wild plants are European or Asian natives (including daisies, clovers and dandelions) (Le groupe Fleurbec 1978). Is this positive or negative judgment of plants serving a purpose? Part of changing the way we perceive the wild green space in our cities might include a change in how we view so-called weeds at the same time.

Some of the submissions for the map were received by amateur botanists, herbalists and wild food enthusiasts who harvest and forage in the city's wild green spaces. Wild City Mapping participated in a few bioblitzes led by Sierra Club Quebec, where volunteer participants armed with guidebooks explore a green space to make a list of all the species they find. The goal is to find out more about the areas and assess their value in terms of biodiversity. Such initiatives encourage citizen participation, regardless of expertise or skill. These accessible, democratic events are a good match for Wild City Mapping, whose focus is on physical engagement with the space and on subjective, individual experiences.

Figure 5.5 Roger Latour shows Plantago Major (Broadleaf Plantain) seeds during a mini
bioblitz in the Lac des Probables lot. Plantain is a European native that is
commonly found in disturbed or compacted soil. As one of the first plants to
colonize poor soil, it contributes to the first steps in soil rehabilitation: its roots
loosen hard surfaces and prevent erosion. ("Plantago")

Photo by Dominique Ferraton

Names and signs

An unmapped, unnamed space is an unknown, invisible space. The simple act of
labelling a space changes this completely: it becomes something that has potential
value or meaning, making it harder to ignore. While they might not yet be found
on conventional maps, some of these wild green spaces have been labelled and
identified in various ways and for different reasons.

The city of Montreal occasionally chooses to re-naturalize or re-wild small areas
of green space. As illustrated below, in this Plateau neighbourhood, a sign was placed
on a small green border beside a dead-end residential street. It reads (translated):
"Leave room for nature! Eco-friendly green space encouraging urban biodiversity."
Beyond its obvious explanation, this official sign serves a few purposes: first, those
who might use the area as a dumping ground or destroy it in some other fashion
might hesitate before doing so; second, those who might see "weeds" as a sign of lack
of care will now perceive them as part of a perfectly planned project; and finally, it
creates some new interest in what might be growing there, since it is automatically
more biologically diverse than standard mowed grass. It is interesting to note that we
often seem to need signs and labels in order to treat a space with respect or to feel
that it is important.

Figure 5.6 A group of participants during Wild City Mapping's "Jane's Walk" in May 2016
Photo by Thomas Kneubühler

Figure 5.7 Lac des Probables, September 2015
Photo by Dominique Ferraton

Artists have often been the ones to identify or tag these spaces. One of the spaces that comes up again and again in discussions about wild green spaces is "Le Champ des Possibles" ("Field of possibilities," or Maguire Meadow as it was first called). Artist Emily Rose Michaud was spending time in this large green space next to the rail line. With the help of community members, she created a land-art piece that reproduced the Roerich symbol on the ground. The Roerich symbol, three circles enclosed by one larger one, is a symbol that was placed on the roof of buildings with cultural value during the Second World War, signalling to pilots not to bomb them. The same idea was taken here: she wanted to signal that this was a place of value. The piece was maintained through the seasons, as she and others gathered and campaigned to keep the space as both a sample of urban wilderness, and a place for leisure, much like a park. She and naturalist Roger Latour were the two initial organizers, and ultimately, they succeeded. This park is now managed jointly by the

Figure 5.8 Sign placed in August 2015. Translation: "What is your perception of this space? Send photos/text to wildcitymapping@gmail.com with the code word DRAGONFLY

Photo by Maia Iotzova

city of Montreal and by a non-profit organization called "Les amis du Champ des Possibles" ("Historique") and maintained as a recreational green space and a space for urban biodiversity.

Several years after this, another artist, Philippe Chabot, installed a large painted sign in an abandoned space not far from the Champ des Possibles. His chosen lot was a relatively small one, but one that held meaning for him since it was part of the view from his balcony. It was also unique in the sense that it held a small wetland, complete with cattails and other marsh reeds. His painted sign was large, almost out of proportion with the space. It depicted a sunset and the name of the space, which he coined: Le Lac des Probables (Translation: Lake of the Likely), linking it by name to the Champ des Possibles, located a few blocks away. The sign was also an ironic reference to posters advertising tourist sites. The large, official sign existed in contrast with the space, which was small, fenced in, and had previously received little attention. Naming the space in such an overt manner also made it easier to talk about: the Lac des Probables became a new entity that could easily be referenced (with its own Facebook page).

The members of Wild City Mapping have also installed plaques or signs at the entrance of many of these green spaces, featuring the collective's logo: a wild carrot growing out of a flat city map. This particular wildflower was chosen for its recognizable silhouette and its abundance in Montreal's wild green spaces. The logo illustrates the ubiquitous and tenacious presence of wilderness in the city. Our sign-making initiative was driven by the same ideas as in the previously mentioned projects: labelling the site designates it as being worthy of reflection and attention. The text included on the signs also invites submissions, which is how many citizens have discovered the project. For those who already frequent the space regularly, it can be a thought-provoking tool, inviting them to think about the space in a new way.

Other spaces acquired names, which became helpful for the purposes of the activists trying to save them as green spaces: Jardin de la Liberté (Freedom Garden), Parc Oxygène (Oxygen Park), Parc des Gorilles (Gorilla Park), to name a few of the spaces that have been the object of citizen initiatives.

Transformation

One of the fascinating aspects of wild urban spaces is their evolution over time. They are often destined to disappear under new residential or commercial buildings, which makes their documentation even more important. Many spaces found on Wild City Mapping's map have since been developed and no longer exist as the wild green spaces they once were. As for the green spaces that do remain, since they are not officially managed or destined to a particular use, they also change over time with each human, animal or vegetable intervention. Plants grow taller, man-made paths change, holes in fences appear and disappear.

This poetic description is a particularly evocative example of the effect that "abandoned" spaces can have on us, and the reasons why these might be important to citizens, whose daily lives are centred around man-made structures with predetermined uses. These open-ended spaces provide a sense of freedom and possibility that is difficult to find elsewhere.

Figure 5.9 The site was more easily accessed a few years ago and at all seasons of the year I
        regularly walked through the site with my dog from Charlevoix to des
        Seigneurs, but last year the fences were rebuilt and improved. Combined with
        the nearby rush to gentrify, condo-ize and art-gallery-ize the area, access has
        now become now more difficult. This is not to say, however, that the site cannot
        be accessed. On a recent visit I found a neatly cut hole in the fencing on the
        west side near the Canal.

Photo and text by Giles Hawkins, 2014

Wild City Mapping is not an activist group; although it does hope for renewed attention and respect for wild green spaces, it does not directly campaign for their preservation. Several groups already do this in various ways, with at least two of them using mapping as part of their technique. The Sierra Club studies the ecology of Quebec's green spaces in order to highlight their importance to the overall ecology of Quebec, including identifying endangered species, making it easier to put pressure on government bodies to preserve them. Their online map lists plant species according to location in Montreal ("Bioblitz Montreal"). Lande, also based in Montreal, facilitates community claiming of abandoned lots, working from an urban planning perspective. Their own online platform maps these lots, each of them labelled with the owner of the space, its size, and how many citizens have currently shown interest in transforming it ("Lande"). Parallels can be drawn between this initiative and the Wild City Mapping project, but the latter does fill a gap: it covers the relationships that citizens already have (or have had) with the space. These subjective, emotional links are essential for any space to acquire meaning.

Figures 5.10a–b   Parc René-Lévesque, May 2008 / August 2015. If you follow the
Lachine Canal in a westerly flow, upriver, past the condos and the
abandoned factories and old bones of industry, you come to a spear of
land sticking out into the St. Lawrence, the charming Parc
René-Lévesque. It's a carefully manicured space with water on all sides,
dotted with sculptures, like the remains of a lost civilization. This is
fitting, because at the very tip of it—you can see it on Google Maps—is
a long ruined jetty, pointing right out to sunset. It's fenced off, but holes
have been cut and the gate doesn't lock anyway.

It's like coming to the ends of the earth. The jetty doesn't stop so
much as it does crumble away and dive beneath the water, like the path
continues on into the spirit world. Trees, grasses, moss, rose bushes,
wildflowers and things I can't name spill out of every crack—the stone is
heaving with water and life. One twilight late in October I came down
and found the barren cement tip swarming with pale moths, fluttering
off over the swirling water like the souls of the dead.

What I love about it, besides the beauty of the greenery and the river
all around, is the fact of its ruin. It's a psychic release to pass from city to
country to nothing, to an end, the place where it all falters and slides into
that lovely flowing abyss. It feels like letting go, and finding out that hey,
everything's still all right. More than alright. There's glory hiding behind
those trembling bushes. And after you've sat for a while at the end of
things and finally turn around, the city seems so much brighter. Less
inevitable, more friendly. Like it's been humanized by its mortality.

Cities always have parts that are crumbling away, but seldom do you
find one so dramatically situated. I worry that someone will come along
and try to clear it out as a boating hazard, but the trees are pretty big, so
it's been like that a long time. And the locals seem to like it as it is...

Photos and text by Kristopher Rosadiuk, 2015

Marginalization

Empty lots and abandoned green spaces are often seen as lawless and ownerless,
spaces where anything is possible and nothing is monitored. This is most definitely
part of their appeal, and also turns them into ideal locations for illegal or illicit
behaviour. When speaking to municipal officers, this is often one of the reasons
given for not allowing these spaces to remain overgrown and "wild." Within these
in-between, marginal spaces are other marginal groups: those seeking shelter, using
these out-of-the-way, wooded areas as homes or temporary spaces on which to place
mattresses or tents. This is not typically addressed when discussing the more romantic
ideas of wildflower-filled fields and spontaneous community gardens. It is also an
aspect that prevents some from entering these spaces, those who are afraid of
trespassing in someone's living space, or who even sense danger, feeling that the
inhabitants pose a threat to their safety. Any decision made by community members
(who have their own homes outside of the space) to "claim" or "repurpose" the
space would most likely drive out any of the current occupants, who have not, so

Figures 5.11a–b Rue De Mentana, July 2014/May 2016
Photos by Maia Iotzova

Figure 5.12 There are many different ambiences that can be seen in this large wild field. There is a section of it which is mainly common reeds (phragmites australis). Another part has different trees, a section has low herbs and another one has small purple flowers (with matching butterflies). I would say that it makes it quite a lovely area to explore. If you go explore, please be respectful of the residents: I have seen informal housing in different parts of the field.

Photo and text by Andréanne Maltais-Tremblay, August 2014

far, been part of these conversations: ultimately preventing any fair speculation on what the best course of action is in these cases. Submissions to our own map also require email or Internet access, which does limit its accessibility and automatically excludes many.

Starting a conversation

One of Wild City Mapping's main goals is simply to start conversations about these spaces, our varying relationships to them, and the different issues surrounding them.

Guiding public walks has been one of the ways to do this. In the spring of 2016, Wild City Mapping participated in the Jane's Walk series, a countrywide series of free, citizen-led walks commemorating Jane Jacobs, the Canadian urban theorist. Two members of the collective led a walk in the Plateau-Mont-Royal neighbourhood, taking participants on a tour of past and present green spaces and addressing issues such as urban ecology, guerrilla gardening, creative land use, and comparing ideas about our perception of these spaces. The participants came with their own past experiences: one of them spoke about the time she spent wandering freely in one green space as a child, before the current condo buildings appeared.

Before founding Wild City Mapping, Maia Iotzova started a series of reflective mapping walks. These focus on providing participants with the time and space to do their own exploring. The mostly self-guided walks request that participants explore a particular space with pens and paper, drawing or writing their own reflections.

In Montreal, the interest in these types of spaces is visibly growing. The more discussions that are had, and the more ways in which these spaces start to be used, the more we will understand what we might need and want from a city and from its green spaces. By collecting personal, individual reflections about these places from the citizens who care about them, we can recognize in a more concrete way what value these spaces can have. The city becomes more accessible and intimate as we start to acknowledge that all it contains can be explored, claimed, or transformed by

Figure 5.13 Photo taken during a reflective mapping activity in the Champ des Possibles in 2009

Photo by Maia Iotzova

each of us. Considering the map and its associated activities as an art project also allows space for new, creative ways of visualizing this data and new ways of seeing these spaces. Ultimately, it allows us to re-imagine what nature in the city can look like.

References

Bioblitz Montréal. "Sierra Club Québec". Available online at: http://montrealbioblitz.com (last accessed 13 July 2016).

Foglia, Richard. "This Is Your Brain on Nature." *National Geographic* (8 December 2015). Available online at: http://ngm.nationalgeographic.com/2016/01/call-to-wild-text (last accessed 15 July 2016).

"Historique." *Les Amis du Champ des Possibles.* Available online at: https://amisduchamp.com/a-propos/historique (last accessed 9 July 2016).

Iotzova, Maia, Marilène Gaudet, Maya Richman and Igor Ron evi (ongoing project). *Wild City Mapping.* Available online at: www.wildcitymapping.org (last accessed 4 May 2017).

"Lande: Cartographier. Accompagner. Transformer." *Lande Montréal.* Available online at: www.landemtl.com (last accessed 13 July 2016).

Latour, Roger. *Guide de la flore urbaine.* Anjou, QC : Fides, 2009.

Le groupe Fleurbec. *Plantes sauvages des villes et des champs.* Montréal, QC: Fleurbec/Éditeur officiel du Québec, 1978.

Louv, Richard. *Last Child in the Woods: Saving Our Children from Nature Deficit Disorder.* Chapel Hill, NC: Algonquin Books, 2008.

"Plantago Major." *North Carolina State University Cooperative Extension.* Available online at: https://plants.ces.ncsu.edu/plants/all/plantago-major (last accessed 9 July 2016).

Part II

Transitions in practice

6 The art of permatravel

Nina Gartrell

Against the background of crisis (economic, ecological, social and cultural), and the rise of "carbon guilt" (Garrard 2013, 177) as a response to anthropogenic climate change, what are we to make of the emergence of "permatravel" as a contemporary travel practice? Is it the viable alternative to unjust and unsustainable modalities of tourism that "permatravellers" aim to cultivate? This paper assesses the achievements and limitations of permatravel through its capture and articulation on blogs, in magazine articles, and in travel memoirs. By focussing exclusively on texts authored by members of the permatravel community this paper cultivates an emic approach to permatravel, focussing on the manner in which permatravellers *themselves* construct, represent and narrate their experiences. My discussion is grounded in an analysis not only of relevant permatravel texts but of my own lived experience of permatravel, which consists of an overland journey from England to Australia that I undertook in 2012–2013.

The purpose of this chapter is to historicize permatravel as an emerging alternative tourist practice, and to summarize what the growing body of literature on permatravel says in regard to the norms and conventions governing permatravel's practice. My aim is to generate a provisional definition of permatravel and to identify a coherent set of practices, motivations and sensibilities around which performances of permatravel cohere. Some of the "expressive choices" (Adler 1989, 1374) made by permatravellers explored in this chapter are: the intellectual and aesthetic orientation of permatravel journeys; the physical activities permatravellers undertake; their preferred modes of transport and accommodation; the social relations created through travel; and permatravellers' use of temporal and financial resources. By examining these issues, I seek to interpret permatravel behavior and begin to consider the role permatravel might play in the transition toward a truly sustainable ecological culture.

Background: "tourist types" and "the art of travel"

Throughout tourism's five-hundred-year history, a colourful and diverse array of "tourist types" has proliferated (Adler 1989, 1366), a process that has, if anything, intensified in recent years. In the most recent decade of the Anthropocene, myriad styles of alternative tourism have emerged, including "ethical travel, environmental travel, green tourism, low-impact tourism, … soft-adventure tourism" (Gilbert 2015,

257); "volunteer tourism" (Lyons and Wearing 2012); "slow tourism" (Oh, Assaf, and Baloglu 2016); "transformational tourism" (Deville and Wearing 2016, 151); and "de-commodified sustainability tourism" (Deville, Wearing, and McDonald 2016). A recent addition to this list is a blended travel practice that I call permaculture travel, or "permatravel." Permatravel is distinguished from other related styles of alternative tourism by its integration of activities associated with permaculture, (gardening, seed-saving and ecological landscape design), with activities traditionally associated with tourism (sightseeing). My fascination with permatravel is admittedly self-interested. I identify as one of the "pioneers" of permatravel, and have a vested interest in seeing the term "permatravel" fly, as I am currently in the process of cultivating a hybrid permaculture travel memoir, titled *Seeds*, as one of the outputs of my doctoral research.

My personal experience with permatravel and permatravel memoir has led me to seek out and engage with a range of other first-hand accounts of permatravel. In this chapter I discuss four separate accounts, including my own, and outline what each account contributes to an evolving understanding of permatravel as a unique method of "worldmaking" (Goodman quoted. in Adler 1989, 1368) and "self-fashioning" (Adler 1989, 1368). In order to determine what is distinctive about permatravel, I loosely apply Adler's (1989) framework of "travel as performed art," and seek to identify some of the key "signifiers" (ibid.) or "factors" (Gilbert 2002, 255) that make permatravel performances unique and different from other distinct styles of travel performance. According to Adler, the art of travel involves "expressive choices" that reflect, among other things, individual travellers' psychological needs, aesthetic preferences, values and desires. Thus I ask: what types of expressive choices do permatravellers make and why?

While a detailed discussion of permatravel's affinities with other related styles of alternative tourism, such as ecotourism and volunteer tourism, falls outside the purview of this paper, I acknowledge that the lineage from which the permatraveller, as a distinct "type" of alternative tourist has emerged, is multiple, complex and hybrid. Permatravellers demonstrate affinities with a range of other "types" of travellers, both past and present, and might be thought of as combining attributes of a number of categories of tourists and travellers: explorers, drifters, gardeners, philosophers, ecologists, environmentalists, cyber-activists, and eco-pilgrims. "Philosopher-gardener" is how permaculture co-founder Bill Mollison (2012, 9) characterises the unique outlook or sensibility of permaculturists. It follows that a permatraveller might be distinguished from other travellers by her facility for merging a philosopher's slow and sensitive contemplation of the laws of the natural world, with a gardener's practical, hands-on approach to stewarding the land. This, at least, is how I personally approached my first ever lived experience of permatravel—as I imagined a "philosopher-gardener" might do.

Permatravel case study number one: "Overland to Oz"

In January 2012 my partner and I embarked upon a pioneering experiment in permaculture-designed travel, or permatravel. The journey was a "flightless" emigration from our home in England, to our new "home" in Australia. For each of us the journey meant something different. For me, it was a journey of home-coming, bringing five years living as an émigré in England to an end. For Richie, a "native" of England, it was a migratory journey. For both of us, however, the journey carried a similar significance. It signalled an end to an era of hedonistic travel, and the start of an attempt to begin travelling in a manner that accorded with permaculture's ethos and design principles.

Several months prior to setting out from England, we had begun speaking of our journey "overland to Oz" as an experiment in permatravel. We believed we were the first to coin the term permatravel and felt appropriately self-satisfied for inventing this witty neologism. Both Richie and I had recently completed a two-week course in applied permaculture design and were enthused by the promise of permaculture. Permaculture educator Stuart Hill's (2011, v) statement that it is time to move permaculture out of the garden and begin applying it "to all that we do" had inspired us. If permaculture could indeed be applied, as Hill proposed, "to all that we do" then why not apply it to travel?

The problem of pioneering

Being "pioneers"[1] in the untried and untested art of permatravel, Richie and I had no idea of what a permaculture-infused travel practice might entail, nor any sense of how to go about implementing one. We decided that the act of designing a permatravel journey would involve a considerable degree of innovation, experi-mentation, trial, and perhaps error. Taking permaculture educator Caroline Smith's (2011, xi) statement about "being humble, dealing with paradox and uncertainty, and making mistakes" as our mandate, we threw ourselves into the process of designing our journey, realizing that whatever design we eventually developed, our plans and methods were likely to alter over the course of time and evolve organically in response to changing circumstances.

Although we had misgivings about *how* to design our permatravel odyssey, we felt sure about the aesthetic and intellectual orientation of our journey: funda-mentally, the concept was to apply "permaculture thinking" (Dawborn 14) to the art of travel. The fundaments of "permaculture thinking" rest on two important pillars: an awareness of and commitment to honouring (a) the ethics of perma-culture and (b) the ecological design principles of permaculture. It was these two frameworks – the ethics and principles – we were attempting to apply to the art of travel.

Permatravel as a purposeful alternative

Five years prior to embarking on our maiden permatravel journey, Richie and I had met and fallen in love in India. We spent the initial two years of our relationship travelling widely and indiscriminately. Our many journeys in Europe and Asia were driven by a hunger to experience as many new things as possible and to immerse ourselves in exotic cultures and ways of life. In response to our growing commitment to permaculture, however, we decided our journey overland from England to Australia should be different from the other journeys we had made in the past – we wanted it to be more purposeful, less hedonistic, and more focussed on "learning" about ecology and self-sufficiency. We wanted several other things too from our new and improved ecological travel practice: to attain a higher degree of autonomy from the tourist establishment than in the past; to attain a high degree of integration with members of host societies (permaculture principle no. 8: Integrate Rather than Segregate); to produce less waste (permaculture principle no. 6: Produce No Waste); to spend less money, and to operate largely from within a gift economy.[2] This spirit of learning, exchange and reciprocity is demonstrated in the introductory letter to WWOOF (Willing Workers on Organic Farms) hosts that we composed prior to setting out:

> Dear _____ [insert WWOOF host's name]
>
> We are a dual-nationality English/Australian couple who are currently WWOOFing our way around the globe from England to Australia. We will be passing through your region in _____ [insert date] and are keen to WWOOF with you. We would like to share our skills and learn more about your culture and way of life. We are passionate about the exchange of skills and acquiring traditional ecological knowledge.
>
> We are attempting to exemplify the ethics of permaculture, and as a result have chosen not to fly. Instead we are using local forms of transportation such as buses, trains and ferries. By avoiding air travel we hope to minimise our carbon footprint.
>
> Having experienced first-hand the joy of creating and tending a garden, we are excited about the prospect of helping other people achieve their vision for a beautiful, abundant and sustainable future.
>
> What we can offer in exchange for food and lodgings:
> • an enthusiastic, open-minded and hardworking approach to life on your farm
> • knowledge and practical help with no-dig gardening, companion planting, foraging, food preservation, compost making, building and maintaining compost toilets, building earth ovens and rocket stoves
> • access to our 600GB database of permaculture resources, including films, documentaries, ebooks and music
> • technical assistance with maintaining your website or blog
> • heirloom fruit, flower and vegetable seeds saved from our garden in Norfolk (England)
> • a place to stay when you visit Australia
>
> In return, we are keen to gain experience in the following:
> • natural building techniques
> • greywater systems
> • aquaculture
> • natural beekeeping
> • animal husbandry

- carpentry & coppicing
- herbal remedies
- traditional recipes (including regional specialties)
- folk lore, stories and traditional ecological knowledge

If you would like to see some photographs of our garden in England or to learn more about our journey please visit: *Patchworkspermaculture* (Richie's blog) and *Typo Traveller* (Nina's blog).

We look forward to hearing from you and hope to spend time with you soon in your garden.

Sincerely,
Richard & Nina

The other change we wanted to make in our travel practice was to shift our focus of interest from capital cities and tourist "sights" to organic farms, ecovillages and urban farming projects – places where we could gain first-hand experience in natural farming techniques and continue to develop the skills that would enable us to achieve a higher degree of self-sufficiency once we were settled in Australia.

In sociological terms our new permatravel philosophy was an attempt to avoid what Cohen (1979, 183) calls "recreational" or "diversionary" modes of touristic experience, and, alternatively, an attempt to embrace an "existential" mode of experience. Tourists engaged in "existential" modes of experience are characterised as "seekers" (Cohen 1979, 189), individuals who feel alienated from their home society, and therefore mobilise travel in a bid to locate an alternative "elective spiritual centre" (ibid. 190). The journey "home" to Australia, amongst other things, was enacted as a quest or permaculture pilgrimage. The objective was to locate, cohabit with, and learn from individuals and communities who shared our commitment to the ideal of "permanent (sustainable) culture" (Holmgren 2011, xix) and who practised "permanent (sustainable) agriculture"; that is to say, communities who provided "their food, energy, shelter and other material and non-material needs in a sustainable way," which is the core of Mollison's (2012, ix) definition of permaculture.

Designing the journey

Prior to setting out from England we entered an intensive period of planning and designing. We selected one of the design methodologies learnt during a two-week Permaculture Design Course (PDC). The design methodology, O'BREDIMET, has its origins in the field of industrial design and consists of nine distinct stages: **O**bservation – **B**oundaries – **R**esources – **E**valuation – **D**esign – **I**mplementation – **M**aintenance – (Re)**E**valuation – and **T**weaking (Aranya 2012, 23). During the initial **O**bservation phase of the design we produced a document known in permaculture circles as a "goals articulation." As the name suggests, our goals articulation was a summary of the goals we hoped to realise over the course of the journey. The overriding goal was to reach Australia without flying, honouring to the best of our ability permaculture's ethos of earth care, people care, fair share. A more detailed breakdown of our goals included:

Earth Care
- to produce as little waste as possible
- to eat locally, seasonally and to make a special effort to source organic produce
- to save, collect and swap heirloom seeds

People Care
- to have fun, enjoy ourselves and stay healthy
- to cultivate authentic and meaningful relationships with places and people

Fair Share
- to prioritise non-monetised forms of exchange
- to distribute our capital in a way that is fair and equitable
- to produce as many yields as possible from our experiences that are of value to others, including garden designs, blog posts, photographs, field journals and video footage (permaculture principle no. 3: Obtain a Yield).

The next step in the O'BREDIMET process was to address the **R**esources at our disposal. Because we had travelled extensively in the past, we already possessed a range of essential resources, including hiking boots, backpacks and a camera. In order to travel more autonomously, however, we needed to acquire several other resources, including a lightweight two-person tent, sleeping bags and a portable device for purifying drinking water. To filter our water we settled on a product called the Lifesaver® water bottle. This resource proved vital to our permatravel practice, enabling us to complete the entire journey from England to Australia without purchasing a single bottle of water.

Other waste reduction strategies employed over the course of our journey were as follows:

- use washable fabric sanitary pads
- carry our own knife and lightweight camping plates, cups and cutlery to prepare our own meals and avoid disposable takeaway containers
- use fabric "eco-bags" to avoid plastic bags
- use biodegradable bamboo toothbrushes
- sparingly use 100% natural, biodegradable toothpastes, shampoo and skin products
- predominantly self-cater from local markets, favouring locally grown, seasonally available, and organic produce
- to forage, where possible, for food
- dispose of biodegradable wastes, such as vegetable and fruits scraps by feeding them to domestic animals (chickens, pigs, camels), thereby turning our food "waste" into a food "resource" for others.

The importance of blogging

Over the course of our journey I published seventy-two posts on my blog, *Typo Traveller*, which I purposely created prior to setting out, as an outlet to "fair share" the cultural capital I was in the process of gaining and to invite feedback on my permatravel practices (permaculture principle no. 4: Apply Self-Regulation & Accept Feedback). Collectively, these posts represent my first attempts to articulate my vision of permatravel as a "new" and innovative style of socially and ecologically responsible travel.

It was an interesting and unexpected turn of events when a blog post I published in Bali, Indonesia attracted the attention of two Australian "yachties." These sailors proved the missing link in our sequence of overland and sea connections, offering us two boat-hitching positions on board their yacht. In exchange for doing our share of night watches, cooking, cleaning and maintaining the boat, we received free food and accommodation. The boat ride from Lombok (in Indonesia), to Darwin (in Australia's Northern Territory) took four weeks to complete. During this time we encountered storms, witnessed smouldering volcanoes, had a collision with a submerged object, and spent over a week in Dili, the capital of Timor-Leste, waiting for our boat to be repaired.

Roughly seventeen months after setting out from England, Richie, myself, and our motley collection of heirloom fruit, vegetable and herb seeds arrived in the port of Darwin and cleared Australian Customs and Immigration. The final leg of our journey was a 3,500 kilometre hitch-hike through the Australian Outback. When we arrived, ten days later, on the front doorstep of my parents' home on the Sunshine Coast we were tired, grubby and triumphant. Our 48,000-kilometre, twenty-one country, seventeen month permaculture pilgrimage was over. We had done it.

The journey continues: assessing the achievements and limitations of permatravel

In terms of the goals we had set for ourselves during the initial Observation phase of our permatravel design, Richie and I had done well. We had succeeded in eschewing air travel! We had relied exclusively on "slow" forms of transportation (permaculture principle no. 9: Use Small & Slow Solutions). We had relied almost exclusively on the free hospitality of WWOOF, Couch Surfing and WorkX hosts for our accommodation. We had collected dozens of varieties of rare heirloom fruit, vegetable and herb seeds, and most importantly of all we had formed dozens of enduring friendships with individuals who, like us, were committed to making the transition from fossil-fuel dependence, toward an ecological culture based on permaculture's ethos of earth care, people care, fair share.

Yet in spite of our many accomplishments, I continued to feel unsettled by some of the compromises we had made. I felt that my lived experience of permatravel fell far short of the *ideal*. Motivated by a desire to clarify the successes and failures of my pioneering experiment in permatravel, I decided to embark on a "new" permatravel journey. Within two months of arriving back in Australia I applied to my local university for a place as a doctoral research candidate. My application was accepted, and I was awarded a government scholarship. The topic of my Doctor of Creative Arts (Creative Writing) research project was "permatravel," and the creative arts product—an innovative hybrid permaculture travel memoir entitled *Seeds*.

First encounters: the permatravel community emerges...

Twelve months subsequent to commencing my doctoral candidacy I had my first encounter with the term "permatravel" outside of my own research. The discovery of a *public* permatravel discourse was both shocking and exciting. Up until this point I had believed Richie and I were the first to coin the term permatravel, and likewise, the only two individuals experimenting in a style of alternative tourism based on permaculture's ethical and design principles.

My online search on the term "permatravel" revealed not one, but two results! The first reference was a post called "The Permatraveler Manifesto" published on *Permatraveler* blogspot. The second was a post entitled "PermaTravel" published on *Uncertainties: a blog about travel, travel without money and gift economies*. These two separate blog posts on the subject had been published within two months of one another. It was my first encounter with the theory of "multiple discovery."[3]

Permatravel case study number two: "The Permatraveler Manifesto"

Anxious to learn what the author of "The Permatraveler Manifesto," Giri Strampello, had written in his pioneering articulation of permatravel, I scrolled down the page. My eyes immediately settled on the following definition:

> Some of you may have wondered, "What is permatravel?" **Permatravel**, a term I have coined after being inspired by the ideals and tenets of permaculture, can be described as a marriage between the individual and the journey. Like permaculture, permatravel is a *design methodology*, comprised of the words permanent and travel. It is a design methodology for consciously crafting one's experience to sustain itself, both in the present and in the future, while wasting as little energy as possible. Starting with the birth of an idea, whose foundations are established in the planning stages and realized throughout the journey, permatravel is both a strategy and a state of mind.
>
> (Strampello 2014)

It was all very intriguing, but what did it mean? It was far from being the coherent declaration of permatravel intention I had hoped for. What, for instance, did the author mean by the phrase, "Imagination is the spark which creates the flame and learning is the fuel the fire needs to survive"? Or, for that matter, "...riding the wave of experience as far as it will take you" (ibid.). Even the notion of permatravel "as a marriage between the individual and the journey" was befuddling. How did the author propose permatravellers should practice "working with surrounding forces" (ibid.)? Did other permatravellers possess Jedi-like powers that I myself had failed to develop?

In spite of my difficulty interpreting the author's meaning, there were several concepts that resonated with my own understanding of permatravel. Firstly, there was the notion that permatravel is a "design methodology." This made sense. Moreover, it harmonised with my own understanding and experience of permatravel as being a consciously crafted travel experience.

Another concept that made adequate sense is that permatravel is a frugal practice, grounded in the philosophy of "wasting as little energy as possible." The emphasis on prudence and frugality synergised with Strampello's notion that permatravel should "sustain itself, both in the present and in the future." Was this an indirect reference to permatravel being a "sustainable" travel practice? In addition to the frugal use of resources, Strampello (2014) identifies another goal of permatravel, "inviting new experiences" and "being open—to ideas, experiences, customs, people…". Might this be an allusion to Holmgren's tenth permaculture principle, "Use and Value Diversity"?

Permatravel case study number three: "PermaTravel"

Having read and re-read Strampello's "The Permatraveler's Manifesto," I turned my attention to the second search result, a blog post called "PermaTravel" written by an individual who published under the alias "anthonymanrique." The most definitive statement I could find in regards anthonymanrique's philosophy of permatravel was this:

> PermaTravel is not necessarily long term travel, but rather cultivates an urge toward a sustainable and compassionate form of travel. It acknowledges the destructive power of the capital-based tourism industry and is actively opposed to it. It deplores resortification and the forced assimilation and partial or full loss of local and/or indigenous culture. Rather, PermaTravel is undertaken in the spirit of a pilgrimage of respect and learning toward and from these cultures.
>
> (anthonymanrique 2014)

Given the nature of the statement, it was abundantly clear that anthonymanrique was theorising permatravel as a conscious *alternative* to exploitative forms of tourism. Sustainability, compassion and cross-cultural learning were three of the key features of the author's particular brand of permatravel.

In terms of transportation technologies, the author states unequivocally that permatravellers should prioritise public forms of transportation, including boats, buses and trains. Human-powered transport technologies are also favoured. For this reason, says the author, permatravel "naturally inclines toward Slow Travel" (anthonymanrique). If there is one form of transportation permatravellers should eschew, says anthonymanrique, it is flying. A further point is that permatravellers should make a concerted effort to contribute to local economies: "choose local (for food, guest-houses etc.), then the money will be going to the right places" (ibid.).

The area of closest symmetry between Strampello's, anthonymanrique's and, coincidentally, my own articulation of permatravel, is the emphasis on the frugal use of resources, reducing consumption, and minimising waste:

PermaTravel encourages thoughtful and compassionate use of the valuable resources that the environment provides for us. It requires an attitude of disdain for waste and cultivates a creative approach to recycling, reduction of consumption and re-use of resources whilst travelling.

(ibid.)

My day of research had yielded some interesting results, but my doctoral permatravel journey was far from over…

Permatravel case study number four: The Art of Free Travel

Twelve months elapsed before my next encounter with permatravel discourse. It was mid-2015. Richie came home from a visit to our favourite independent bookstore carrying a brand new copy of a book whose publication I had been eagerly awaiting: *The Art of Free Travel: A Frugal Family Adventure*, co-authored by Patrick Jones and Meg Ulman, two members of an Australian permaculture-art collective known as "The Artist as Family."

Although the journey portrayed in the memoir differed significantly from mine and Richie's, Jones and Ulman had explicitly referred to it as an example of "permaculture travel" in an article published in a 2015 issue of *Pip* (the Australian permaculture magazine). The journey portrayed in *The Art of Free Travel* consists of a 400-day cycling-camping trip up the east coast of Australia, and back again, undertaken not only by Jones and Ulman, but by their two sons, Zephyr and Woody, and their dog, Zero. The authors conceive of their journey as part of "a transition from what Australian writer Deborah Bird Rose calls "man-made mass death" to "environmental accountability" (Jones and Ulman 2015b, 93).

The protagonists' decision to adopt bicycles as their primary mode of transportation is a conscious effort to eschew polluting transportation technologies. It also turns out to have profound implications in terms of the journey's aesthetic orientation. The mode of perception induced by riding bicycles, says Jones and Ulman (2015b, 3), is one of "going slow." The journey's slowness induces feelings of intimacy with the local environment that would have been impossible were they to journey by car.

Cycling and camping are two of the most important physical activities in Jones and Ulman's permatravel practice. Like cycling, camping enables the protagonists to enjoy a more ecologically connected and "creaturely"[4] (Jones 2013, viii) experience of themselves as human animals immersed in their environment. Other physical activities that play an important part in Jones and Ulman's particular style of permatravel are foraging, hunting and fishing. One of the purposes of their journey is to gather data for a book they propose to publish on "free tucker." This book is one of the many yields they aim to produce as a by-product of their permatravel practice.

As the title *The Art of Free Travel* suggests, operating within a gift economy is central to Jones and Ulman's articulation of permatravel. Although the family possess a small budget that they use to access goods and services such as food, accommodation, bicycle repairs, and car hire for a portion of the return leg of their journey, they succeed admirably in subsisting on a meagre daily budget of AUD\$30 per day, which is roughly the equivalent to the GBP15 per day that Richie and I subsisted on over the course of our overland journey from England to Australia.

Jones and Ulman's commitment to using gift economies has significant implications in terms of the social relations they create through their permatravel practice. Freed from the normal encumbrances of what Cohen (1984, 380) calls the "tourist-local relationship" with its emphasis on the "commoditization of hospitality," Jones and Ulman find themselves engaging meaningfully in other peoples' lives, and are frequently and serendipitously invited to stay with members of local communities, or are accommodated by Warm Showers hosts who offer free accommodation to cyclists. Jones and Ulman dutifully repay their hosts by doing various tasks. These acts are framed as "barter" (Jones and Ulman 2015b, 53) and include anything from cooking a meal to running a backyard workshop on how to slaughter a rooster.

Findings and discussion

So what do the four permatravel case studies examined in this chapter reveal about the sensibilities, practices, motivations and behaviours of permatravel practitioners? Although the four separate accounts of permatravel examined in this chapter are heterogeneous, there is enough of a "shared coherence" (Adler 1989, 1371) between them that we might feasibly talk of them as constituting "a body of travel performance" (Adler 1989, 1372). The case studies' "shared coherence" can be traced to a number of factors:

1   Permatravellers seek a high degree of autonomy from the tourist establishment, and furthermore, a high degree of integration within the communities they visit. Permatravellers show a marked preference for cohabiting with locals (as opposed to lodging in tourist hostels or hotels) and make thorough use of hospitality networks like Couch Surfing, WWOOF, and Warm Showers. Wild camping is also a common practice among permatravellers.

2   Permatravellers prioritise non-monetised forms of exchange and operate largely within a gift economy.

3   Permatravellers demonstrate high levels of technological literacy. They maintain high levels of internet usage whilst on the road and actively engage with social media technologies to enable their permatravel activities. Blogging is an important permatravel activity.

4   Permatravellers tend to adopt an "existential" mode of experience. "Existential" journeys have an affinity with pilgrimage, and so too does permatravel. The alternative "elective centres"[5] that permatravellers tend to seek are communities that exhibit high levels of self-reliance, possess traditional ecological knowledge, and who model harmonious relationships with local environments.

5   In contrast to their well-defined travel goals, permatravellers have loose itineraries and cultivate an open-ended relationship with time.

6   Permatravellers' foci of interest include the homes, farms and gardens of WWOOF, Couch Surfing, and Warm Showers hosts, community gardens,

organic farms, botanical gardens, farmer's markets, Indigenous communities, ecovillages, national parks, beaches and other wilderness areas.

7   Permatravellers possess a thorough understanding of and commitment to permaculture's ethical and design principles. This is an important factor that distinguishes permatravellers from other types of alternative tourists. It follows that an individual who is **not** conversant with the ethics and principles of permaculture cannot embrace nor practice permaculture travel. The permaculture principles that display the highest degree of relevance for permatravellers are: Use and Value Diversity, Produce No Waste, Apply Self-Regulation and Accept Feedback, Obtain a Yield, Integrate Rather than Segregate, and Creatively Use and Respond to Change.

8   Permatravellers prioritise "slow" forms of transportation, such as buses, trains and ferries. They embrace hitch-hiking, boat-hitching, and human-powered transportation such as walking and cycling. Permatravellers have a vexed relationship with flying, and attempt to eschew flying altogether.

9   Permatravel is a frugal practice. Permatravellers seek ways to minimise their expenditure of resources, from fossil fuels to finances. Although permatravellers seek to consume less, they also tend to produce many yields. Permatravel is a highly generative practice. The emphasis is on gaining multiple yields from the resources expended. Yields from permatravel practice include "intangible" yields such as lived experience, self-knowledge, wisdom, friendship, skills, competencies and traditional ecological knowledge (TEK), in addition to "tangible" yields such as photographs, seeds, video footage, and written accounts of permatravel experiences (for instance blog posts and permatravel memoirs).

10 A central goal of permatravel is to cultivate meaningful, reciprocal, and enduring relationships with members of host communities. To these ends, permatravellers approach human and non-human others with an attitude of respect, reciprocity, and fellowship.

11 Permatravellers engage in diverse activities, including cycling, walking, wild camping, producing permaculture designs, hitch-hiking, boat-hitching, art production, political activism (for instance participating in rallies, marches and blockades), volunteering, teaching, foraging, gardening, hunting, fishing, WWOOFing, Couch Surfing and blogging.

This is by no means an exhaustive list of the attributes or sensibilities of permatravellers. It is simply a start. I hope this list will provide a solid platform for further investigation of the permatravel phenomenon, and galvanise individuals who are currently engaged (or considering engaging) in permatravel to continue to perfect their art of permatravel.

With reference to the above points, I propose a definition of permatravel that is non-essentialising and accommodates plural and diverse expressions of permatravel and permatravel practices. It is as follows:

permatravel: 1. an alternative travel practice embodying the ethics and principles of permaculture.

Notes

1 My use of the term "pioneer" in this context is not intended in the sense of being an individual involved in the colonial enterprise of exercising dominion over foreign lands, but in the *ecological* sense of being a "pioneer plant": a hardy and adaptive organism that colonizes degraded or disturbed soil and enables succession, thereby making previously inhospitable terrain more habitable for other (usually more highly developed) organisms who come after them.

2 The term "gift economy" defines a system "based not on the exchange of money, but on cooperation and generosity, shared goods and services, and mutual help and support" (Molz 2013, 215).

3 Multiple discovery is, "a term used in the scientific community whenever two or more scientists in different parts of the world come up with the same idea at the same time. (Calculus, oxygen, black holes, the Möbius strip, the existence of the stratosphere, and the theory of evolution – to name just a few – all had multiple discoverers)" (Gilbert 2015, 61).

4 In Jones's glossary of terms he defines "creaturely" as "instinctive, intuitive and animalistic characteristics" (Jones 2013, viii).

5 The term "elective centre" derives from Cohen's study of the ideology and practice of backpacking. In "Backpacking: Diversity and Change" he discusses the historical background within which backpacking emerged, and argues that it was a response to the major social and political upheavals of the 1960s. During the 1960s, disenfranchised young people, "Impelled by the alienation from the home society" went out in search of "an alternative way of life or 'elective centre'" (Cohen 2003, 105). These youthful travellers were the precursors of contemporary backpackers.

References

Adler, Judith. "Travel as Performed Art." *American Journal of Sociology* 96.6 (1989): 1366–1391.

anthonymanrique. "PermaTravel." *Uncertainties*. Available online at: http://uncertain-tiesblog.wordpress.com/2014/04/21/permatravel (last accessed 1 August 2014).

Aranya. 2012. *Permaculture Design by Aranya: A step-by-step guide*. East Meon: Permanent Publications.

Cohen, Erik. "Backpacking: Diversity and Change." *Journal of Tourism and Cultural Change* 1.2 (2003): 95–110.

Cohen, Erik. "A Phenomenology of Tourist Experiences." *Sociology* 13 (1979): 179–201.

Cohen, Erik. "The Sociology of Tourism: Approaches, Issues, and Findings." In *Annual Review of Sociology* 10 (1984): 373–392.

Dawborn, Kerry. 2011. "The New Frontier: Embracing the Inner Landscape." In Kerry Dawborn and Caroline Smith (eds) *Permaculture Pioneers: Stories from the New Frontier*. Hepburn: Melliodora Publishing, pp. 2–15.

Deville, Adrian and Stephen Wearing. 2013. "WWOOFing Tourists: Beaten Tracks and Transformational Paths." In Y. Reisinger (ed.) *Transformational Tourism: Tourist Perspectives*. Oxfordshire: CAB International, pp. 151–168.

Deville, Adrian, Stephen Wearing, and Matthew McDonald. "WWOOFing in Australia: ideas and lessons for a de-commodified sustainability tourism." *Journal of Sustainable Tourism* 24.1 (2016): 91–113.

Garrard, Greg. "The unbearable lightness of green: air travel, climate change and literature." *Green Letters: Studies in Ecocriticism* 17.2 (2013): 175–188.

Gilbert, Elizabeth. 2015. *Big Magic: Creative Living Beyond Fear*. London: Bloomsbury.

Gilbert, Helen. 2002. "Belated Journeys: Ecotourism as a Style of Travel Performance." In Helen Gilbert (ed.) *Transit: Travel, Text, Empire,*. New York: Peter Lang, pp. 255–274.

Hill, Stuart B. 2011. "Afterword: Four Key Features of Permaculture (applicable to 'everything'); and an Opportunity for the Future (also applicable to 'everything')." In Kerry Dawborn and Caroline Smith (eds) *Permaculture Pioneers: Stories from the New Frontier*. Hepburn: Melliodora Publishing, pp. 324–333.

Holmgren, David. 2011. *Permaculture: Principles and Pathways Beyond Sustainability*. Hampshire: Permanent Publications.

Jones, Patrick. "Walking for food: Regaining permapoesis." DCA thesis, University of Western Sydney, 2013.

Jones, Patrick and Meg Ulman. "Artist As Family: The Art of Permaculture Travel." *Pip* 4 (2015a): 32–35.

Jones, Patrick and Meg Ulman. 2015b. *The Art of Free Travel: A Frugal Family Adventure*. Sydney: NewSouth Publishing.

Lyons, Kevin D. and Stephen Wearing. "Reflections on the Ambiguous Intersections between Volunteering and Tourism." *Leisure Sciences* 34 (2012): 88–93.

Mollison, Bill. 2011. *Introduction to Permaculture*. Tasmania: Tagari Publications.

Mollison, Bill. 2012. *Permaculture: A Designers' Manual*. Tasmania: Tagari Publications.

Molz, Jennie G. "Social Networking Technologies and the Moral Economy of Alternative Tourism: The Case of Couchsurfing.org." *Annals of Tourism Research* 43 (2013): 210–230.

Oh, Haemoon, George A. Assaf, and Seyhmus Baloglu. "Motivatations and Goals of Slow Tourism." *Journal of Travel Research* 55.2 (2016): 205–219.

Smith, Caroline. 2011. "Introduction." In *Permaculture Pioneers: Stories from the New Frontier*, edited by Kerry Dawborn and Caroline Smith. Hepburn: Melliodora Publishing: ix–xix.

Strampello, Giri. "The Permatraveler Manifesto." *Permatraveler*. Available online at: http://permatraveler.blogspot.au/p/the-permatraveler-maifesto.html (last accessed 9 May 2016).

7 Momentum in the age of sustainability

Building up and burning out in a transition town

Emily Polk

I was enthralled with the Transition Town movement from the first moment I heard about it—from a starry-eyed professor in graduate school who praised the young social movement for its grassroots, community-based approach to enacting solutions to the complex problems wrought by climate change. Indeed the movement, which began a decade ago in Totnes, England, to help communities "transition" to "a low-carbon, socially-just, healthier and happier future" (Transition Network), has since spread to more than 1,120 Transition initiatives in 43 countries. The Transition model, freely accessible on its website, offers tips, tools, strategies, suggestions, and advice on everything from initiating a Transition Town, to building a resilient food system, to starting a cooperative business (Hopkins and Lipman 2009; Hopkins 2011). Fiercely apolitical, with a focus on a solutions-based, positive framing, (Chatterton and Cutler 2008; Connors and McDonald 2010), the movement grew so quickly and with so much fanfare, I wondered whether it was going to be able to sustain itself long-term. I also wondered – as a mother with a young child, working full time, trying to finish school, with no extended family nearby, limited financial resources, and a deep desire to *do something* – could I also participate? And more than that: would I have the momentum to participate long-term without getting burned out?

My own Transition Town, Transition Amherst, was situated in a small river valley in Western Massachusetts that is also home to several colleges and one major university. For a year and a half—from the time it was registered as an official initiative on the website to the moment it informally disbanded—I attended all of the meetings, taking notes, helping to organize and promote events, volunteering at the local sustainability festival, and genuinely enjoying the company of around a dozen thoughtful people who cared deeply about making their community more resilient. The meetings were held in the farmhouse of a young family who had recently moved to the area. Some of my greatest memories from that time are from the moments before and after the meetings, as I made my way up to the house, listening to the wind blow through the pines at the edge of the farm, smelling the crisp cool air tinged with the wood smoke of a neighbor's fire. I always took a moment to gaze at the stars burning through a silky black sky and to look up at the old wooden door of the farmhouse, on the other side of which I knew I would find warm tea and fresh bread and a mix of voices sharing their stories, visions, and goals for the meeting.

I was moved, especially in the early days of the initiative, by the sense of possibility and by the notion that courageous people, united by a desire to make their community more resilient, were taking a few hours out of their evening to build one together. Those early days felt so hopeful and I drew upon that hope for sustenance throughout the following year. But my participation ended up being a complicated experience for me. I did not have the capacity (resources, time or support—see above) to engage as fully as I would have liked and thus did not always feel like I had a right to speak up or try to influence decisions and choices when, in retrospect, I might have.

I had also decided to make my participation part of a research project that would ultimately be an ethnography of my Transition Town. I let everybody know that I thought the research could ultimately be used by Transition Amherst and I was grateful for their approval. This ethnography would end up informing the bulk of my dissertation, which would ultimately help me to get a job that was likely far away from this town. During my time with Transition Amherst, I was sensitive to these complexities and contradictions. What did it mean to focus my energy on supporting the resiliency of a town that I might end up leaving? I also did not want my analysis to be compromised by my personal attachments and friendships, which depended largely on emotional connections and less on factual quantifiable data, and yet I knew that the success of these initiatives often depends on such connections. I note this complexity, not only because it ultimately informed my own sense of burnout, but also as a way to suggest that the factors that influence burnout for participants are highly personal and contingent upon individual contexts and circumstances.

As the increasingly violent impacts of climate change make the need for grassroots action more urgent, this essay has offered an opportunity to take a more personal look at my own experience with the Transition movement and involvement with my Transition Town. I ended up writing an academic book about the Transition movement—I was honored by the Press's offer to publish but regretful of the fast turnaround. Were I to go back and write it again, I would take more time to distinguish between the processes and practices of imagining, developing, and creating alternative and more resilient eco-systems and the very arduous and complex practice of sustaining them. Now that I have passed through the other side of my burnout, I think I would have been more patient with my own frustrations and limitations and made kinder selections about how and when I quoted people. This piece has allowed me to do that in some ways while expanding upon that Transition Town ethnography with additional research on burnout from the movement. Finally, I hope to share in this essay some of the factors that contributed to and compromised the long-term sustainability of my Transition Town, with a particular focus on connecting its long-term viability to the burnout experienced by many of us.

Ultimately for my Transition Town, a lack of clear communication and sufficient time to work through disagreements and conflicting visions, plus the absence of effective leadership, made it difficult to resolve tensions and to avoid a sense of disconnect and frustration. This eventually led to members feeling exhausted and unable to continue to participate. I think some of the above mentioned factors can be anticipated and mitigated against, and this essay seeks, in part, to explore how and when a group might actively do that work in order to sustain itself long-term.

Although researchers have studied the concept of burnout as an erosion of a positive psychological state (Schaufeli et al. 2009) often accompanied by mental exhaustion (Schaufeli and Buunk 2002), the majority of research has focused on the workplace, with only a small body of literature focusing on sustaining participation in social movements (Chen and Gorski 2015). In February of 2016, however, the Transition Network chose to focus its newsletter on the causes and consequences of burnout, suggesting that the experience—for both individuals and groups—is a significant issue. Indeed Sophie Banks, who helped to develop the "inner transition" aspect of the movement (Transition Network), noted that more than half of all Transitioners she spoke with said they had experienced or were at risk of experiencing burnout, which she described as a state of severe exhaustion where recovery takes a long time (Banks 2016). Several authors featured in the newsletter suggest that the risk of burnout is particularly high for people who are driven by a sense of urgency and anxiety in the dire face of multiple global crises, and must negotiate the inverse relationship of the high demand for such work with the often low resources to support it. The strain is amplified by the passionate and personal investment people have in the work (Johnstone, 2016).

As I note in the book (Polk 2015), The Transition model does offer several general tips for how groups might sustain their momentum. According to the *Transition Companion* (Hopkins 2011, 172), initiatives can get stuck because they don't plan for succession. Members feel that the same faces are always appearing at events, and there are no new participants; problems go unaddressed between members of the group: anger, disappointment, frustration cause suppression of feelings; funding to support the continued development of projects is low, and members feel that there is too much "processing" and not enough "doing." This last—akin to that infamous phrase attributed to Oscar Wilde, "socialism takes too many evenings"—was certainly part of the problem for Transition Amherst. Many members (myself included) talked about the limited amount of time we had to participate, and the limited amount of time available at a bimonthly meeting to make decisions and coordinate activities. Tensions arose and momentum declined when members wanted to discuss and establish group processes and others argued that there simply was no time, given the projects and goals of the group (Polk 2015).

Each member of Transition Amherst had different goals, visions, skills, and resources to contribute. Ideally, this is what makes a Transition initiative thrive because everybody is bringing something new to the table. However, the lack of strategy and group process within Transition Amherst caused frustration for some members. We were tasked, for example, with questions about which events Transition might co-sponsor in the community, which causes Transition Amherst might support financially, and who might speak for the group to various media outlets to promote Transition activities. Such decisions often involved long and arduous discussions, largely because there was never any agreed-upon process for how such decisions would be made. Tensions arose between those who wanted to devote more time to developing governance structures and members who wanted to devote the majority of the meeting time to organizing practical projects with and for the community. Cindy,[1] a member in her fifties said: "I think the integrity and the intention behind those meetings was really deep and admirable. I guess I'm left feeling like along the way there were people whose feelings were hurt in that group and who didn't feel heard and never had the chance to be heard. I don't feel settled about it" (Polk 2015, 119).

Tellingly, the Transition model very rarely uses the term "leadership" in any of its communication materials online or offline. Transition US offers a "Governance Toolbox" which includes tips for effective facilitation, including: helping the group to define its goals and objectives; assess its needs and create plans to meet them; provide processes that help members to use their time efficiently; guide discussions; and support group members in feeling heard. The toolbox does not explain, however, how a facilitator can do the above, and/or how to negotiate the challenges that arise when the above does not happen. And Transition Amherst struggled with the question of leadership. The facilitator was responsible for assuming a leadership role at the meeting; however, there was nobody to hold others accountable to or make people responsible for fulfilling their commitments to the group long-term. It was generally assumed that people who came to the meeting with ideas for projects and events would lead the organization and development of them (Polk 2015, 113).

This lack of leadership was made most apparent when we began planning our "Great Unleashing," an event that every Transition Town is encouraged to host as a way to introduce the initiative to the larger community and celebrate the town's history. Countless logistical decisions needed to be made and I grew increasingly silent around them. I had not lived in Amherst as long as the others had so did not have the same historical or familial connections. I was consumed with caring for a baby (who was still nursing every couple of hours) and overwhelmed with teaching and other research projects, conferences, and daily survival tasks (grocery shopping, shoveling snow off my car and the driveway). I never spoke to the group about feeling overwhelmed and unable to contribute, I just didn't speak up when it came time to make decisions or volunteer to take on leadership roles with regard to planning the event. Gradually the loudest voices in the group—i.e. the ones with the most time and the strongest opinions—took over.

Roger Reed, a carpenter in his sixties, concurred that it was the strongest voices that eventually held sway. He suggested that the absence of effective leadership was directly tied to the group's inability to communicate with each other and resolve conflict:

> The way I've seen it happen more often than not in the Transition Group is that there's disagreement to the point where if a decision isn't made everything's going to fall apart. There was so much unending discussion and lack of making decisions... At one point it was the strongest voices, strongest egos that held sway on how decisions were made. They were sort of accepted by everybody else but I don't really feel that we had come to a consensus necessarily so that everybody was fully on board.
>
> (Polk 2015, 116)

Reed's comment amplifies a marked tension that underscored the group's work together. This was the tension between (a) acknowledging the amount of time it takes to establish and apply processes of consensus that result in everybody feeling heard and participating fully in decisions and (b) the feeling that, in the face of limited amounts of time, resources, and the urgency of the issues, time should be spent on fulfilling actual goals set forth during meetings, not spent discussing group processes. Without an effective leader to negotiate the limited amount of time and/or the tensions, the group began to lose its cohesiveness and momentum.

During this time, my own capacity to take on a leadership responsibilities was compromised by the fact that I was negotiating my role as an ethnographic researcher and an active Transition Town participant. I wasn't always certain when I had a right to speak up and when it was my responsibility to sit back and observe the Transition process unfolding. I note this now because I formally interviewed all of the participants in the Transition Town immediately after the group disbanded and many of them were quite vocal and articulate about how they experienced the tensions and frustrations that led to their burnout. I included many of their quotes in my book, partly as a way to figure out my own experience. But in hindsight, I would not have included so many negative ones and I would have been more clear about my own positionality (and biases) as a participant observer.

I also would have done a better job underscoring that all of the participants in Transition Amherst were guided by good intentions and a genuine desire to build and nurture a more resilient community. I do not mean to suggest that the conflicts that arose were easily avoidable or resolvable. In fact, it may just be the opposite. I hope to illuminate the struggles of one Transition Town as a way to suggest that even the most generous and altruistic people are not immune to the conflicts that cause burnout while doing the difficult work of sustaining an initiative. Indeed, Sophie Banks notes that burnout is the dirty secret of the environmental movement (Banks 2016). The factors that contribute to it as well as the consequences that follow from it are important to unpack if we are going to be successful in imagining a sustainable alternative to our current systems.

Of course, in a place like Amherst, a college town with a large population of sustainability-minded people, other groups were already doing projects compatible with Transition goals. While most people knew others, for example, who were involved with CISA (Communities Involved In Sustaining Agriculture)—a non-profit working to strengthen farms and engage the community to build the local food economy—and Pioneer Valley Local First—a membership-based organization, working to encourage people in the area "to *think local first* so that they *buy and bank local first*"—Transition Amherst never coordinated any activities directly with them. Similarly, the University of Massachusetts, where I was getting my doctorate, had a series of sustainability-oriented activities and events; however, we were never able to build consistent partnerships with them. The Transition movement, which operates at a "town" level, would have benefited from more coordinated efforts with such groups, in terms of sustaining the group's momentum and avoiding individual burnout. During my time with Transition Amherst, active and sustained coordination with other groups was never discussed consistently as a collective group, although they were considered privately and in one-on-one interviews. The group as a whole worked very hard to apply the global model to the community of Amherst, but aside from providing links to the other groups on its website transitionamherst.org, we did not consider in any systemized way how our work could be coordinated with other groups already doing similar work. I am just as much to blame for this as anybody. I was so excited to be welcomed into the group initially, and so enamored with the global Transition model that it did not occur to me how important it was to work with others even if it was not an event that was labeled a "Transition" activity or directly hosted by our initiative.

In doing research for the book project, I did discover examples of Transition groups that seemed to be more successful in navigating these challenges, particularly around group decision-making processes and how to sustain momentum long-term. Sustainable NE Seattle (one of the longest-running Transition initiatives), has established its own model for governance, which it has shared in a webinar. The planning and coordination of Sustainable NE Seattle projects were left up to individual subgroups. The steering committee, however, consistently met twice a month and the central focus of those meetings was on keeping up the momentum. The model therefore allowed for the central group really to commit to sustaining the group, while the smaller groups were empowered with the planning and coordinating of individual projects, thus distributing power, control, and leadership. But even as this model of governance might seem to emphasize leadership at the expense of more collaborative processes, the group also emphasizes the basic importance of civility. Members admitted that while they didn't always see things eye to eye on a project, they put their friendship first. "We don't second guess each other," said one member. "People don't question or veto each other—if someone wants to do it we trust them." Their one rule: "Whatever is said must advance the conversation. So we don't really have a formal model, we just have a conversation with people we trust." (Sustainable NE Seattle webinar, 2013, cited in Polk 2015).

Even in the most well-organized and civil of groups, however, individual burnout can take its toll. Toward the end of my time with Transition Amherst, many participants expressed a sense of personal burnout with the initiative, suggesting the importance of prioritizing and preparing for the emotional and psychological toll that service to such an initiative takes. Roger Reed said:

> It always goes back to how do you find time to do all this. So I think when we got to a point when it seemed like all of the effort we put in had reached a conclusion I think people were relieved and were willing to just sort of drop everything and if something else was going to happen somebody else would pick up the ball and it wouldn't have to be them. I include myself in that group. I was fatigued after... and I was only involved for eight months! I was fatigued at the end of it and really willing to just say boy I'm glad that's over and not worry about anything else.
>
> (Polk 2015, 124)

Reed raises here the problem of sustaining the group in the face of the burnout of the individuals in it, suggesting that strategies for finding that next person who will "pick up the ball" have to be part of a Transition Group's agenda.

Though I do not have quantitative information on the diversity of community members who attended Transition Amherst workshops and activities, I found, overall, that Transition Amherst did not have a strategy for contacting and incorporating new members, except, for example, to have people sign their name and email to a signup sheet at an event, after which their name was added to a general Transition Amherst listserv. Outreach was largely limited to advertising on the website or Facebook page and face-to-face communication with friends.

The fact that Amherst is a "university town" has its advantages and disadvantages in terms of sustaining a deep sense of community and long-term participation in a Transition Town. With one large university and two colleges, there are more than 40,000 students who occupy a temporary residence within the town (Planning Amherst Together 2007). Their involvement with Transition Amherst would likely be limited to an academic school year with limited transportation opportunities unless they had a car. The new ideas and energy have the potential to fuel participation and engage the community, however, the high turnover means that people are less able to invest in the initiative long-term.

Interestingly, while the Amherst group struggled with the time commitments required to sustain its momentum, it did not struggle as much with money. According to the Transition Network, the lack of sustainable funding is one of the primary reasons that an initiative loses momentum and stops its activities. Carolyne Stayton, Executive Director of Transition US, the Transition movement's hub for the United States, has said that the next step for making Transition Towns sustainable is making sure "money comes into it," either by collaborating on fundraising with other initiatives, having a fiscal sponsorship or non-profit status (Polk 2015, 127). Transition Amherst did have its own bank account with several hundred dollars in it. Money for Transition-related activities such as promotional materials for events and/or to rent out rooms in the library was either taken out of the account or subsidized by members coordinating the event, suggesting perhaps that a Transition Town might be more productive with members who have the personal resources to sustain it. In our case, though, if time is money, money, unfortunately, did not translate into time, which seemed to be the more crucial commodity.

Individual and group burnout is one of the dirty secrets of the environmental movement—or indeed any movement that relies upon the good will and commitment of the individuals who contribute to it. One of the central purposes of this essay is to call attention to the importance of anticipating it, understanding why it happens and the importance of developing strategies for dealing with it. It is important to note that all of the factors and variables that influence the momentum of a group and its long-term viability are connected to each other. In my own experience with my Transition Town, I found that, important as the problem of limited time was, it might have been mitigated by more consistent and stable leadership within the group. Such leadership would have enabled effective facilitation of meetings, where a consistent decision-making process was defined and agreed upon; balance could be negotiated between time spent on planning actions and developing group processes; and time spent discussing the group's projects and building deeper connections with one another based on the values that brought them to the group in the first place. Such leadership might have helped us to situate our efforts in the larger community, allowing us to develop strategies for reaching out to more diverse groups of people as well as nurturing community-building opportunities within the group itself.

All of these suggestions do not negate the fact that time is still such a severely limited resource for so many of us. Indeed negotiating, planning for and thinking about ways to sustain an initiative and avoid burnout takes time away from those who want to spend it digging up dirt for a community garden or offering a workshop on beekeeping. But perhaps, at the end of the day, it does not have to be either/or, but *both*. Perhaps, by focusing with a sense of self-care and community-care on both the product and the process of the work, we might find a balance that can sustain us individually and collectively. Resilience specialist Chris Johnstone suggests in a recent interview posted on the Transition Network:

> There's content in terms of what do we do, but there's also process which is how do we do it. How do we change the quality of our meetings? It's seeing that how we do things is as important as what we do…We can judge what we do by the end result. Also we [can] say—Can we do it in a way that is nourishing? Can we do it in a way that is attractive? When we start asking those questions… it really changes things.

Eventually I did get that university teaching job 3,000 miles away from the small river valley where Transition Amherst was born. Today I teach courses focused on communicating climate change, social justice, and writing about the wilderness. I take my students to community gardens in underserved communities and coordinate public teach-ins to give them platforms to share their activism and their research. I help advise students with their sustainability efforts and continue to volunteer and write and publish as much as I can. Time still remains my most elusive resource, but the work feels particularly urgent as a new kind of darkness and uncertainty moves over us after the 2016 U.S. presidential election. Although I am not active in a Transition initiative, there is not one week that goes by when I do not think about something that I learned from my experience there. I prioritize the labor of building community and trust with my students before we begin the hard work; I check in with them throughout our time together to make sure we are communicating clearly and needs are being met; I try to get them to see how their research can be connected to other research, how we can take our work outside of the classroom and apply it in ways that make the world better. I try to model compassionate leadership by holding them accountable and facilitating meaningful learning spaces. We talk about how all of us have felt burnout at one time or another, and about how hard it is to maintain momentum with limited resources in the face of such big challenges. We share different strategies for sustaining our passion and our curiosity and even our optimism. Somehow, in the talking itself, we are energized again, even if only for a moment.

Sometimes I think about all of those nights when I stood outside the wooden door of the old farmhouse in a quiet river valley, before a Transition meeting, knowing that on the other side, there was a room full of people who were making time to work and dream and imagine a better, more resilient community. There are so many of us on the other sides of those doors in communities all over the world.

There are so many of us trying to figure out a way to keep on doing the work even when we are tired of it, even when it all seems too hard.

I try to remember no matter where I am, to take a deep breath and pause. Then I go in.

Note

1 Names have been changed to protect the identities of Transition Town members.

References

Chatterton, P. and Cutler, A. 2008. "The Rocky Road to a Real Transition: the transition towns movement and what it means for social change." *The Trapese Collective*, 41.

Chen Weixia C. and Gorski, P. 2015. "Burnout in Social Justice and Human Rights Activists: Symptoms, Causes and Implications." *Journal of Human Rights Practice* Vol. 0 Number 0, 1–25, Oxford University Press.

Connors, P. and McDonald, P. 2010. "Transitioning communities: community, participation and the Transition Town movement." *Community Development Journal*, Vol 46 No 4, 558–572.

Editorial: "Sophy Banks on Balance or Burnout?" Available online at: https://transition-network.org/news-and-blog/editorial-sophy-banks-on-balance-or-burnout (last accessed 1 August 2016).

Interview with Chris Johnstone: "Burnout is a risk where people are passionate about what they do." Available online at: www.transitionculture.org/2016/01/13/interview-with-chris-johnstone-burnout-is-a-risk-where-people-are-passionate-about-what-they-do (last accessed 7 August 2016).

Hopkins, R. 2008. *The Transition Handbook: From Oil Dependency to Local Resilience.* UK: Green Books.

Hopkins, R. 2011. *The Transition Companion: Making your community more resilient in uncertain times.* UK: Green Books.

Hopkins, R. and Lipman, P. 2009. "Who we are and what we do." *Transition Network.org*, 1–24.

Planning Amherst Together. 2007. PERSPECTIVE: Context, History, and Planning Heritage, 1–18. Available online at: www.amherstma.gov/DocumentCenter/Home/View/1626 (last accessed 1 February 2013).

Polk, E. 2015. *Communicating Global to Local Resiliency: A Case Study of the Transition Movement.* Maryland, MD: Lexington Books.

Schaufeli, W. B. and P. Buunk. 2002. "Burnout: An Overview of 25 Years of Research and Theorizing." In M. J. Schabracq, J. A. M. Winnubst and C. L. Cooper (eds) *The Handbook of Work and Health Psychology.* Chichester: Wiley, 383–425.

Schaufeli, W., Leiter, M. and Maslach, C. 2009. "Burnout: 35 years of research and practice." *Career Development International.* Vol. 14, 204–220.

"Sophie Banks Reflects on 10 years at the heart of Transition". Available online at: http://transitionnetwork.org/news-and-blog/sophy-banks-reflects-on-10-years-at-the-heart-of-transition (last accessed 2 August 2016).

Transition US Governance Toolbox. Transition United States, 1–11. Available online at: www.transitionus.org/sites/default/files/TransitionUS_HowTo_GovernanceTool box_v2.0.pdf (last accessed 1 February 2013).

8 "Fracking is stoppable, another world is possible"

Claire Males

"Fracking is stoppable, another world is possible" was a regular chant during protest marches against fracking lorries at the Balcombe Community Protection Camp at Lower Stumble, located on a wide grassy verge of the B2036 road in summer 2013. The community of activists, local residents, and earth defenders who protested were there to fight for the same planet but a very different world: one more environmentally balanced and less exploitative. The community that formed along the roadside was open to anyone, was based on consensus community meetings, claimed itself alcohol- and meat-free, organised itself haphazardly around campfires and borrowed gazebos, and had electricity through solar power. This movement occurred in Balcombe in response to the proposed hydraulic fracturing (fracking) operation that the company Cuadrilla had begun several miles outside the village.

Aged nineteen and driven by the idea we could save the planet through direct action, I spent ten weeks protesting between August and October as part of the camp community. This chapter, informed by my own experience and conversations with other participants, argues that a messy prototype of the imagined "other world" that many desired actually existed at the protest site itself. In response to a local environmental threat, over several months people built and strengthened a purely grassroots community. Balcombe was one of many protest camps that have been organized along these lines in the UK and elsewhere, and I hope to illustrate how the camp itself can act as a catalyst for action.

The protest was called a blockade, derided by the media, and heavily policed. Given that semi-legal practices occurred, I offered the interviewees the choice to change their names to protect anonymity. Many were, however, proud and happy to have their voices represented. A protest site in opposition to a government and corporate project makes for volatile and emotive subject matter. But here I draw on the more constructive elements of the camp, the memory of which may otherwise become buried under the majority of press reports and recollections ("How summer" 2014),[1] which have focused on the disruptions and on the outcome of the fracking project. My focus, then, is not on fracking but on the people who were opposed to fracking and the wider activist community united by shared ethical and political ideals. Those who are concerned about risky methods of fossil fuel extraction are often also those who seek a more far-reaching alternative to a fossil fuel-reliant society. It is not just the singular issue of fracking or carbon or climate change that people opposed; rather, activists felt that in life in modernity, people, animals, plants, and the earth itself are facing an increasingly interconnected bleak situation. The single issue of fracking thus opened up a wider discussion and a space for alternatives to be lived.

Terms such as "off-grid," "environmentally conscious," and "alternative lifestyle" have varied definitions. There are myriad criteria – petrol consumption, organic food, solar power – that one could use when attempting to discern how far particular situations evidence green credentials. My instinct here is to represent the mentality, record a picture of the ideas that circulated, and trace the fates of those that pursue them. I take the approach firstly that the terms "eco" and "off-grid" should be broadened to include the self-perception of those participating. If a group of people express that they wish to live off-the-grid and go to lengths to do so, it indicates a popular groundswell worthy of attention. Total self-sufficiency will always be hard to achieve in modern urban and rural England, as the country is relatively overpopulated and there is minimal free land. Engagement with the wider system is inevitable through employment and legal battles over the free spaces that do exist, but people are consciously attempting to disentangle as far as they can. And, to my mind, any community that makes attempts to self-sustain, that is influenced by environmental concerns and enabled through the basics of lifestyle, solar panels, living outdoors, and DIY practices, is evidence of a mentality that seeks an alternative to a world relying on fossil fuels and ecocidal practices.

Balcombe as "another world"

I cannot, of course, list the collective beliefs of every individual at Balcombe; however, themes did emerge, as the commitment to protecting the environment united people regardless of their backgrounds, and common practices helped materialize collective values, leading to the idea that the camp represented "another world." The songs sung by a group can indicate a sense of the values held by the people singing them, and the chants and slogans which the protesters shouted whilst "walking the lorries" (part of the blockade, to slow down the fracking operation) can be used as insight into the ideals and philosophies of the protest community at Balcombe. The chant which inspired the title of this essay is an example, that "Another world is possible." "Frack free Sussex" was one of the original slogans, which, over time, shifted to become "frack free planet," or "stop fracking everywhere." This reflects the different priorities for protesters, as many were local to the immediate area of West Sussex; however, soon "frack free everywhere/planet" became more popular, reflecting a rejection of not-in-my-back-yard-ism.[2] The media attempted to exaggerate any possible division between the protesters and residents; however, these were minimal, with 95 per cent of the Balcombe residents strongly against fracking (Frack Free Balcombe 2015, 3).

Another popular chant that people shouted while marching against the lorries carrying out the fracking operations was "There are many, many more of us than you." This was chanted directly to the police and communicated that the protesters felt united ideologically as part of a wider, loosely connected family of activists. The particular tune and chant had been popularised at anti-fascist counter demonstrations, where the mechanics of the protest created a situation with two groups opposing each other, one left wing and the other right wing. In Balcombe there were no counter-protesters in support of fracking, so the police became the opposing group, which then went on to be imaginatively outnumbered by the song.

The police presence at camp was controversial and multi-faceted. During marches it would sometimes turn violent; at times they would make random arrests of individuals thought to be agitators. This led to the evolution of the slang term "snatch squad" to describe when the police's actions were deemed arbitrary kidnap. Participant Emma recalls:

> In that respect, Balcombe was a catalyst. I always thought of myself as a middle class member of society, not a protester. But then I saw the police acting like unfeeling robots, then I would see the media report something completely different. And I realised that they were lying. Until then I trusted the BBC: that was a turning point for me when I realised the dominant narrative was broken, and we had to work to create a new one.
>
> (2017)

In more peaceful moments there were occasional friendly interactions with the police, leading to disagreements between protesters about whether anyone should talk to the police in a casual manner because the state was perceived by the majority to be the enemy. Some still insisted on engaging the police in conversation in order to educate them about fracking. From this we can gauge that while the collectively held values were antithetical to those of the government, this feeling was expressed at different degrees of enthusiasm by individuals.

Many people who protested at Balcombe were keen to emphasise that they felt they were fighting *for* something, not *against* something, acting with a positive impulse rather than as a negative reaction. Camp members began to refer to themselves as "protectors" as opposed to protesters. Balcombe participant Emma explains her thinking about this terminology:

> I believe that to save life on earth as we know it, we need to oppose the dominant narrative and replace it with a new one. We are not protesters, we are protectors, we are protecting the safe water supply, and the planet.
>
> (2017)

Banners depicted wildlife, trees, plants, and water sources, reflecting the concern that fracking would damage the natural aquifers in the area. Slogans such as "only when the last tree and fish are dead will you realise you can't eat money" appeared on signs and placards. A YouTube video of the camp shows a protester saying, "There is only one planet; there is no planet B. If they destroy this one, then where do we go? That's why I am here" (Truthferretfilms 2013). The Balcombe protesters felt a strong allegiance to the health and welfare of the planet; in this case, it was the aquifers and reservoirs in West Sussex, but such concern is what arguably unites and defines all environmentalists. As Laura recalls, "Balcombe was a place for people who all cared about the bigger picture. Yes, everyone disagreed with fracking, which is why we were there, but that bigger picture is what connected us" (2016).

Alongside the urge to stop the potential damage to the water table (and house prices) caused by fracking, a wider ethic was committed to pursuing a real alternative. Natural gas is another fossil fuel, and many people are growing uncomfortable with the degree of fossil fuel dependence and would rather get power from renewable sources. I certainly recall a strong sense that the work of protecting the earth was bigger than Balcombe, and that by being there and objecting to fracking, we were all part of a thriving and radical alternative.

The camp at Balcombe as an off-grid community

The protector ethos that characterized Balcombe was built, too, into the very material practices of the day-to-day running of the camp. The camp operated under a DIY ethic and was organised in a grassroots manner. Tents, handmade benders, foraging, community kitchens, recycled structures and donated materials are examples of low-impact practices that took people back to the basic skills that are part and parcel of off-grid living. The camp was set up to help people live outside, in order to be as close to the fracking drill as possible, and being a mobile community reminded everyone of basic questions of water and power supply. The main barriers to the camp as a model for realistic, long-term, off-grid community building were the facts that, as a protest camp, it was supported by donations that created an unexpected abundance of food and provisions; and also that fracking as a common enemy united and attracted people, giving people an occupation that was entirely circumstantial.

Balcombe was characterized by a campfire lifestyle, as people cooked and ate around communal fires, sharing food and responsibilities. Around the camp were several communal "tea tents," which combined a campfire with chairs and where everyone was welcome to sit and talk. A gazebo with the fracking information leaflets was adjacent. These tea tents became symbols of hospitality, for, in-between the lorries, meetings, and road block actions, an ample selection of tea was constantly being prepared. Drinking tea communally is representative of the wider ethic and practice at Balcombe; anyone who sympathised with the movement was welcome to come, and new visitors especially were offered tea. These casual moments of conversation in an open domestic space allowed all protesters to connect, and this was one of the main ways in which the Balcombe protest became such a hub of activity.

Petrol generators or solar panels provided electricity for the internet and lights. The solar power electricity tent was a much-lauded aspect of Balcombe life, as it was a chance to demonstrate the sustainable alternative. Meals were cooked in standalone kitchens and people would take turns to cook breakfast, lunch and dinner, and then to wash up. Each morning a bell would ring to give a fifteen-minute warning of a meeting, open to anyone, at which it would be determined who was on meal duty that day. Laura recalls,

> I was involved in the kitchens and helped to prepare meals. Things were always changing as new people would arrive and bring new ideas. Sometimes there were arguments about what to cook; it was not easy. But dinner was prepared,

three meals a day were cooked, and everyone was fed, which is amazing if you consider most people were strangers before coming to Balcombe.

(2016)

The food came from many places, and local farmers donated surplus seasonal vegetables, which led to a sometimes less-than-varied diet. Seasonal eating is certainly one pillar of a more sustainable alternative world, but it was an adjustment for those previously used to being sheltered from the season's effects by the supermarket supply chain. As Steve recalls, "There were a lot of courgettes. People started complaining, asking why there were courgettes again. Even I remember complaining about that!" (2016). Those who continued such a lifestyle after Balcombe were soon rudely acquainted with the winter weather, but their first introduction at Balcombe was through courgettes.

Some bushcraft practices also emerged, enabled by the surrounding forests and fields. Roadkill pheasant and squirrel would be cooked, and damsons and apples growing wild were foraged. This abundance was facilitated by the season, as wild fruit is not available all year round. Such practices widened the skillset of protesters, offering tools for a more sustainable and local engagement with food. Admittedly, though, a problem of ecosystem supply would emerge were the Balcombe verge to become a full-time encampment. These resources might become scarce if all two-hundred-odd people foraged daily.

Most of the infrastructure for the meeting space, the kitchens, and the sleeping space, was acquired through donations. For example, Stuart and Emma, who live on a smallholding ten miles away, recall donating pots and pans, benches, and a water container. Occasionally large donations of clothes and food from individuals or groups that supported the blockade would arrive, and these would be shared out among the protesters. Some money for running the camp came from sympathetic businesses like Lush[3] and these funds would also go towards supporting the direct actions and paying the court fines accrued through illegal road blockades.

With such an abundance, camp life took on a utopian feel. Once the infrastructure was built, goods arrived and were circulated without anyone needing their own money to survive. This meant people were free to plan actions and to march in front of the lorries without needing to think about where their food and shelter was going to come from. This also created the space for skills to be taught, learned, and practised in-between the lorry marches.

The standard nylon camping tents everyone began sleeping in were not adequate for long-term living, so alongside them, new kitchens and shelters were built, called "benders." Benders were remembered by some as a folk tradition of travelling people's shelters, and historical records can confirm that this had been a traveller practice for centuries. Benders were constructed from branches cut and pegged to the ground, then framed with a tarpaulin, and then insulated with layers and layers of fabric and whatever people had to hand. People traditionally used willow, but in Balcombe they used beech from the local woods as it was more common. Benders were new to some, and soon more people were learning how to build them, a key example of how the protest infrastructure circulated traditional skills.

The camp population varied as people would come and go, staying for various periods. On a normal day the population was between 60–200 residents, swelling up to 3000 on a single day of action organised by Reclaim the Power.[4] Bearing this in mind, it is worth pointing out that the camp was remarkably united in that coordinated actions happened, dinner was always cooked, and everyone was happy to pitch in. It was a community in which people wanted to make work, queue for dinner, and do their own washing up. In the most base and earthy example of camp organisation volunteers built the compost-based toilets, organised council waste collection, and members of the camp would elect to change the toilet paper and clean the toilets daily. Reliance on the local council for waste collection could be criticised by some radical thinkers as compromising how far the camp was off-grid and independent, but given the ad hoc organisation and potential for relations to sour, the cooperation that enabled this must be viewed as a positive.

Ideologically, much of the infrastructure was influenced by the Occupy movement, a form of popular protest against neoliberalism that arrived in the UK in 2011. Occupy advocated a broad-brush style of protest where the lifestyle was the lynchpin of the revolution, and the principle was to build a new community of activists in a public place where anyone could join in and voice their concerns (Chomsky 2012). Many Balcombe protesters had been involved with and informed by these practices, and these veterans of Occupy worked alongside seasoned protesters who had been involved in other road blockades in the 1990s (Wall 1999). In contrast, other protesters were new to protesting and visited either out of curiosity or through their pure objection to fracking, which led to a real diversity among participants. As Balcombe "protector" Stuart described it, "What I liked about Balcombe was that it had a real, genuine diversity, yet everyone communicated. You would have blue-rinse Tories sat eating dinner with hard-line tree-climbing activists... it was surreal" (2017). Balcombe has been remembered as being festive and easy for people to take part in. Some, particularly those involved in subsequent anti-fracking protests, which took place over the winter in far harsher conditions, have criticised the camp for having the appearance and atmosphere of a carnival, with camping, circus toys, banner painting, and children's areas giving it a gaudy air at times. This assertion is only partially accurate – it overlooks, for example, conflict and stress caused by fracking and police – but the fact that Balcombe was able to take on the relaxed, utopian air of a festival meant that it was more accessible and welcoming to a wide range of people: precisely the kind of campfire culture that the protest aimed to cultivate.

Despite its many successes, however, the camp at Balcombe was not utopian; it could never be said to be self-sufficient or off-grid, as it was financially supported by organisations that wanted to oppose the fracking. Alongside this, contradictions emerged as people drove petrol cars, or ate food sourced from the supermarkets, sometimes skipped (salvaged from a bin) or from local farms. The main kitchen was vegetarian by default, yet it soon emerged that not all people shared this ethic and several alternative "meat kitchens" emerged, with people having covert, meat-eating sessions with an air of convoluted secrecy.

A similar pattern happened with alcohol; a meeting early on decided the camp would have a better reputation if it was dry (alcohol-free), yet many would have a drink in the evenings, either in defiance or in ignorance of this rule. This did cause problems but after a while most realised it was simply not worth having arguments about personal choices, as the daily marches provided a moment of unity, and disagreements would mostly be forgotten. Rules like the dry camp were hard to enforce because in a grassroots community there is no means to do so.

"Ad hoc" is a perfect term to describe how, in a community of individuals, contradictory strands of eco-philosophy emerged to coexist. Many people who joined the camp had goals of pursuing a more environmentally balanced world. They arrived to express their concerns about fracking, and were able, while protesting, to practice a form of communal living with shared responsibilities. These practices made the camp into more than a blockade, for the practices of using solar power, cultivating "campfire mentality," and building a communal organisation offered an on-the-spot guide to more sustainable living. It may not have been low-impact living in a pure sense, but for many, protest camps like Balcombe were an opportunity to experience significantly less-impact living.

Beyond Balcombe

Of equal importance to what happened at Balcombe in 2013 is what happened afterwards. Once the fracking drill was taken down in late September, people began to contemplate what to do next, as some no longer wanted to go back to how they lived pre-Balcombe. Three years on, there are several positive changes visible, as well as some familiar problems resurfacing. Many people kept protesting at other sites all over the country, such as Barton Moss in Greater Manchester, Horse Hill in West Sussex, and Upton in Cheshire. Some stayed in the local area and started on new projects or continued ongoing ones, based on or strengthened by the network they were able to access through Balcombe. The village started an initiative to produce its power through communal solar panels (Mathiesen 2015), a movement inspired by the environmentalism of the anti-fracking protests.

Community forming

A number of Balcombe participants had begun to look on the camp as a home, as it had provided everyone's basic needs for over two months. Following the protest, many hoped to continue the low-impact practices that they had learned. At first, a short-term stay on an eco-friendly holiday camp and farm in East Sussex was arranged as a retreat, on the provision that the protesters help with some of the end of the season work. This then coincided with a Transition Sussex event at the same location, at which the former protesters were welcomed free on the condition that they gave instructional talks at the event. There was a sense that those involved in the protest had gained a prestige among the wider local community, having devoted their time to being "protectors."

Following this, a group negotiated with several sympathetic local landowners to build small temporary communities in the local area, each lasting between six and eighteen months. These were organised in a similar manner to the Balcombe life in terms of using campfire cooking, and benders built using wood, tarpaulin, and recycled materials. At times these arrangements were chaotic, and all existed under verbal agreements with the landowners, making them vulnerable and limiting how far the group could pursue off-grid projects that rely on stability, such as livestock. People's motivations for continuing the lifestyle were a mix of pragmatism and ideology, for they had come together as friends with common values of protecting the environment and living as a community, and this was something they decided they wanted to continue.

Laura recalls her experience of this period:

> I remember the camp donations getting smaller and smaller and I realised I had to start standing on my own two feet again. We were living in a bubble and I started having to learn quickly how to do things like make a fire for myself, that before someone else in the camp would have done. Everyone else were blokes. I was the only woman, and they seemed to know what to do. But I thought if we stayed as a camp then we could change things, we could regroup. There was such a good network.
>
> (2016)

Jamie sums this up when looking back three years on:

> I realised that all I wanted to do was find like-minded people who wanted to live off-grid. I went along to Balcombe for a day, stayed for some months, and have been living off-grid ever since. I lived in my van in 2013, but have since sold it and now I have lived in yurts, in benders, in woods, with friends I met at Balcombe. I have less and less possessions, and I want less and less.
>
> (2016)

The group size would fluctuate, and in the winter the numbers were low, but in the summer of 2014 "activist camps" were held at these sites, taking advantage of the stability provided by verbal agreements to live on the land. In this form, the "campfire lifestyle" lived on, and the people that lived there were able to work through problems without the constant chaos of the protest camp. People had a place to go where they could live outside and pursue a lifestyle which involved a closer relationship with the earth, taking steps to be further off-the-grid and more self-reliant. Laura again:

> I started out finding things very hard. There is a lot of manual labour involved when you have to carry you own water, chop your own firewood. You don't realise how unfit you are until you have to do it. At first I could only carry half-loads of water... then by the summer of 2014 I was carrying the full 25-litre container easily. I got stronger gradually.
>
> (2016)

The sites this group found were, although more than the ten-week rush of Balcombe, always short-term. There was talk of arranging a lease and raising funds to continue on one piece of land; however, these conversations did not work out, as the landowner felt the land to be worth more than the amount the group could collectively raise. What many of these stories have in common is the lack of means for the community members. Those on a low income with no savings become subject to the whims of verbal agreements and possible evictions. Financial means do not equate to skill and knowledge, and it is important to consider how those with less means have managed to continue off-grid without owning land.

Laura and Steve presently live across two yurts and a caravan in a field that is a temporary, squatted traveller site, again subject to eviction threats, court appeals, and possession orders. They have accepted that the best course of action is to become mobile because there is a sense of futility in any attempt at permanent living:

> after building into a site, making a life, then being asked to leave and evicted with nothing… there's only so many times you can do that. You don't want to, after a while, and start to accept the things you won't change.
>
> (Steve 2016)

> We are now trying to work out how to make sure our life can fit into trailers and caravans, because if we are evicted we don't know how long we might be on the road until we find a new place. I want to get chickens, but we would need to find a safe way of transporting them from site to site.
>
> (Laura 2016)

Steve and Laura's yurts, caravans and trailers have the advantage of being relatively easy to dismantle and move. Travellers are often not permitted to build any structure with wood and nails, which means many of the skills the land squatters have developed, such as building structures, have to be replaced by a new creativity and willingness to be adaptable. The lifestyle can be considered off-grid or self-sufficient (if again the reliance on petrol and diesel is overlooked, as most people, including Steve and Laura, work part-time and so need to travel to and from work). There are solar panels for power, and tanks for water; in the summer most of the living space is in a field, and in winter it is indoors where warmth becomes the prized com - modity. There is maximum time outdoors; life is dictated by the seasons; and everything to be done – fetching water, insulation, or firewood – has to be done by hand. The rights of those seeking off-grid lifestyles and the rights of travellers are becoming more allied as both face similar problems, being subject to evictions and legal uncertainty in a world where land for development is more and more highly valued. Steve and Laura will have been evicted from the land they presently inhabit by the time this essay is published.

It was not always a smooth transition for people to make from a protest site to an off-grid community. Some spent over three years moving between protest sites and became used to the rules and norms that permit people to occupy a space as activists. Some Balcombe protesters became used to the dynamics of having a common enemy of fracking and the police, and became disruptive.

While Steve and Laura abide by the general consensus of the community they now live in, such as the agreement not to build structures with wood and nails on the land, others did attempt to build more permanent structures, finding it difficult to adapt to life outside of a protest camp.

Runnymede

Other protesters from Balcombe went to a site in a forest further west in the Thames Valley at Runnymede. Inspired by the story of England's historical Diggers,[5] the collective at Runnymede saw themselves as attempting to reclaim disused land. The occupation was intentionally political, settled along principles that the land had been squatted by activists who sought to peacefully change society through lifestyle. Runnymede residents had joined the camp at Balcombe, and protectors were in turn welcome to visit there. A verbal agreement allowed this site until the bailiffs claimed it back in 2015 after a struggle and conflicted eviction. Runnymede was forest-based, with a chicken coop, vegetable gardens, solar panels, campfire cooking, and cob-and-straw kitchen. People slept in shacks built completely out of recycled materials, and most of the food was from local supermarket bins. Skipping is a form of urban foraging, a necessity for many on low incomes, and at times it has been lauded for combating supermarket waste; it is a common practice among many protesters and squatters because of the abundance of food available and the relatively low risk attached. Runnymede is a good example of a squatted land-based site, where anyone was welcome, that mixed protesting with daily life and saw the lifestyle itself as a protest. Those who could never afford to even rent were able to take the initiative and build their homes for free.[6]

The Crossing

Emma and Stuart Goodwin are in a different position to the other stories I have explored, as they own a plot of land in East Sussex, which they have begun to turn into a small farm called "The Crossing." Their relative stability enabled them to support the camp structure at Balcombe, and they have since continued their project, growing organic food to help the local community of Forest Row become more self-sufficient. They are attempting to become a force for positive environmental balance through the use of biochar stoves which help store carbon back in the soil, and through regenerative agriculture. As their land is based on a hill above the village, it could become a natural flood defence by planting native hedges, encouraging wildlife, and aquaculture. People are welcome to come and learn the associated skills either as a work exchange or for special teaching days. The Goodwins are working towards a project which will be beneficial to the environment, and they are also able to make money from the land to sustain themselves.

A project like The Crossing faces a multitude of planning permission hoops to jump through, and bureaucratic roadblocks, and Emma and Stuart are currently raising funds for a legal bill in response to a challenge from the council, which is a costly distraction from their farming and regenerative work (Goodwin 2016). Their project is a thoughtful response to the age of crisis, and they are not faced with eviction, giving them freedom to work on revolutionary environmental practices. In a hypothetical world where any motivated people have land and resources to work with, The Crossing is an example of what could be done, yet even then it is not smooth sailing.

How far did the anti-fracking movement help create a new world?

The anti-fracking protest movement is part of a wider environmentalist response to the global crisis. A protest camp is a chaotic, semi-legal situation, fuelled by sympathetic donations, yet through community-led decisions and people taking the initiative, Balcombe functioned, fed people, and coordinated actions against fracking for approximately thirteen weeks. The fracking drill's imminent presence galvanised a new community into working together, opening the door for many into the world of environmental protesting, blockades, and, for some, into off-grid living.

Balcombe reminds us that real social and ecological (or permacultural, to borrow the terms of the anthology in which this essay appears) change must be accessible for people of any income, and not just reserved for those who can afford courses, membership fees, or festival tickets, let alone their own piece of land. No social or environmental change will be truly permanent if it is only accessible for those with greater economic means. There are many criticisms one can make of the ad hoc routes to community building, as they are never without their problems, disagreements, hardships and contradictions, but spaces like Balcombe and the sites that followed were open to anyone who agreed with the shared values. The question of establishing permanent spaces wherein alternatives might be lived remains crucial. The skills can be taught, the funds raised for the solar panels and the water containers, and the interpersonal disagreements will be worked on with time, but if the natural spaces are simply built over, or made too expensive, only allowing for temporary situations, the crisis will be extended too. In recounting these events, I have endeavoured to show the possibilities that emerge when people can access and experience an open community that works together with a common goal. The camp at Balcombe provided one of these, and, for a short time, secured a venue in which people could share ideas and work on making another world more possible.

Notes

1   "How summer fracking protest unfolded in Sussex village," *BBC News*. Last modified April 17, 2014, www.bbc.co.uk/news/uk-england-sussex-26765926.
2   For an exploration of the acronym NIMBY see Devine-Wright (2011).
3   Lush is a cosmetics company that supports animal rights and environmental protests in the UK.
4   Reclaim the Power is a movement that organises mass-participation direct actions mostly against fossil fuels.
5   See the Runnymede "Diggers" community website https://diggers2012.wordpress.com.
6   The popular BBC documentary series, *Britain's Spending Secrets*, featured some members of the Runnymede community.

References

"Britain's Spending Secrets." 2015. Television. London: BBC, 2015. Documentary television series.

Chomsky, Noam. 2012. *Occupy*. London: Penguin UK.

Devine-Wright, Patrick. (ed.) 2011. *Renewable Energy and the Public: From NIMBY to Participation*. New York: Routledge.

Emma and Stuart. 2017. Personal conversation at The Crossing, Forest Row, July 27.

Frack Free Balcombe. 2015. "FFBRA Newsletter Number Thirty Four." Available online at: www.frackfreebalcombe.co.uk/page126.php (last accessed 10 September 2015).

Goodwin, Emma. 2016. "The Crossing's Fight for Regenerative Farming." *Permaculture Magazine*. Available online at: www.permaculture.co.uk/articles/crossings-fight-regenerative-farming (last accessed 20 July 2016).

"How summer fracking protest unfolded in Sussex village." 2014. BBC News. Available online at: www.bbc.co.uk/news/uk-england-sussex-26765926 (last accessed 17 April 2014).

Jamie and Steve. 2016. Personal conversation at Capel site, March 29.

Laura. 2016. Personal conversation at Capel site, July 29.

Mason, Rowena. 2012. "Fracking: Coalition gives go-ahead to controversial shale gas drilling." *The Telegraph*. Available online at: www.telegraph.co.uk/news/earth/energy/gas/9741802/fracking-Coalition-gives-go-ahead-to-controversial-shale-gas-drilling.html (last accessed 13 December 2012).

Mathiesen, Karl. 2015. "The 'fracking village' that wants to go 100% solar." *The Guardian*. Available online at: www.theguardian.com/environment/2015/jun/05/the-fracking-village-that-wants-to-go-100-solar (last accessed 5 June 2015).

Shankleman, Jessica. 2014. "Fracking protest village Balcombe raises funds for solar power." *The Guardian*. Available online at: www.theguardian.com/environment/2014/mar/27/fracking-protest-village-balcombe-solar-power (last accessed 27 March 2014).

Steve. 2016. Personal conversation at Capel site, July 28.

The Runnymede "Diggers" community website. 2016. Available online at: https://diggers2012.wordpress.com (last accessed 29 July 2016).

Truthferretfilms News Network. 2013. "Police Snatch Squad in Action Balcombe Fracking Targeted Individuals No Warning CL376." YouTube video. 30 mins 50 secs. Available online at: www.youtube.com/watch?v=J1y_Ff7mutc (last accessed 11 August 2013).

Wall, Derek. 1999. *Earth First and the Anti-Roads Movement: Radical Environmentalism and Comparative Social Movements*. New York: Routledge.

9 The problem with money

Possibilities for alternative, sustainable, non-monetary economies

George Price

Part 1: What is the problem?

There may have been a time when money was a relatively harmless or neutral inanimate object, void of any intrinsic character (good or evil), but now—in this time like no other before it—things have changed. The problem with money—in our current dire dilemma, as the Earth and all who dwell therein are facing the likelihood of the worst catastrophe in human history—is the power that money has been given to perpetuate the engines of the monstrous machine that has actually created the imminent catastrophe.[1] The economic systems that most humans in the world today live under are dependent upon the continued production and consumption of things that are actually toxic to our personal and environmental health. The personal human health issues brought to us by junk foods, junk pharmaceuticals, and toxic petro-chemical agriculture are better-known and more widely acknowledged than the environmental and climate destruction issues, even though the threat from climate disaster is more dire. That monstrous machine, the money-driven, toxic industrial production and consumption system, brings us phenomena like the disappearance of glaciers, Arctic ice, and permafrost; the accelerating releases of methane; the increased frequency of droughts and other extreme, abnormal, unpredictable weather patterns; the daily mass extinctions of species of animals and plants; rising seas engulfing small islands; new migrations of people and other species as "climate refugees"; and many other evidences of climate destruction that continue to accelerate beyond the rates that scientists predicted just a few years ago. The prevailing systems are dependent upon keeping us enslaved through financial debt and cultural brainwashing, which includes convincing people that there is no possible better system, and that the best we can hope for is to mildly tweak the system we have, working through the "proper channels." But those channels are corrupt governments that are also enslaved by the multinational industrial corporate elites. These systems are designed, structured, and intentionally maintained to perpetuate themselves and continually bring the imagined "benefits" of disproportionate material rewards *and political power* to a very small percentage of the people of this planet. Under these conditions, our continued entrapment in currency-based artificial economies continues to push us further away from any possibility of resolution to this crisis.

Money itself has become the corporate industrial monster's ultimate weapon, as well as the shackling chains by which the "1%" has the rest of us in bondage. It is monetary economic systems (whether you are under the pseudo-socialist system in China or the capitalist system of the U.S.A, or any other unsustainable mega-nation or empire) and our subjection to them that give these corporations, governments, and banks their leverage and their force. It is the very fact that they have us physically and legally in debt to, and psychologically bound to, these corrupt, unnatural, arbitrary and *unnecessary* monetary systems that makes people go to work in toxic, destructive places like the tar sands of Alberta or the Bakken "oil fields," the Monsanto laboratories, or the Fukushima nuclear plant. It is money and the leverage of the monetary systems, especially debt and credit, but also the psychological fear that stimulates ruthless competition (for profits or jobs), that makes even the best of the politicians in this world either completely subject to the will of the corporations, or impotent in their attempts to stop them. It is money that perpetuates the commercial brainwashing of the mostly submissive, unquestioning, unimaginative, stupefied human societies and makes us believe that we've "gotta have it," "can't live without it," and therefore must ruthlessly compete with each other and submit to the system, even when it orders us to compromise our consciences and participate in activities that we know are wrong, or even deadly. The powers of the money world, especially bosses and banks, have perpetuated fear and insecurity about the potential "disaster" of not having enough money, while simultaneously convincing people that there can be no other way to live than in submission to their system and their rules. But, more importantly than all of the above, these monetary systems also alienate us from the true source of all wealth and all life—the natural world—and deceive us into thinking that these human-crafted strange objects we call "money" are the real wealth that we must covet and pursue endlessly—and that "there is no other alternative."

Is the continued use of money and the deadly, life-sucking bondage of our current economic systems really inescapable or perpetually locked-in? One thing that most humans do not realize, in part because the pursuit of money is so normalized and unquestioned and, in part, because very few people talk about or teach this, is that we humans lived fairly well, for the most part, during the 97.5 percent of our existence (pre-Mesopotamia, pre-unsustainable empires) that we lived without money.[2] We are still the same species and this is still the same planet (all changes considered), so, if we did it before, why can't we do at least something like that again? If we can relearn some of the ancient, life-nurturing and life-sustaining ways and combine them with any clean, sustainable technologies that we have created since the time that our indigenous ancestors[3] departed from those ways, we can also reorganize ourselves into small, cooperative, nature-directed, egalitarian, democratic, sustainable societies (and larger allied networks of such societies), and free ourselves from any need for, or attachment to, monetary systems. That may seem improbable to most people who have known nothing but the current prevailing social constructions, and who have been grossly misinformed about the real lifeways and circumstances of small-scale, sustainable indigenous societies (both past and present). To that I will simply say that there is much for us all to learn about Earthways and our untapped human potential to live harmoniously with nature. There are also questions about current human population size and ecosystem carrying-capacities that we probably cannot resolve definitively without actually making the attempt to redirect ourselves toward true sustainability and begin (or continue, for those who are already on this path) the learning processes. We would also need to have many serious democratic discussions about which familiar modern technologies and "conveniences" we would need to give up, either temporarily or permanently. What other viable (for the long-term) choices do we have?

What I am talking about here is actually the ultimate form of "going on strike" and the ultimate boycott. By creating such alternative economic systems, in harmony with Earth's systems, and getting enough of the human population, worldwide, to join these systems, we could then effectively disarm the corporate industrial/financial death machine and stop the destruction of our planet. Our independence from these destructive socio-economic systems, their currencies, and their toxic products, which we would no longer need, will make their industries unprofitable, and eventually crash their economies, removing all of their leverage over us and the biosphere, and simultaneously breaking all of the chains by which they have had us bound for so long! That would be a true declaration of independence! The independence gained from our worldwide boycott of the system could lead to a restored *inter*dependence, or reciprocity, with all parts of the natural systems of life, for our interconnected, mutual benefit. We can and *must* unite our energies, minds, and abilities and come up with alternative, Earth-based, non-monetary economic ways and technologies, and wean ourselves from the use of toxic machinery and products, in the small window of time that remains in which we are still able to save life on Earth. I would rather do this, and take the matches out of the hands of these corporate "arsonists," who are, in essence, burning up our planet, than to continue with futile and inadequate efforts to put out the innumerable individual fires through our acts of protest and attempts to pass regulatory laws. While patient pursuit of gradual, incremental change, "working through the proper channels" might have been a reasonable, pragmatic method of attaining progressive social evolution in ages past, we are now in a time like no other that our species has known, and a crisis that demands much more immediate and drastic action. I strongly doubt that the purveyors of the global ecological and economic crises, who continue to increase the tightness of their grip on the U.S. and other national governments, through laws like "Citizens United" and treaties like the controvrsial Trans-Pacific Partnership (TPP), would allow us to simply vote away their power through democratic political processes. Historically, that is just not what empires do. For the many reasons that I describe here, I am persuaded that we must "vote with our feet," with our actions and with how we choose to live on this Earth, and that the actions I propose here, and many actions that are already in motion around the world, really do have the potential to make the changes that must be made.

I realize that this path will initially seem too daunting to most of us modern humans, and also undesirable to many of our species who are so alienated from nature and acclimated to the unnatural "modern way of life." But, as more and more people tune in to alternative sources of information and become aware of worldwide phenomena like the accelerating impacts of climate change, accelerating wealth inequality, politicians who answer only to corporate lobbyists, increasingly brutal, militarized police states, and a host of other societal ills that they also find troubling, they are becoming more open to the idea that radical social change may actually be necessary. Among the greatest fears that we humans carry are the fear of the unknown and the fear of the loss of what is familiar, what we have prepared for and already committed ourselves to—in short, the only way of life that we really know. Consequently, those amongst us who are the most deeply invested in the "success" of the current system, who see their own personal success as deeply intertwined with the perpetuation of the status quo, and in many cases feel that their investment in the system has actually rewarded them significantly, will have an especially difficult time hearing any of this. Some of us may not feel significantly rewarded by or fond of the system at all, but have been persuaded to accept the idea that there is no way out, or no realistic alternative to the dominant, entrenched patterns of "modern life."

As awareness of the deteriorating global circumstances brings people to start looking for possible alternatives, there is something even more powerful and compelling than fear of catastrophe that will motivate them to engage in that pursuit. I call it "the appeal of the potential good," or the anticipation of great pleasure and relief from a heavy, oppressing burden, accompanied by the possibility of a life of real joy and peace. This appeal manifests itself most and proceeds to increase when people begin to view and experience actual models of ideal, alternative, nature-based, non-monetary, sustainable economic communities. I will now devote the rest of this chapter to describing some examples of such models that are already in existence, around the world.

Part 2: Models and possibilities for new, sustainable economic lifeways

Perhaps the best and most widely visible examples of the development of sustainable community-based economics that can enable independence from the commercial, industrial market system can be found within the organic farming-based local food movement. This movement has many of its roots in the "back to the land" and "grow your own" movement of the late 1960s, but the twenty-first century has seen a real surge in this kind of action and thought, perhaps even more serious or earnest than the old `60s and early `70s phase. The movement for growing our own food, rather than purchasing it, is not as large as the complementary local food movement in which people try to buy as much of their food as possible from local farmers. That is probably due to the difficulty of finding time for farming and gardening with as much time as people have to put into the work that they do for money, in this increasingly competitive and insecure job market. In 2014 there were 8,268 farmers' markets in the U.S., which was a 180 percent increase from 2006. The U.S. Department of Agriculture (USDA) reports: "In 2012, 163,675 farms (7.8 percent of U.S. farms) were marketing foods locally, defined as conducting either direct-to-consumer (DTC) or intermediated sales of food for human consumption, according to agricultural census data" (2015, 7, 5). "Intermediated sales" refers to practices like local grocery stores and restaurants purchasing and selling food raised by local farmers. USDA reports confirm that the local food movement has caught the government's attention, but the reports only cover market concerns regarding the movement—issues of profitability and monetary trends—and demonstrate no interest in the increasing number of people growing their own food for direct consumption, rather than for money. In my own experience, as an organic food grower since 1970 and a permaculturalist since the mid-1980s, it seems to me that the permaculturalists are the food growers and wild food caretakers who are the least interested in growing food for money, and most interested in doing those activities as part of a quest for alternative, sustainable ways of life.[4]

Although we vary somewhat in our individual approaches to it, by definition we permaculturalists are committed to allowing our local ecosystems to guide and shape our interactions with the land and water, instead of us shaping those spaces only as we see fit. We are engaged in caretaking and preserving the native food and medicine plants and trees on our lands: planting and cultivating only those crops that are compatible with our ecosystems. We treasure biodiversity and have a profound respect for everything that belongs to the land and water we live with. All the living things that belong here have an equal right to be here and many vital purposes. They fit together and reciprocate each other and have been doing so since long before we humans arrived. It is our goal to fit in with those life-giving natural systems, to be a reciprocating part of it all—not to force the ecosystem to fit into the unnatural world of modern humans and their artificial, money-driven ways of being. We would not enter into a land-water system and say, "this looks like a good place to grow _____, and we should do so because growing that crop here can bring us much money." When first coming to live in a place of land and water, we would seek to learn what that place asks of us—what good could we do for that place so that it can continue freely to share its gifts of life with us and the other species who are a part of that place? How do we become a useful, helpful part of it all? How can we rightfully belong to any particular place? Knowing these natural systems are greater, healthier and more real-life-giving than any human-created economic system, we plant our compatible crops right alongside and interspersed with the native crops, wherever there might be enough room and water. Although we sometimes move water around to service the crops (irrigation), we realize that it is best to plant seeds or transplant plants into the naturally wetter places where nature will bring water to the plants, if possible. There are many other ways in which the harmonious methods of permaculture take shape and merge with the various ecosystems, worldwide. These methods are both ancient and new, rooted in the ways of First Peoples going back to the ages before the advent of unsustainable mega-societies.

So, if most people in the local food movement—with the exceptions of subsistence permaculturalists, home gardeners and some non-monetary trading done in community garden spaces—are still selling their crops for money, where do we find examples of people who are doing other things for the purpose of freeing ourselves from the monetary systems? One would think that some good models for moneyless local economies could be found in the barter fair movement. Bartering has always been a part of human non-monetary economic interaction, but began to spread more widely as an active form of resistance to the industrial capitalist system in the early 1970s, with large outdoor gatherings often called names like "The Barter

Faire" (that spelling of "Fair" reflects the previous "Renaissance Faire" movement). Barter fairs were kind of like "counterculture" swap meets, with an intention of economic sharing and exchange, avoiding the use of money. Over the years, the commitment toward not using money at the barter fairs waned and so did the barter fair movement. One of the first and biggest of the counter culture barter fairs, the "Barter Faire," of Okanogan, Washington, founded in 1974, eventually dropped the word "barter" from its name and is now called the "Okanogan Family Faire." Whereas originally everything was (mostly) moneyless and free, now "vendors" pay for spots and customers pay for admission tickets, just so they can go in and shop there, making it even more money-oriented than most swap meets or art festivals. Some bartering does occur at the few remaining barter fairs, but mostly between the vendors. The old barter fair movement may have faded away, but the good news is that bartering is by no means dead. It is actually thriving and growing, and the primary locale for this new bartering movement is on the internet. There is also a new, twenty-first century upgrade of the old outdoor barter fair movement, an international phenomenon called, the "Really, Really Free Market" (RRFM), which holds much more promise as a movement for actual systemic economic change than the old hippie barter fairs did.

Before I return to describe the RRFMs in more depth, I will first comment more on the phenomenon of online moneyless trading. In a short essay by Christopher Doll, a research fellow at the United Nations Institute of Advanced Studies, titled "Can We Evolve Beyond Money?," the author describes how the internet has created the infrastructure for greater, more widespread possibilities for economic sharing and moneyless "collaborative consumption":

> ...the internet has reduced the friction costs of searching for what is available and massively enabled peer-to-peer transactions to be done on a far wider scale than has ever been seen before... If, as it is frequently argued, Generation Y is the first generation of digital natives and sharing is their norm, could it be that collaborative consumption rather than consumer capitalism will be their norm? If so, what will the next generation bring?
>
> (2011)

Two generations of humans who are now used to all of this free access—to ideas, to goods, and to services—have made it more possible than ever to enable and organize people for substantial, systemic transformations of all kinds, including worldwide, non-violent economic revolution. (Even so, there are other environmental and health-related costs to using the internet and the electronic devices for accessing it that we will eventually need to weigh out when we debate what technology to keep and what to leave behind.) There is a useful compilation of bartering and swapping websites in an article by David Quilty, titled "36 Bartering and Swapping Websites—Best Places to Trade Stuff Online."[5] There are many more than just these 36 sites out there, something which is revealed in the comments after the article, as person after person writes about sites that the author missed. Some of these sites allow for some use of money, but most are focused on barter and sharing. Some of the sites have a socio-political agenda for avoiding the use of money, while many others seem to be just trying to help people save money or mitigate circumstances related to poverty. As the social-change advocates interact more with the simply economically straddled people on these websites, seeds of revolutionary thinking are most certainly being sown. Every time a person experiences economic benefit without the use of money, a new sense of what might be possible is further developed and strengthened.

From my perspective, the two most interesting websites on the list, which do the most toward addressing the pertinent systemic issues and working toward creating the possibility for an international boycott of the system, are Freecycle and the Freegans. Freecycle (www.freecycle.org) describes their organization as "...a grassroots and entirely nonprofit movement of people who are giving (and getting) stuff for free in their own towns. It's all about reuse and keeping good stuff out of landfills." Founded in Tuscon, Arizona in 2003, by a recycler named Deron Beal, Freecycle is now a very large network (5,289 groups in 32 countries, and 9,105,322 members) of local, volunteer-run sites.[6] Connections are made for giving and receiving online. There are two categories of posts, "Wanted" or "Offer." Users have to be registered members to reply to posts and make arrangements for contacting each other. Membership is free "and everything posted must be free, legal and appropriate for all ages."

The Freegans organization is a little more direct and explicit about their revolutionary motivation for abandoning the prevailing economic system. Here is a brief excerpt of their description of themselves from their web page:

> Freegans are people who employ alternative strategies for living based on limited participation in the conventional economy and minimal consumption of resources. Freegans embrace community, generosity, social concern, freedom, cooperation, and sharing in opposition to a society based on materialism, moral apathy, competition, conformity, and greed. Freeganism is a **total boycott** of an economic system where the profit motive has eclipsed ethical considerations and where massively complex systems of productions ensure that all the products we buy will have detrimental impacts, most of which we may never even consider. Thus, instead of avoiding the purchase of products from one bad company only to support another, we avoid buying anything to the greatest degree we are able.[7]

One of the strategies that they are well-known for is "dumpster diving," (aka "urban foraging"). But, rest assured, the Freegans are engaged in much more than dumpster diving. Their wide range of activities include: freely distributing and recycling the wide variety of good quality disposed products that they find in waste bins; creating free organic soil for gardeners by composting the spoiled food and other organic matter that they find; creating and freely distributing biofuel from disposed restaurant cooking oil and other vegetable oil; repairing and redistributing broken mechanical items and equipment; they "occupy and rehabilitate abandoned, decrepit buildings" to provide homes for the homeless and create community center gathering places; creating organic urban free food gardens on vacant lots; foraging for wild plant foods and medicines; sharing surplus vegetables, fruits and nuts produced by local farmers, and several other related activities. Freegans work with other recyclers and with other like-minded organizations, such as Food Not Bombs, homeless shelters, and the Really, Really Free Markets. The Freegan website gives much information and many links about what they believe and what they do, but does not give personal information or a history of how their movement began. Also, to be clear, even though the Freegans have a great website, by which they connect many sustainability activists, most of what they do is done offline, in the streets and various public and private spaces. Freeganism has spread internationally and there are now Freegan groups in the U.S., France, Brazil, Norway, Greece and Lebanon.

Also taking place on the ground, the Really, Really Free Markets are not actually barter markets, because no direct exchanges are allowed there. No money, no deals, no selling, no trading, just "Take what you need, and bring what you don't." A chalkboard sign put up at one of the RRFMs says, "Do not compete for an item. This is a no-money market. No trade, swap, barter, or sale." Participants can offer their skills and services, as well as material goods, and the events are held in public parks and other public spaces. The RRFMs are examples of what is known as a "gift economy" (Vaughan 2011), in which every material need is met for free, based on a perspective that there is truly "enough for everybody," if we properly take care of and manage our abundant resources. Of course, such a perspective can only be successfully applied if we eliminate resource insecurity and the cultural tendency towards greed, which raises the question of what happens when a greedy, insecure, or capitalistically well-conditioned person goes to a RRFM? I'll leave that question unanswered for now, partly because I suspect that it has a wide variety of possibly valid answers. The compatibility between Freegans and the RRFMs is glaringly obvious and it is easy to see why they collaborate so well and why so many Freegans are involved with organizing and running RRFMs. These intertwined movements both seek to stop the destructive and wasteful effects of the capitalist system and introduce people to different forms of economic practice, as well as of human interaction. The first RRFM occurred in Christchurch, New Zealand in 2003, and the idea sprang forth from a meeting of the free food/anti-hunger organization, Food Not Bombs. That same year, two more RRFMs were held, one in Jakarta, Indonesia, and the other in Miami, Florida. Since then, RRFMs have been held in dozens of U.S. cities, and Canada, Australia, Malaysia, Taiwan, England, South Africa, and Russia. The movement is very popular in Russia and has spread through many cities there (Moynihan 2009).

Although there are many more examples of non-monetary economic practices and organizations that are working towards that end, I will just mention one more here: time banking. The time bank idea was conceived and developed in the early 1980s by Edgar Cahn, a professor at the University of the District of Columbia School of Law. Cahn calls time banking "an alternative currency system in which hours of service take the place of money," and provides this further explanation:

> [time banking is] a mode of exchange that lets people swap time and skill instead of money. The concept is simple: in joining a time bank, people agree to take part in a system that involves earning and spending "time credits." When they spend an hour on an activity that helps others, they receive one time credit.

When they need help from others, they can use the time credits that they have accumulated.

(Cahn and Gray 2015)

In the 21 years since Edgar Cahn founded TimeBanks USA, time banking has spread to more than 30 countries, including "China, Russia, and various countries in Africa, Europe, North America, and South America." In the United States, there are "about 500 registered time banks, and together they have enrolled more than 37,000 members. The smallest of them has 15 members; the largest has about 3,200." Time banking is easily facilitated by a computer database that enables members to register the skills or services that they can offer and find people who can provide them skills or services that they might need. Hours of time credit and time debt are also kept on the database and each local community time bank has their own database. Cahn and Gray describe the growth of time banking since Cahn founded TimeBanks USA over twenty years ago:

> Today organized time banking takes place in more than 30 countries— including China, Russia, and various countries in Africa, Europe, North America, and South America. In the United States, there are about 500 registered time banks, and together they have enrolled more than 37,000 members. The smallest of them has 15 members; the largest has about 3,200. In the United Kingdom, time banks have enrolled about 32,000 members, and more than 3,000 organizations have registered to use one of the major time banking software platforms. Worldwide, time bank databases document more than 4 million hours of service. (And that figure understates the true scope of time bank participation: Survey data indicate that at least 50 percent of time bank members do not record their hours of service regularly.)
>
> (Cahn and Gray 2015)

That last remark, in parentheses, contains evidence of a very powerful phenomenon that occurs frequently in these moneyless, community-connecting, local economic activities: the intrinsic rewards, like finding your own skills valued by others, making connections and friendships through giving and receiving, and developing social trust or "social capital," become more valued than the extrinsic rewards from receiving services or material gain. Examples of that profound experience are expressed over and over by people involved in freeganism, the RRFMs, time banks, Food Not Bombs, Freecycles, and many other community-based, alternative economic efforts. Christopher Doll describes "social capital" very well:

> What is intriguing about collaborative consumption is that the credit rating upon which so much of our access to goods and services currently depends will be replaced by a new rating—our own personal trustworthiness rating. That is to say, our access to goods becomes, in part, a function of our social capital rather than our financial one. This is an incredibly powerful concept in helping us understand personal wealth in broader terms and indeed, what we might use in place of money. Social capital accumulates over time: the more

you share properly, the higher your rating rises, which in turn promotes good social conduct. This is all good in theory, provided that personal freedoms and identities aren't compromised in the process.

(Doll 2011)

It is in this process of cultivating "social capital," or what I would simply call "relationships of trust," that we find the personal accountability within moneyless systems. People naturally want to be trusted and accepted and they want to interact with other people whom they can trust and rely upon as dependable and caring persons. What also becomes clear when observing and considering how these systems actually succeed, is that they function best at the local, small community level, rather than in the context of the anonymity of a sprawling, unsustainable mega-society. Hopefully, what the development of local, moneyless, life-connected economic systems will do for us and our planet is restore much of what we all had 5,000 years ago, before the advent of mega-societies, empires and money.

Even though I live on a farm 37 miles north of the town of Missoula, Montana, I belong to the Missoula Time Bank. I recently interviewed two of my friends, Susie Clarion and Carol Marsh, who were part of the small core group who founded the Missoula Time Bank (MTB), back in the Spring of 2013. There are now 126 members in the MTB and 2,157 hours exchanged, as recorded in the database, but Carol told me that she and others sometimes fulfill requests for services and then do not record it in the database, again reflecting the perspective that the experience of the transaction, or interaction, is often reward enough in itself. In the MTB we also have what is called a "Community Chest," through which we can donate some of our hours for community service group projects, like building houses with Habitat for Humanity. My friends also pointed out another lesson they have learned through their time bank experiences: it is just as valuable to ask for and receive services as it is to give. We spread that good feeling of having our gifts and skills valued by others through being available to receive from others. Mutual benefit and reciprocity are major values in the time bank system, as expressed in this quote from the website:

> The question, "How can I help you?" changes to "How can we help each other build the world we both want to live in?" Time banking is based on equal exchanges. Everyone benefits because every member both gives and receives.[8]

As Susie Clarion said to me,

> Providing services through the time bank is not just doing a job. It is the interaction and bonding, the listening and teaching which are the true values of the time bank experience. What people seem to enjoy most about their time bank experiences is making good friends.[9]

When I peruse these sorts of examples of alternative, non-monetary, community-based economics which are already in place and spreading, I become more confident that an international boycott of the current prevailing economic system is possible. We are already creating the infrastructure of what can replace it and the momentum is building. That may be cause for inspiration or even celebration, but I caution all who might be willing to go forward with this movement: there is good reason to publicly temper our exuberance and to welcome public skepticism. If this revolutionary strategy sounds unlikely or impossible to most modern humans, consider this: it would have to be laughable to work. Any non-violent revolutionary strategy which intends to bring to a halt the destructive forces of our current political and economic systems and replace those systems with their opposite—life-supporting, sustainable, Earth biosphere-led, humane, just, interconnected and mutually, equally beneficial to all living beings, new international network of local, ecologically-specific economic systems—has got to be laughable, scoffed at and easily dismissed by the oligarchs and the tools who serve them, if we don't want our movement to be brutally squashed and destroyed before it can reach its fulfillment. If they hear about what we are doing, we want them to laugh, mock us, call us "crazies," question our intelligence, dismiss us as fools, and then ignore and forget about us. "They think that they can grow all of their own food and medicines, make their own clothes, build their own houses and other structures, transport themselves sufficiently without fossil fuels, create their own electricity, and boycott all of our industrial products! That's insane! And get people all over the world to do that? That's even crazier!" Yes, that's what we want them to think and say to themselves. Right. Nothing to see here, Comfortable Ruling Class. Just go on with your obliviousness and your delusions. Entertain yourselves and spend your money while it is still worth something. Then, one day, you will come to us waving your silly, worthless currencies in your hands, asking us to feed you and clothe you, or give you shelter, and we will say, "That is not how we do things here, in this new world. We belong to life and to each other. We take care of this living world that gives us life together. We work together, play together and share everything. Freely we have received and freely we give. If you are ready to learn and experience what it means to truly live, come and join us." We won't know what is possible until we give this revolutionary transformation our greatest, unified (or at least mutually supportive) effort. There might be many more people, worldwide, who are ready for this (*including those who do not yet realize that they are ready for this!*) than we have been led to believe.[10]

Notes

1   For a detailed description of the present crisis, with source links, see George R. Price, *Thinking About the Unthinkable,* in Learning Earthways, https://georgepriceblog. wordpress.com/2013/12/28/thinking-about-the-unthinkable.

2   Due to space limitations for this anthology, I am unable to develop this point fully for this article, but have developed it further in a similar article, "The End of Money," which can be found on my blog, *Learning Earthways,* https://georgepriceblog.wordpress.com. For further study of this topic, see Sahlins, Lee, Thomas, Korten and Eisler.

3   All first humans, from whom we all are descended, were indigenous people who lived sustainably with the natural world.

4   A good overview of the permaculture movement and many details about the practice can be found on the blog, Permies.com (https://permies.com). The information exchange in the well-used discussion forums on the blog is extremely useful.

5   David Quilty, "36 Bartering and Swapping Websites—Best Places to Trade Stuff Online," posted on Money Crashers website, www.moneycrashers.com.
6   On the Freecycle website it says, "the Freecycle concept has since spread to more than 110 countries," but their trademark is registered in 32 countries.
7   http://freegan.info.
8   Missoula Time Bank website, www.missoulatimebank.org.
9   Interview with Susie Clarion and Carol Marsh, July 30, 2016, Missoula Montana.
10   For those who may wonder why I did not mention Jacque Fresco's "Venus Project" in an article about moneyless economies, especially since that is usually the first thing that comes up when you Google search "moneyless economies" and the first example many people think of regarding that topic, I'll just say this: I think that the Venus Project is too focused on human technology as a solution and it is not really centered on Earth sustainability.

References

Cahn, Edgar S. and Christine Gray. 2015. "The Time Bank Solution." *Stanford Social Innovation Review*. Available online at: https://ssir.org/articles/entry/the_time_bank_solution (last accessed 4 May 2017).

Doll, Christopher. 2011. "Can We Evolve Beyond Money?" Available online at: https://our world.unu.edu/en/our-world-3-0-can-we-evolve-beyond-money (last accessed 4 May 2017).

Eisler, Riane. 2011. *The Chalice and the Blade: Our History, Our Future*. New York: Harper-Collins.

Korten, David C. 2007. *The Great Turning: From Empire to Earth Community*. Oakland, CA: Berrett-Koehler Publishers.

Lee, Richard B. 1979. *The !Kung San: Men, Women and Work in a Foraging Society*. Boston, MA: Cambridge University Press.

Low, Sarah A. et al. 2015. *Trends in U.S. Local and Regional Food Systems*, AP-068, U.S. Department of Agriculture, Economic Research Service (January).

Moynihan, Colin. 2009. "An East Village Market Where Everything Is Free Faces an Uncertain Future." *The New York Times* (January 28).

Sahlins, Marshall. 1972. *Stone Age Economics*. Chicago: Aldine/Atherton, Inc.

Thomas, Elizabeth Marshall. 2006. *The Old Way, A Story of the First People*. New York: Farrar Straus Giroux.

Vaughan, Genevieve. 2011. "Shifting the Paradigm to a Maternal Gift Economy." Paper delivered for Women's Worlds. (Ottawa, July 7). Available online at: http://gift-economy.com/articlesAndEssays/shiftingparadigm.pdf (last accessed 4 May 2017).

Part III

Revolution disguised as gardening

10 A war against weeds

Combating climate change with polycultural pacifism

David Carruthers

To understand the profound importance of regenerative agriculture, the kind of farming that builds natural capital, we need to see it not as a fringe or retrograde activity—'unable to feed the world,' as conventional agronomists would claim—but as a heroic and undersung achievement in the face of overwhelming institutional neglect, cultural dissipation, economic monopolies and dire ecological challenges from chemical, nuclear and genetic pollution, climate change and an eroding resource base in the land and in society.

Peter Bane, *The Permaculture Handbook*

We don't have a very good vocabulary to describe what other species do to us, because *we* think that we are the only species that really *does* anything. But, to the extent that you can put yourself in the place of these other species, and look at the world from their point of view, I think it frees us from our sense of alienation from nature, and we become members of the biotic community.

Michael Pollan in Gray's film adaptation of *The Botany of Desire*

As the Second World War hurtled headlong toward its twice-punctuated end, *Time Magazine* was already plotting the postwar practices of American agriculture, scheming of a near-future repatriation of the battlefield into the farmer's field. An article dated 19 February, 1945, "The War Against Weeds," forecasts a militarized agriculture that declares weeds its "No. 1 enemy" (67) and introduces to the public the possibility of employing incendiary and chemical weapons, flamethrowers and DDT, against pests of all kinds. And, while the suggestion of such an aggravated agriculture merely, almost ludicrously, participates in the combative rhetoric everywhere in vogue in the throes of war, this *lingua belli*, the language of war surrounding industrial monoculture sings particularly true, not only to the radical transformation of agricultural practice from the 1940s forward, culminating in and extending beyond the ineptly named Green Revolution, but also of a truth more insidious still about the inevitability of oppressive expansionist policies to industrial monoculture, an invasion agriculture.

As permaculturist Toby Hemenway offers in his ambitious talk, "How Permaculture Can Save Humanity and the Earth, but Not Civilization," delivered 12 February 12, 2010 at Duke University, addressing the most obvious question of why so many of the world's once-great civilizations set up shop in some of the most arid wastelands, one need only inspect any of them, from the once-Fertile Crescent of Mesopotamia to the white desert hills of Greece and toward the Great Dust-Bowl Plains of Canada and the United States, to identify a cycle of violence—toward the land, then its people, and ultimately an *evil* outsider—perpetuated by relatively short-term agricultural solutions to the everlasting problem of sustenance-acquisition that result in potentially permanent drought and desertification. This destructive habit, the addiction to agriculture,[1] subdued today only temporarily by some quick petroleum fix by which we trade inevitable desertification for worse chemical intoxication, is, then, not only the *modus operandi* of Empire, but its primary mover.

Evaluating the relationship of war to agriculture and climate change, alongside permaculture's adoption of invasive species, this chapter examines the violence inherent in industrial monoculture and its postwar practices, with especial attention to the intersections of colonial and agricultural discourses of *invasion*, to propose the alternative of perennial polyculture as a viable solution to the many social and environmental consequences of climate change. Using living concepts endorsed and practiced by permaculture, I propose the growing movement of local, sustenance agriculture—including the practices of heirlooming, seed-saving, and co-planting—offers a viable, resilient alternative to large-scale industrial monoculture, thereby fostering a healthy relationship with the land and its occupants that promises not only to avert large-scale ecological crisis driven by unsustainable agriculture, but proven by the likes of Geoff Lawton and other permaculturists, to repair and recover lands already devastated by drought and its inevitable conflict.

Late in 2015, the International Center for Agricultural Research in Dry Areas' (ICARDA) seed bank at Aleppo, "one of the world's most unique seed banks [located in] Syria's largest city" (Condon 2015), designed with the intent of providing safe haven for some 143,000 accessions of species essential to the agricultural production of the Fertile Crescent, was breached by two armed groups, resulting in ICARDA's relocation of 13 percent of these accessions and the first official 'withdrawal' from the seed bank at Svalbard, Norway—nicknamed the Doomsday Vault—some mere seven years after its construction (ibid.). At the time of this manuscript, rebel fighters continue to occupy Aleppo's seed bank, permitting its operation in exchange for provision of food rations, citing an 'unwritten agreement' that

> guarantees that [the rebels] have food, since prices in Syria have skyrocketed, and [the dryland institute has] no problem with this arrangement, because, at the very least, it guarantees the continuation of our research farm, since allowing it to go fallow could ruin it as a research station.
>
> (ICARDA's director general Mahmoud Solh quoted in Badr 2014)

Testament to the agricultural cause of conflict is the report last year, in the *Proceedings of the National Academy of Sciences*, that the Syrian civil war was affected by a five-year drought in the region due to global climate change (Kelley et al. 2015).

An educational web-comic, "Syria's Climate Conflict," written by Audrey Quinn and illustrated by Jackie Roche, narrates the cause of the conflict and stages the environmental risk of climate change in terms accessible to a popular audience, explaining that

Between 2006 and 2011, over half of [Syria] had suffered under the worst drought on record. This drought was more intense and lasted longer than could be explained by natural variations in weather. This was climate change. Nearly 85% of livestock died. … Nearly a million rural villagers lost their farms to the drought. They crowded into overcrowded cities like Daraa. In the cities, the water problem became even more dire. There weren't enough jobs. … So, a group of teenage boys expressed their frustrations [by spray-painting a slogan borrowed from revolutions in Cairo and Tunis:] 'The people/want/to topple the regime!'

(2014)

The boys' incarceration and torture provoked mass protest against the tyranny of the Assad regime, met with state violence ultimately catalyzing the conflict, ongoing today, involving some nearly twenty nations and implicating others with a steady influx of climate refugees.[2]

Here at Aleppo, not only does the climate-caused military conflict in Syria jeopardize sustenance agriculture by dispossessing people of their traditional lands, but it also threatens the very failsafe measures put in place to overcome such losses. The occupation and dispersal of the seed bank at Aleppo would seem to be so much collateral damage not confined to the Syrian conflict, but belonging to a grander theatre of war—a climate war.

That climate change is a major contributor to armed conflict around the world should come as little surprise to many observers, today, and to some fewer, still, in the future, as it only escalates in the coming years. And, yet, many permaculturists— including Geoff Lawton, whose large-scale restoration polyculture projects in such desert countries as Jordan, Afghanistan, and Saudi Arabia have earned him world renown—regard unsustainable agriculture—contributing as it does some 13 percent of global greenhouse emissions (CAIT 2015), and because of the imminent risk of it producing near-irreversible desertification—as a more immediate threat to the biosphere than other sources of greenhouse gas emissions contributing to global warming (Lawton 2014). Geoff Lawton's project of 'greening the deserts' exhibits the capacity for permacultural methods of ecosystemic design to combat climate change while also repairing its most devastating effects. These methods, including slowing and storing water through berms and swales, and stacking species to build permanent, regenerative, surplus-producing perennial polycultures, engineer the microclimatic conditions that offset the rising temperatures produced by carbon emissions and capture carbon and water from the air while desalinating soils eroded by chemical fertilizer (Mackintosh 2015).[3]

Exhibiting the intrinsic alliance between militarized discourse and agricultural practice, a massive 1941 propaganda campaign produced by the British Ministry of Information in conjunction with the Ministry of Agriculture, romanticizing the urban agrarian, promoting the 'Victory garden,'[4] and encouraging citizens to "Dig for Victory," teaches children that "food is just as important a weapon of war as guns" ("Dig" 2009). In the short film, accompanying this grave voiceover is the extreme close-up image of the smooth glistening surface of a squash inspected by a diligent child patriot, fading to the image of a military weather balloon, sharing the same glossy sheen as the fruiting body, being hoisted into the air by soldiers. Then, a bereted platoon tills rows between leafy greens, artillery cannon poised skyward in the near background. And, although the visual analogy, here, is a false one—neither is a weather balloon a weapon, nor a gun a gourd—the sequence, suggesting that men, women, and children alike take up arms in the form of plowshares in the war effort, is a powerful one. Such a reminder, however, that warfare, in quite a provocative way, is in its very essence just such a 'food fight,' of vegetable weaponry—one recalls the adage, attributed in equal measure both to Napoleon and Frederick the Great, that "an army marches on its stomach"—attests to an intimacy, more deeply rooted, still, between the vegetable and the weapon, agriculture and warfare, greater than that for which our wartime propaganda campaign can account.[5]

Rather, however, than merely munitions for the machinery of war, fuel for a standing army or its reserves,[6] so also is local food farming a weapon *against* war— the reacquisition of the infinite means of (re)production.

There is a moral imperative to garden in wartime—more than 40 percent of Second World War food production in America occurred in the family garden, accounting for more than one million tons of produce ("Dig for Victory")— providing that food is, in fact, a weapon. And, of course, this *is* war.

Tao Orion, in her *Beyond the War on Invasive Species* (2015), traces the origin of the colonial rhetoric of plant *invasion* to Charles Elton, who had "lived through World War II in England, where he worked to ensure that England's strictly rationed food supplies were safe from rodents, including three invasive species of rats and mice that had been introduced to Europe in the eleventh century" (13). Elton's 1958 publication, *The Ecology of Invasions by Animals and Plants*, "argued that organisms flourishing in regions where they did not evolve should be considered invaders that pose imminent harm to their introduced ecosystems" (quoted in ibid.). Gilbert Caluya traces Elton's thought to the influence of "one-time secretary of the British Eugenics Education Society" (2014), Oxford's Sir Alexander Carr-Saunders, whose 1922 *The Population Problem* attributed overpopulation "to primitive peoples reproducing at higher rates because of lower mental and physical capacity, which in turn endangered the standard of living among the higher races" (ibid.).

This obviously xenophobic rhetoric of *invasion*—Elton's mapping of his experience of *animals* alien to an island nation onto an ecological understanding of *plant* 'behaviour' more generally—remarks not only upon one zoologist's analogizing and *zoomorphizing* by grafting animal extensions onto the plant kingdom, but also testifies to a tendency, greater still, of scientific inquiry's adulteration by adoption of cultural phenomena: attitudes, *mythoi*, predilections, stories disguised in the Trojan Horse of its pretense toward objectivity and truth.

One needn't pry too hard into Elton's thought to perceive the human in it; indoctrinated by the myth of national statehood with mettle twice-tested, it is no great wonder that his contribution to the ecological sciences held a mirror to its *society* in its historical moment more so than it did to *nature* and the world. In the introduction to Elton's *Ecology*, he writes, "It's not just nuclear bombs and war that threaten us. There are other sorts of explosions, and this book is about ecological explosions" (Elton quoted in Orion 2015, 14)—a sensationalistic Cold War era analogy equating nuclear and population *booms*, investing the latter with an immediacy and scale of violence disproportionate to any real risk of ecological invasion by borrowing from the ready-made fear of nuclear *annihilation*: and this amidst the sudden overgrowth of a baby *boom* in our own primate species due to the end of the war.

It should be noted, here, however, that the *conservation* efforts resultant of Elton's fraught understanding of ecosystems should not be discarded wholesale, on the grounds of being founded on an analogy (and a false one, at that). They should, instead, like the vegetable *invaders* they work to suppress, be evaluated on the grounds of their effective impact on the environments they work to preserve: gauging the actual benefit against actual harm. I hope not to trivialize the actual and immediate destructive impact of many invasive species—too countless to list here, but some of the most impactful including the emerald ash borer, the zebra mussel, and the European rabbit—nor do I hope to undermine the cognitive association of invasive species with their colonial hosts, as a reminder of some hundreds of years of cultural and ecological oppression at the behest of the invasive species of European imperialists.[7]

Such conservation practices, however, run a severe risk of standing in for the *natures* they work to recreate and preserve: they serve as synecdoche, the part standing in for the whole, for the global biosphere. The implication, then, in these popular conservationist activisms, by extending the *agrilogistical* division, the "thin rigid boundaries between human and nonhuman worlds" (Morton 2014) delineating the 'pristine' nature of the conservation *area* from its surroundings, is a presupposition that the remainder beyond the perimeter is not to be conserved. The decision to erect finite zones worthy of protection implicitly grants free ecocidal reign over every area beyond the scope of the protected boundary. If "[a]grilogistics is the smoking gun behind the (literally) smoking gun responsible for the Sixth Mass Extinction Event" (ibid.), then the thin red line of the conservation area border is the license that declares open season on the rest of the planet. Unless such protections can be afforded indefinitely to the planet as a whole, and especially to those areas most at risk—including everything from old-growth rainforests to desertified battle-grounds—the conservation area, governed predominantly by its war against weeds, stands as an artifact signifying a nature already lost at its conception: Catriona Sandiland's *melancholy nature*, "incorporat[ing] environmental destruction into the ongoing workings of commodity capitalism" (2010, 333).

Such a provisional, metaphorical understanding of plant migrations as akin to the migrations of animals (and, more particularly, people), already contradicting its own logic by paradoxically asserting *place* as both a characteristic *inherent* to the biological organism and an *arbitrary* limit able to be transgressed, pivots upon the conflation, (quintessential to all manner of totalitarian thinking) between *nature* and *nation*—etymological cognates descending from the Latinate root (*nascor, nasci, natus sum*: to be born)—that grants rights based on *nascence*, privileging in-born qualities over acculturated ones, and binding the occupation of territories by the state with a *birthright* to them. Anthropocentric invasion ecology takes, or *mistakes*, plant and animal kingdoms for human ones, superimposing the regulation of the state onto the biopolitical maintenance of ecosystems (thereby transforming ecosystems into artificial reproductions thereof by setting the human above its nature). It is dictated by the same xenophobic political rhetoric that disallows climate refugees access to vital resources—a suspicious political assessment of risk based on the imagined potential for and not actual production of harm.

Exhibiting this tenuous conflation of *invasion ecology* between the capacity for plants to spread and their ability to effect harm, Brendon Larson, in *Metaphors for Environmental Sustainability: Redefining Our Relationship with Nature*, reminds us

> that the use of the invasion metaphor in the field of invasion biology derives from political geography, and ecologists have opined that initial concerns about invasive species arose from related concerns about Nazi invasion [... and] that these cultural associations also confound scientific inquiry; the term *invasion* is misleading because it conflates spread with impact, when preliminary data suggest that species that spread are no more likely to have a significant influence than those that expand very little.
>
> (2011, 163)

My own position, however, is that the ease with which the metaphor of invasion arises from agricultural thinking, perpetuating the toxic logic of *agrilogistics* during and after the Second World War, suggests more than a seemingly-arbitrary, historical mapping of the conditions of war onto the conceptualization of agricultural and conservation practice. It suggests a necessary relationship between war craft and large-scale commercial farming: that the violence always-already in-built to monoculture renders itself transparent only after the great cost of imperial warfare resulting from its practices has entered the popular imagination through historical myth-making. Two World Wars have revealed a violence already persistent within the system of unsustainable agriculture. The spade reveals itself as such only after the earth has been scathed; agriculture reveals itself, through these ready-made metaphors of invasion, as always-already weaponized only after the world had witnessed war on the scale of no other.

Not only, however, does this rhetoric of *invasion* when applied to ecological systems obfuscate any observational understanding of the actual impact of *foreign weeds* on those systems, but it also bolsters a certain fear of the exotic that homologizes plant and human others, thereby creating a safe space for the displacement of xenophobic impulses onto a pristine nature. W. O'Brien, cited in Larson's *Metaphors*, demonstrates,

> The commonly perceived separation of natural and human spheres that allows us to view derisive anti-foreign rhetoric as 'benign' when applied to nature [such as the war on invasive species], but as 'malignant' when applied to humans [such as refusing asylum to climate refugees], cannot be sustained because the images they conjure and the meanings they carry are inseparably entangled, and thus one can never be certain what sentiments lie behind an expression of concern about 'the exotic.'
>
> (2011, 183)

Larson continues, "A war against exotic invaders cannot be isolated within the realm of invasion biology. ... A war against invasive species thus supports veritable war, indirectly, by implicitly endorsing and reinforcing the logic of war" (ibid.).

More sinister still is the fact that, as Larson also identifies, the rhetoric surrounding actual warfare is becoming ever more sterilized in its presentation to the public— for instance, the devastating effects (including psychological) of drone warfare on civilian populations being masked and trivialized by such euphemistic terms as *collateral damage*, or killing missions medicalized as *extractions* or *excisions* (Weber 2014)—in such a manner as to conceal the death and brutality essential to it, while the violent language of the enemy threat being countered in the 'war against weeds' grows ever more sensationalistic and brutally damning (Larson 2011, 183). Such a displacement of the very real horror of war onto a minor, manageable (often non-)threat precludes any appropriate public response to the injustice of on-going imperial occupation. Semantically, the rhetoric of invasion surrounding plants and their migration occupies a cultural position, a field in the common dialect that would otherwise occupy itself with meaningful discourse on the nature of warfare, military *occupation* and *invasion*.

This identification of the hyperbole of the discourse of invasive ecology is not, of course, to argue that invasive species cannot pose very real risks to 'natural' ecosystems. Permaculture co-founder, David Holmgren, is very careful, in his "Weeds or Wild Nature," to clarify, warning:

> I have always emphasized the distinction between animals (especially vertebrates including fish) and plants when considering the potentially problematic introduction of these organisms to new environments: clearly top predators are the most problematic of all introductions. That being said, prohibitions on culture of (for example) Redfin perch in central Victoria is meaningless when this species has been naturalized in all streams and most dams for at least a century.
>
> (2013)

While the introduction of novel *animal* species into an hitherto-unknown environment provides a greater potential for risk than the introduction of non-native *plant* species, the ideological and political campaign against special invasion is too often myopic and ineffectual to maintain its privilege in the popular imagination, policy, and environmentalism today.

The most problematic issue with the rhetoric of *invasion ecology* is its sheer arbitrariness. Most every vegetable consumed by the globalized family was imported to its place of cultivation, at one time or another, in an act of *ecological imperialism* (Crosby 2015), without much consideration for its status as endemic. Virtually every plant found in our decorative gardens evolved elsewhere. It is naturally this distance, between the flower border and the treeline, that overdetermines the beauty of the decorative. The same exoticism is invested in the natural selection of a flower bed as it is in the wild nature beyond. And yet, in this *agrilogistic* model of relatively ineffectual environmental action, they should never meet.

Demonstrating the ease with which otherwise *invasive* species are *naturalized*, not only into ecological systems, but, more importantly, into ideological ones, Michael Pollan, in *The Botany of Desire*, identifies the apple, so iconic to American culture, as a species introduced by European colonists—one essential to early frontierism and the westward migration of late peoples across the continent (2001, 12; 16). And yet, none but the Amerindian would contest the apple, the *big* apple, as being anything less American than apple pie.[8] Tao Orion, however, in an appendix to her book, itemizes over one hundred *known* varieties of transoceanic plant migrations occurring *before* globalization and the modern colonial era, with much debate surrounding the continental origins of many species there before and thereafter,[9] suggesting some bastardization already inherent in the purification project of invasion ecology—that akin to the maintenance of the double standard of virginity against women or the eugenic myth toward the purity of races.[10]

Not exclusive to plant invaders, even those distinctions of animal specimens most obviously novel to a clime find themselves on tenuous footing when pressed. The zebra mussel, for instance, a popular invader of our Great Lakes Basin, notoriously purifies fresh water, even siphoning off heavy metals and chemical pollutants (Orion 2015, 129). This is both a risk and a benefit, promising to purify lakes and streams while threatening higher species through bioaccumulation. Abe Cabrera, environmentalist writer and researcher, identifies the human culpability in these and other *invasions*: "due to pollution, an invasive organism takes advantage of the polluted environment to become an apparent menace, only to recede again once the environment recovers" (2016).[11] Any real and immediate danger to the freshwater system, however, seems to come at the dismay of boaters and cottagers, of lake-based industry and tourism, due to the *Dreissena polymorpha*'s chokehold on drainage and uptake pipes, their unsightly and costly effects on docks, ships' hulls and propellers, rather than on the health of these freshwater ecosystems (Orion 2015, 129).

Not one species is yet threatened to extinction by this mollusk, although many are affected by its added competition (ibid.).[12] And it is an *invasive*, due mostly to the ostentation of its effects, rather than on a measure of any real ecosystemic harm. As early as Linnaeus, the gypsy moth (pejorative in the Latin as much as the English) had been called "a destroyer unequal," "Lymantria dispar" (Linnaeus 1758)—and this was already in its 'native' environment. Such intersection in naming, between the moth's common and taxonomical nomenclature, implicitly assimilating the Romany wanderer as a destructive force, exhibits this very same xenophobic impulse, othering the animal and the man in the pairing. Similarly, Asiatic bird flu and swine flu, the Spanish influenza: these *pests* are always bound in the naming to their *othered* origins.[13]

Catriona Sandilands identifies real ecological harm to plants and pollinators with the invasion of the *Cynanchum rossicum* (the so-unfortunately-named dog-strangling vine)—especially the already-threatened monarch butterfly by gravely imitating its milkweed habitat. It also threatens other vegetation by overcrowding and changing the chemical composition of soil. However, Sandilands also identifies the cause of the spread of the invasive vine as the preservation of a borderline—by "highways, hydro corridors, railways, ongoing industrial agriculture, encroaching suburban development, and the looming presence of a large disused landfill" (2013, 95)—because the vine favours the forest edge and, as many *invaders* do, disturbed soils. The permaculturists, as does Sandilands here, reconsider the terms of invasion as 'space created,' demanding they themselves become better gardeners to occupy the zone, fulfill the need of the space, with some better other organism.[14]

Contesting this over-reactive pejoration of *invasion*, David Holmgren advises that the permaculturist reconsider the terms by which one refers to these *non-native* species, reclaiming them as *naturalized* and *naturalizing, spreading*. This neutral descriptive nomenclature evacuates the categorization of *alien* species of its anthropomorphized status as an *invader*, instead demanding that harm be evaluated on grounds beyond a plant's capacity merely to spread, or it being discovered 'out of place' (2013). Other ecologists, including Julie L. Lockwood, Martha F. Hoopes, and Michael P. Marchetti (2013), likewise evaluate the terminology of *invasion*, identifying its use as problematic. Their assessment of invasive species, however, limits this problem solely to the breadth of the term's scope. Used to refer variously and contradictorily to native and non-native, transported, established, spreading, and impactful species, alike, the term invasive lacks specificity; likewise, it is used synonymously to other pejorative terms, such as alien, colonizing, escaped, exotic, foreign, immigrant, noxious, nuisance, pest, tramp, transient, waif, and weed (Lockwood et al. 2013, 3), that demonize species wholesale, precluding any observation of the potential ecosystemic benefits offered by an invader or acceptance of the imminence of ecosystemic change in the Anthropocene. The authors limit their own use of *invasion* to identify "those species that found their way out of their native range and into a novel non-native location via human actions" (2013, 2)—anthropogenic spreading.

Note, however, that this indefinite definition of *invasion* disregards any consideration of *impact*; by such a measure, all equine species are *invaders* to the New World,[15] alongside most decorative grasses furnishing suburban lawns[16] and 33 percent of all earthworms (Blakemore 2008), not to mention any and all humans, some 15,000 years ago, some 500 years ago, and today.

Such a plagued, pestilent (mis)understanding of ecosystems, *invasion ecology*—an oxymoron—in its denial of ecosystemic change, its preference toward homeostasis rather than diversity and complexity, founds itself upon an archaic, chthonian conceptualization of evolution, wherein species develop autonomously, autogenetically from the earth of the place, without desire or capability to spread, or to be spread upon. Furthermore, this conceptualization of *invasion* is based on observations particular to island ecosystems, originating with Britain and then superimposed onto continents considered mere larger islands. So, too, does *invasion ecology* analogize animal behaviour and migration onto plant 'behaviour.' Such figurative understandings—whether synecdoche, metonymy, or metaphor—preclude the objectivity toward which the biological sciences pretend and colour, mar, adulterate, and obfuscate observational understandings of naturalizing species.

The permaculturists, including David Holmgren, in a somewhat radical, comprehensive ecological understanding, recognize the component structures of ecosystems, allowing the designer to build them from the ground up, with little concern for nativity or spread. This is a more dynamic understanding of the codependence of species based on the 'lock and key' relationships provided by the concept of *ecological fitting*, proposed by Daniel Janzen (1985), who augments the traditional co-evolutionary explanation of species adaptation to suggest that many species have migrated into ecosystems, *post factum*, based on transferrable *fitness*. Janzen observed, in the Costa Rican rainforest, that many species had migrated there late in the geological record—they were, at one time, *invaders*—and yet still contribute to the vitality and resilience of their system, augmenting its biodiversity. *Invasion*, Janzen's concept attests, is a normal component of healthy, 'natural' ecosystems.

Ecosystems, the permaculturists including Tao Orion understand, tend toward complexity:

> In highly functional natural systems, every function is supported by multiple elements. In such places, life-provisioning processes or functions, like nutrient cycling or water filtration, are carried out by diverse species, every one doing its part. This way, if one species is affected by disease, fire, or another disturbance, their service to the rest of the ecosystem is taken up by other capable species. Because living systems tend toward complexity, if only one or two species are thriving where there once were many, it's important to look at the underlying ecological factors that may be contributing to the lack of diversity.
>
> (2015, 189)

Many *invaders*, then, have the potential to contribute toward ecosystemic complexity while filling an ecological niche; they are, in fact, both the cause and effect of a vital system's tendency toward biodiversity.[17]

The permaculturists, evolving out of the environmentalism of the late-twentieth century, take the anthropogenic spread of non-native species through globalization as an inevitability. Their position, then, is to counter the risks of harmful or unwanted *naturalizing* species by designing every aspect of a perennial ecosystem, building and priming it in such a way as to guarantee its autonomous succession indefinitely. Weeds and pests, for the permaculturist, are not species to be demonized or eradicated but to be observed and accounted for through comprehensive understandings of the niches made available by their boot-strapped system. Slug populations, for instance, can be regulated by constructing habitats that are inviting to predatory snakes; harmful insect populations can be tempered by building bat houses; impactful *weeds* can be prevented by filling their *zone* with something more conducive to the vitality of the ecosystem.[18] To the permaculturist, more is more.

The real risk, then, of the arbitration of the introduction of *some* novel species as invaders while others are blindly accepted, even praised for their benevolence—their beauty, their flavour, their nutrients, their utility, their medicine—especially when such arbitration is rarely made on the grounds of actual harm,[19] is that those who are most culturally and ecologically colonized by such name-calling when it is enacted as policy are most often the last consulted when it comes to making such influential decisions. The pejoration of *cannabis* as a similar 'weed,' for instance, to be culled from the garden of the state, and any cultivators criminalized, is just such an obvious example of a plant with exceptional properties, medicinal and otherwise, traditionally condemned on such feeble, xenophobic foundations as to call into question the prohibition of all plants.[20]

Ecology regarding naturalizing, naturalized, or spreading species as *invasive* does violence to nature and cultivation alike, as it compares the act of gardening to the conduct of military defence. The curation and arbitration, the design, then, of otherwise wild organic space, becomes based upon principles of exclusion and homogeneity, uniformity rather than inclusion and heterogeneity, diversity. In conservationist environmentalisms, this monoculturalism favours not one particular species of plant, but instead a singular ecosystem preserved in a synchronic state: a project akin to Samuel Johnson's eighteenth-century lexicography, attempting to rescue and preserve

> the *English* language, which, while it was employed in the cultivation of every species of literature, has itself been hitherto neglected, suffered to spread, under the direction of chance, into wild exuberance, resigned to the tyranny of time and fashion, and exposed to the corruptions of ignorance, and caprices of innovation.
>
> (1755)

Notice, here, how uncannily similar is the language between the rhetoric of *invasion ecology* and Johnson's aims to preserve the corruption of his mother tongue. And, while it is most obvious to linguists today that such a noble effort by purists to stabilize the word, futilely attempting to preserve it from corruption in the uncouth mouths of the undereducated mob, roots itself in classist and xenophobic sentiments, and thus runs contrary to the forces that govern language and drive its ongoing evolution (rather than its corruption or decline), the ecological sciences and, particularly, invasion ecology have until late remained impervious to the same self-scrutiny that would identify its origins as steeped in cultural presuppositions that do damage to scientific inquiry and the pursuit of knowledge.

Akin, then, to the understanding of structuralist linguistics that supplanted conservation efforts such as Johnson's, permaculture, under the auspices of Janzen's *ecological fitting*, promotes a type of structuralist ecology, identifying the interplay between species and basing its understandings of an ecological environment as a system of difference—an emphasis on the comprehension of the *langue* of an ecological system in order to design and implement the *parole* in such a manner as to promote the dynamism and vitality of the novel, arbitrated system.[21]

Invasion ecology, like its paternal grandfather, monoculture, adhering to Morton's *agrilogistics*, aims to preserve an artificial, synchronic, static 'snapshot' of an ecosystem (at great costs, both economical and ecological), rather than to foster the diachronic conditions tending toward maximum (re)production, resilience, versatility, complexity, and abundance, and all of these emerging from maximum diversity. In this way, invasion ecology, and its resultant conservationism, serves only to honour the memory of a nature already abandoned to the conditions of late capitalism; it "hangs the trees in a tree museum," so to speak, and dredges up the corpse of the environment for its occasional viewing, despite its threadbare shroud and meagre remnants. And this, the most prevalent environmentalist effort (by governments, anyhow) to honour a dead nature.

Furthermore, corroborating this spectral quality of the unadulterated natures toward which conservationisms aspire, Jodi Frawley and Iain McCalman, in their *Rethinking Invasion Ecologies from the Environmental Humanities*, suggest,

> ecologists tend to conjure up perfect ahistorical pasts, which contemporary scientists, managers, and communities then work to recapture (Alagona et al., 2012). All too often nostalgia has subsumed a reality that is much more ambiguous. Research grounded in the experiences of people engaged in grappling with changed or changing environments often proves more complex, revealing that new ecosystems may be detrimental to some actors, while others can be energized by these same disrupted, hybrid or changing environments (Davis et al., 2011).
>
> (2014, 6)

And, yet, motivated by more than a nostalgic drive toward an idealized, pure and static nature, such conservation environmentalisms are also, and primarily, propelled by economic factors: allowed by their affordability relative to other activisms and tempered by the demands placed upon the land by industry.[22]

David Holmgren explains the pervasive impetus of governments and non-profits favouring an invasion-ecology approach to environmental activism:

> this positive agenda [conservationism] was massively amplified by a simultaneous negative campaign against all naturalizing plants (and animals) as 'environmental weeds' and vermin. Compared with other active campaigns of the environmental movement against nuclear power, genetic engineering, coal mining or even native forest logging, the demonizing of naturalized species was not up against established powerful interests, and found a psycho-social resonance in the general population that could relate to the idea of pest plants and animals. A war against 'environmental weeds' or simply invasive species was a natural extension of the war against agricultural weeds that had its origins with the beginnings of agriculture and civilization.
>
> (2013)

Besides being the most affordable and least resistant means of environmental activism at the political level, *invasion ecology* has come to stand in for the very nature it presumes to preserve through national, provincial, municipal, and more local friends' interests. This is not to suggest, in any way, that I or those others within detest the parks system and its efforts; it is, however, to address the artificiality of conservationism's interest but also to identify these efforts as an extension of a toxic *agrilogistics*, and to recognize the limitation of those same interests as steeped in a combative rhetoric that does violence to nature and understanding alike.

The peace effort then, is led by the local, independent activist, the permaculturist, the gardener: blue helmets on the front lines in back yards, everywhere—heels dug in at the seed bank at Aleppo, stationed in Afghanistan, Vietnam, and China, stocking trenches with raised *hugelkultur* beds stacked under the model of *ecological fitting* from clover up to canopy. The United Nations Trade and Environment Review declares that:

> The world needs a paradigm shift in agricultural development: from a 'green revolution' to an 'ecological intensification' approach. This implies a rapid and significant shift from conventional, monoculture-based and high-external-input-dependent industrial production towards mosaics of sustainable, regenerative production systems that also considerably improve the productivity of small-scale farmers.
>
> (2013, i)

This, the most radical position, suggesting a complete overhaul of global agro-economic systems toward producing food in the places it's most needed, is also the simplest. Masanobu Fukuoka, perhaps the grandfather of permaculture, promotes a Zen do-nothing, or slow gardening wherein he outsources the labour of a system onto its components (1978)—mind, these, too, include a small team of student volunteers—with his no-till, no-prune, organic polyculture.

This agroecological, polycultural position, however radical, is growing. With some 2,313 permaculture projects—small-scale, local, eco-utopian spaces, both rural and urban, governed by the permaculture ethics of "people care; earth care; and fair share"—profiled on the *Permaculture Worldwide Network* website,[23] and many more projects and practitioners unlisted and active—more than a mere community of like-minded environmentalists—permaculture constitutes a veritable global movement of those working to transform agriculture away from its *agrilogistic* inheritance and toward low-input, high-yield, co-operative community projects that share the fruits of their labours. Rather than looking back nostalgically toward an (a)historical ecological past, however, permaculture looks forward toward a perpetually sustainable future while also employing the tricks and techniques gleaned from pre-modern practices. Employing Keyline design of water storage, constructing passive solar housing from recycled materials, using efficient rocket-mass heating, growing on raised *hugelkultur* beds, integrating both domestic and imported vegetation for sustenance and fuel, and much, much more—permaculture takes the do-it-yourself initiative to the extreme, aiming to design self-sufficient systems that meet the needs both of the environment and its human members.

Such agroecology, supplanting other conventional methods of environmental activism, such as governmental initiatives of conservationism, that toe the party line of *agrilogistics* and allow for business as usual elsewhere, take the anthropocenic position for granted, identifying the obsolescence of a *purification* project toward ecosystems and accepting the hybridized *naturescultures* that exist under the looming presence of anthropogenic climate change and the sixth mass extinction event. As such, the permaculturist pursues a policy of stewardship that emphasizes integration of human elements with natural ones, not afraid of mixing these domains to produce novel ecosystems that serve the people and the planet in equal measure, with some disregard for whether a species originated in one place or another.

The promise, at least in theory—in the production of microclimates that offset an increase in average temperatures; the design of forests that serve to trap and store water in otherwise arid environments; the creation of self-perpetuating ecosystems that sink carbon from the atmosphere; and the harnessing of regenerative energies such as biomass and passive solar—is to circumvent the catastrophe caused by a reliance on fossil fuels, both by reducing demand on them and combating the devastating effects of this demand, and, in case both these fronts fall to the enemy, to have recourse to food, water, and fuel in a post-everything apocalypse.

Indirectly, then, by working to reduce the 13 percent of global carbon emissions produced by unsustainable industrial agriculture and the desertification due to these rising temperatures, the salination of soils by chemical fertilizers, and soil erosion through the removal of biotic material, permaculture also declares war against war by preventing the conflict inevitable to monocultural practice. Rather than declaring a war against weeds—a crusade that even Monsanto-Bayer could spearhead—that perpetuates the toxic logic of industrial agriculture (facetiously, *aggroculture*), it is time for us to take up our vegetable arms to design "sustainable, regenerative production systems" (United Nations 2013) that meet our societal needs while nurturing our biome and redistributing the spoils of peace.

Notes

1   Timothy Morton, in his *Dark Ecology* and elsewhere, identifies this 'addiction to agriculture' as essential to the concept of *agrilogistics*. In a rather informal blog post, Morton provides a "quick and dirty" definition of the concept: "An agricultural program so successful that it now dominates agricultural techniques planet-wide. It arose in the Fertile Crescent 12,000 years ago. Toxic from the beginning to humans and other lifeforms, and now responsible for a huge amount of global warming. It led to industry, the other huge global warming factor. Though toxic, it has been wildly successful, because the program is even more compelling than Candy Crush. It operates blindly, just like a computer program. It promises to eliminate anxiety and contradiction—social, physical and ontological—by establishing thin rigid boundaries between human and nonhuman worlds, and by reducing existence to sheer quantity. Agrilogistics is the smoking gun behind the (literally) smoking gun responsible for the Sixth Mass Extinction Event" (2014).

2   The United Nations High Commissioner for Refugees (UNHCR) estimates "that even by the most conservative predictions up to 250 million people will be displaced by the middle of this century as a result of extreme weather conditions, dwindling water reserves and a degradation of agricultural land. Many people will also be forced to flee their homes to escape fighting over meagre resources. [... I]n real terms this meant that the number of displaced would rise by a minimum of six million each year due to climate change" (Sunjic 2008).

3   For more information on Geoff Lawton and the Permaculture Research Institute's project of 'greening the desert,' cf. the short documentary film, "Permaculture Greening the Desert" (Mackintosh 2015). Similarly, cf. originator of 'holistic land management,' Allan Savory's TED talk, "How to fight desertification and reverse climate change" (2013), for further evidence of the successful restoration of desertified regions.

4   "According to the Royal Horticultural Society there were nearly 1.4 million allotments in Britain by the end of the war, which produced 1.3 M tonnes of produce. The

government estimated that around 6,000 pigs were kept in gardens and back yards by 1945. Along with state investment in failing farms, the campaign led to the UK halving its reliance on food imports" (Gibbs 2013). Incidentally and aptly, the local sustenance farming of the wartime Victory garden, a rather permacultural initiative, demonstrates the viability of a prototype of small-scale domestic agriculture and its potential to supplant globalized industrial monoculture systems.

5   *Smithsonian Magazine*, citing John Stolarczyk, curator of the 125-page virtual World Carrot Museum, and a 1998 Johns Hopkins study, debunks the myth of the carrot as a super-vegetable promised to improve eyesight and even grant night-vision, attributing its origins to a British Ministry of Information campaign promoting the ration in surplus while also concealing the invention of Airborne Interception Radar (AIR) on Allied aircraft. The carrot does, then, in its own special way, grant nocturnal vision to those in flight, if only by keeping this information from the enemy. One such poster reads, "NIGHT SIGHT *can mean LIFE or DEATH*: EAT carrots and leafy green or yellow vegetables... rich in Vitamin 'A', essential for night sight" (Smith 2013).

6   America spent some seven billion, alone, in 2015 "to stop poppy production in [an] Afghanistan" plagued and powered by opium, who "supplied the world with 90 percent of the heroin" in that year (Saifee 2016), not limiting, then, the movement of armies to their bellies, but also to their coursing veins and vegetable arms.

7   For a comprehensive study of ecological imperialism, cf. Alfred W. Crosby's title of the same name, *Ecological Imperialism: The Biological Expansion of Europe, 900–1900* (2015).

8   "Even Ralph Waldo Emerson, who knew a thing or two about natural history, called it 'the American fruit'" (Pollan 2001, 6).

9   One such example of many includes the disputed endemicism of the genus *Datura*, its origin, itself, migrating from Europe to India with Siklós' study of the pre-Colombian Vajramahabhairava-Tantra of the 11th century CE (1993).

10 For more on the latter, cf. Wallace's work, "The Pit Bull and the Child" (2015), on the indiscriminate genocide of the murkily half-bred pit bull through breed-specific legislation, and Schuster on the Nazi project of resurrecting the Ur-bull through artificial selection, in his work on "German Animal Studies, Extinction, and the Holocaust" (2016).

11 An article in *Science*, "Musseled-Out Native Species Return to the Hudson" (Kessler 2011), and another in the *Star Tribune*, "Zebra mussels decline on Lake Mille Lacs" (Smith 2014), would seems to confirm this possibility for invasive populations to peak and stabilize in time.

12 It is important to reflect that *competition* does not necessarily indicate an ecosystemic *threat*. In fact, competition is indicative of the vitality and resilience of a given system: the greater the biodiversity of a system, the greater its internal competition. For further study on the benefits of competition to ecosystems, cf. the restorative effects of the reintro-duction in 1995 of the grey wolf to Yellowstone National Park, putting pressure on the *native* threat of an otherwise glutting elk population, thereby stabilizing the river system, preventing soil erosion risking desertification, and reforesting overtaxed regions ("Wolf").

13 This is not to argue, however, that one ought not to name a harmful species with nomenclature that denotes its harmful nature. Though, this is rarely as simple as it sounds. Consider, for instance, *Atropa belladonna*, the deadly nightshade named after the Classical Fate responsible for cutting the thread of the fabric of life. Its toxic alkaloid, *atropine*, has many medicinal functions, including slowing the progress of myopia in children, resusci-tation from cardiac arrest, and treatment of insecticide and nerve-gas poisonings. Ralph Waldo Emerson, in *Fortune of the Republic*, reminds us that "a weed [is a] plant whose virtues have not yet been discovered."

14   I presume, only, that Sandilands' suggestion, too, in identifying the manufacturing of the conditions to invasion, is that industry seek some better design while environmental action reconsiders the *causes* of invasion beyond merely demonizing particular species for being discovered, somehow, out of place.

15   Kirkpatrick and Fazio, in "Wild Horses as Native North American Wildlife" (2010), ask, "Are wild horses truly 'wild,' as an indigenous species in North America, or are they 'feral weeds'—barnyard escapees, far removed genetically from their prehistoric ancestors?" arguing for the *naturalization* of the 'feral weed' after some five hundred years since invasion.

16   Even, the most popular, *Kentucky* bluegrass (*Poa pratensis*), so-inspiring of its own regional musical genre, is disappointingly-yet-not-surprisingly endemic to the Old World (Bush 2002).

17   It might be argued that many invaders have the potential to replace biodiverse ecosystems with monoculture, as is the myth behind the invasion of the purple loosestrife (*Lythrum salicaria*) in Ontario. However, Canadian ecologist Claude Lavoie, cited in veteran ecologist and senior research fellow in the Department of Animal and Plant Sciences at the University of Sheffield in England, Ken Thompson's *Where Do Camels Belong?: The Story and Science of Invasive Species* (2014), corrects, "stating that this plant has 'large negative impacts' on wetlands is probably exaggerated. The most commonly mentioned impact (purple loosestrife crowds out native plants and forms a monoculture) is controversial and has not been observed in nature (with maybe one exception). There is certainly no evidence that purple loosestrife 'kills wetlands' or 'creates biological deserts', as it is repeatedly reported."

18   These and some seventy more permacultural design solutions to habitat, energy, agricultural, and ecosystemic challenges are presented by Paul Wheaton in his instructional keynote speech at the S. California Permaculture Convergence (2013).

19   Consider, for instance, the devastation, both cultural and ecological, upon the colonial introduction of sugar cane to the Caribbean, or the Great Famine resultant of potato introduction to Ireland. Ron Benner, in an interview in *Gardens of a Colonial Present*, explains in detail, "I mean, look at the Irish, and the introduction of the potato into Ireland in the early 1700s, and the *infestans*—the fungus that attacked the potato plant [between 1845 and 1852]. Of course, I don't call it the potato famine; it really should be called the English famine because there was plenty of food in Ireland to feed the people. In fact, at the height of the famine [...] some First Nations people, the Sioux perhaps, had heard about the famine and wanted to help out by donating all this corn; but people didn't yet know what to do with it, and it was all wasted" (Fischer 2008, 107).

20   Richard Nixon's aide, John Ehrlichman, explaining the motivation behind America's "War on Drugs," in a 1994 exposé for *Harper's Magazine*, reveals, "The Nixon campaign in 1968, and the Nixon White House after that, had two enemies: the antiwar left and black people. You understand what I'm saying? We knew we couldn't make it illegal to be either against the war or black, but by getting the public to associate the hippies with marijuana and blacks with heroin, and then criminalizing both heavily, we could disrupt those communities. We could arrest their leaders, raid their homes, break up their meetings, and vilify them night after night on the evening news. Did we know we were lying about the drugs? Of course we did" (Baum 2016).

21   One might contend, here, with the successful argument that contemporary ecology, as a discipline, permaculture or no, already adheres to a structuralist methodology, with its emergence from the systems thinking of the late 1970s, coming out of cybernetics and informatics, defined by its "paradoxical self-reference, a 'thetic in' [...] that will always constitute a 'blind spot' and generate an 'outside' for its own (or any) observation" (Wolfe

2010, xix). The point, here, however, is that *invasion* ecology, in practice, betraying its roots in systems theory with its denial of an outside, by resisting migration and novelty, is not.

22 The ongoing logging of Algonquin Provincial Park, in Ontario, for instance, is just such evidence of the latter.

23 Some of the most impressive of these projects: David Holmgren's Melliodora Farm of Central Victoria, Australia; Geoff Lawton's Zaytuna Farm of New South Wales, Australia; and Bill Mollison's Ragman's Farm of Gloucestershire, UK.

References

Badr, Hazem. "Syria's ICARDA falls to rebels, but research goes on." *SciDev.Net*. Available online at: www.scidev.net/global/r-d/news/syria-s-icarda-falls-to-rebels-but-research-goes-on.html (last accessed 22 May 2014).

Bane, Peter. 2013. *The Permaculture Handbook: Garden Farming for Town and Country*. Gabriola Island: New Society Publishers.

Baum, Dan. "Legalize It All: How to win the war on drugs." *Harper's Magazine*. April, 2016. Available online at: http://harpers.org/archive/2016/04/legalize-it-all (last accessed 5 May 2017).

Blakemore, R.J. 2008. "American earthworms (Oligochaeta) from north of the Rio Grande – a species checklist." Available online at: www.annelida.net/earthworm/American%20Earthworms.pdf (last accessed 5 May 2017).

Bush, Tony. "Kentucky bluegrass (*Poa pratensis L.*)." *Plant Fact Sheet*. United States Department of Agriculture Natural Resources Conservation Service. February 5, 2002. Available online at: www.plants.usda.gov/factsheet/pdf/fs_popr.pdf (last accessed 5 May 2017).

Cabrera, Abe. "Invasive: Nature in the Anthropocene." *Hunter/Gatherer: A Journal for Rewilders*. August 29, 2016. Available online at: http://wildism.org/hg/article/invasive-nature-in-the-anthropocene

CAIT Climate Data Explorer. "Historical Emissions." *World Resources Institute*. Available online at: http://cait.wri.org (last updated June 2015 – last accessed 5 May 2017).

Caluya, Gilbert. 2014. "Fragments for a Postcolonial Critique of the Anthropocene: Invasion Biology and Environmental Security." In Jodi Frawley and Iain McCalman (eds) *Rethinking Invasion Ecologies from the Environmental Humanities*. New York: Routledge, pp 31–44.

Condon, Michael. "Syrian seed bank saved after occupation by armed forces threatens unique collection of ancient grains." *ABC*. September 21, 2015. Available online at: www.abc.net.au/news/2015-09-21/syrian-seed-bank-saved/6792590 (last accessed 5 May 2017).

Crosby, Alfred W. 2015. *Ecological Imperialism: The Biological Expansion of Europe, 900–1900*. 2nd ed. New York: Cambridge University Press.

"Dig For Victory." British propaganda film commissioned by The Ministry of Information, 1941. *YouTube*, uploaded by Imperial War Museum, March 20, 2009. Available online at: www.youtube.com/watch?v=H_Gs7Vik75k (last accessed 5 May 2017).

Fischer, Barbara. 2008. "An Interview with Ron Benner." In Ron Benner (ed.) *Gardens of a Colonial Present*. London, ON: Museum London, pp. 101–117.

Frawley, Jodi and Iain McCalman. 2014. "Invasion Ecologies: The nature/culture challenge." In Jodi Frawley and Iain McCalman (eds) *Rethinking Invasion Ecologies from the Environmental Humanities*. New York: Routledge, pp. 3–14.

Fukuoka, Masanobu. 1978. *The One-Straw Revolution*. Emmaus: Rodale Press.

Gibbs, Margot. "How 'Dig for Victory' campaign helped with the War." *The Telegraph*. April 16, 2013. Available online at: www.telegraph.co.uk/news/earth/environment/9996180/

How-Dig-for-Victory-campaign-helped-win-the-War.html (last accessed 5 May 2017).

Gray, Edward. 2009. *The Botany of Desire*. Documentary film. Kikim Media.

Hemenway, Toby. "How Permaculture Can Save Humanity and the Earth, but Not Civilization." February 12, 2010. Lecture delivered at Nicholas School of the Environment, Duke University, Durham, NC. *YouTube*, uploaded by nocholasschoolatduke, September 22, 2010. Available online at: www.youtube.com/watch?v=8nLKHYHmPbo (last accessed 5 May 2017).

Holmgren, David. "Weeds or Wild Nature: A Permaculture Perspective." *Permaculture Research Institute*. November 12, 2013. Available online at: www.permaculturenews.org/2013/11/12/weeds-wild-nature-permaculture-perspective (last accessed 5 May 2017).

Janzen, Daniel. "On Ecological Fitting." *Oikos* 45, no. 3 (1985): 308–310.

Johnson, Samuel. 1755. "Preface." *A Dictionary of the English Language*. London.

Kelley, Colin P. et al. "Climate Change in the Fertile Crescent and Implications of the Recent Syrian Drought." *Proceedings of the National Academy of Sciences* 112, no. 11 (2015): 3241–3246.

Kessler, Rebecca. "Musseled-Out Native Species Return to the Hudson." *Science*. January 21, 2011. Available online at: www.sciencemag.org/news/2011/01/musseled-out-native-species-return-hudson

Kirkpatrick, Jay F. and Patricia M. Fazio. "Wild Horses as Native North American Wildlife." *Animal Welfare Institute* (January 2010). https://awionline.org/content/wild-horses-native-north-american-wildlife (last accessed 5 May 2017).

Larson, Brendon. 2011. *Metaphors for Environmental Sustainability: Redefining Our Relationship with Nature*. New Haven, CT: Yale University Press.

Lawton, Geoff. "Reversing Desertification with Gabions." *Permaculture Research Institute*, February 15, 2014. Available online at: www.permaculturenews.org/2014/02/15/reversing-desertification-gabions (last accessed 5 May 2017).

Linnaeus, Carl. 1758. "Lymantria dispar." *Systema Naturae*. 10th ed. Stockholm: Laurentius Salvius.

Lockwood, Julie L., Martha F. Hoopes, and Michael P. Marchetti. 2013. *Invasion Ecology*. 2nd ed. Hoboken, NJ: Wiley & Sons.

Mackintosh, Craig. "Permaculture Greening the Desert." Documentary featuring Geoff Lawton and the Permaculture Research Institute. *YouTube*, uploaded by SDA-Network, February 25, 2015. Available online at: www.youtube.com/watch?v=2xcZS7arcgk (last accessed 5 May 2017).

Morton, Timothy. "Agrilogistics: Quick and Dirty." *Ecology Without Nature*. Blog post. July 9, 2014. Available online at: http://ecologywithoutnature.blogspot.ca/2014/07/agrilogistics-quick-and-dirty.html (last accessed 5 May 2017).

Morton, Timothy. 2016. *Dark Ecology: For a Logic of Future of Coexistence*. New York: Columbia University Press.

Orion, Tao. 2015. *Beyond the War on Invasive Species: A Permaculture Approach to Ecosystem Restoration*. White River Junction: Chelsea Green Publishing.

Permaculture Worldwide Network. 2016. Permaculture Research Institute. Available online at: https://permacultureglobal.org (last accessed 5 May 2017).

Pollan, Michael. 2001. *The Botany of Desire: A Plant's-Eye View of the World*. New York: Random House.

Quinn, Audrey. Illustrated by Jackie Roche. "Syria's Climate Conflict." *Mother Jones*. Web-comic. May 2014. Available online at: www.motherjones.com/politics/2014/05/syria-climate-years-living-dangerously-symbolia (last accessed 5 May 2017).

Saifee, Jessica. "The War on Opium in Afghanistan." *The Huffington Post*. May 5, 2016. Available online at: www.huffingtonpost.com/jessica-saifee/the-war-on-opium-in-afgha_b_9828506.html (last accessed 5 May 2017).

Sandilands, Catriona. "Dog Stranglers in the Park?: National and Vegetal Politics in Ontario's Rouge Valley." *Journal of Canadian Studies/Revue d'études canadiennes* 47, no. 3 (Fall 2013): 93–122.

Sandilands, Catriona. 2010. "Melancholy Natures, Queer Ecologies." In Catriona Sandilands and Bruce Erickson (eds) *Queer Ecologies: Sex, Nature, Politics, Desire*. Bloomington, IN: Indiana University Press, pp. 331–358.

Savory, Allan. "How to fight desertification and reverse climate change." Presentation. *TED2013: The Young. The Wise. The Undiscovered.* Terrace Theatre, Long Beach, California. February 23, 2013. Available online at: www.ted.com/talks/allan_savory_how_to_green _the_world_s_deserts_and_reverse_climate_change/transcript?language=en#t-551438 (last accessed 5 May 2017).

Schuster, Joshua. "German Animal Studies, Extinction, and the Holocaust." Presentation. *Making Common Causes: Crises, Conflict, Creation, Conversation*, Biennial Conference of the Association for Literature, Environment, and Culture in Canada, June 18, 2016, Biological Sciences Building, Queen's University, Kingston, ON.

Siklós, Bulcsu. "*Datura* Rituals in the Vajramahabhairava-Tantra." *Curare: Journal of Medical Anthropology* 16 (1993): 71–76.

Smith, Doug. "Zebra mussels decline on Lake Mille Lacs." *Star Tribune*. August 27, 2014. Available online at: www.startribune.com/zebra-mussels-decline-on-lake-mille-lacs/ 272813081 (last accessed 5 May 2017).

Smith, K. Annabelle. "A WWII Propaganda Campaign Popularized the Myth That Carrots Help You See in the Dark." *Smithsonian Magazine*. August 13, 2013. Available online at: www.smithsonianmag.com/arts-culture/a-wwii-propaganda-campaign-popularized-the- myth-that-carrots-help-you-see-in-the-dark-28812484 (last accessed 5 May 2017).

Sunjic, Melita. "Top UNHCR official warns about displacement from climate change." *UNHCR: The UN Refugee Agency*. December 9, 2008. Available online at: www.unhcr.org/ news/latest/2008/12/493e9bd94/top-unhcr-official-warns-displacement-climate- change.html (last accessed 5 May 2017).

"The War against Weeds." *Time* (February 19, 1945): 67–68.

Thompson, Ken. 2014. *Where Do Camels Belong?: The Story and Science of Invasive Species*. London: Profile Books.

United Nations Conference on Trade and Development. "Key Messages." *Trade and Environment Review 2013: Wake Up Before It Is Too Late*. Available online at: http://unctad. org/en/publicationslibrary/ditcted2012d3_en.pdf (last accessed 5 May 2017).

Wallace, Molly. "The Pit Bull and the Child." *TOPIA: Canadian Journal of Cultural Studies* 33 (2015): 183–205.

Weber, Elisabeth. "Living Deaths." *A matter of lifedeath, Mosaic's* annual conference, October 2, 2014, University of Manitoba, Winnipeg, MN. Keynote address.

Wheaton, Paul. "Permaculture Keynote – S. California Permaculture Convergence." Keynote address. San Diego, CA. *YouTube*, uploaded by Paul Wheaton, August 23, 2013. Available online at: www.youtube.com/watch?v=6vZPTPIHO8w (last accessed 5 May 2017).

"What is a Victory Garden?" *The National WWII Museum*. Available online at: www.national ww2museum.org/assets/pdfs/victory-garden-fact-sheet.pdf (last accessed 19 September 2016).

Wolfe, Cary. 2010. "Introduction." In *What is Posthumanism?*, edited by Cary Wolfe, xi–xxxiv. Minneapolis, MN: University of Minnesota Press.

"Wolf Reintroduction Changes Ecosystem." *Yellowstone Park*. Last accessed November 30, 2016. www.yellowstonepark.com/wolf-reintroduction-changes-ecosystem

11 Regeneration

Loss and reclamation in African–American agrarianism

Leah Penniman

Acknowledgments

I offer a low bow of gratitude to my mother, Adele Smith-Penniman, for inspiring me to be an agent for social change with her example as a leader in the civil rights movement. I thank my father, Keith Penniman, for instilling in me a love of nature and respect for stillness. Blessings upon the memory of granddaddy Samuel C. Smith and all those in my Haitian lineage who showed the world how to defeat colonial oppression. Deep love to my spouse, Jonah Vitale-Wolff and our children Neshima and Emet Vitale-Penniman. Together we have built a family committed to the love of land and of justice.

In the summer of 2005, our young black-Jewish family moved to the South End of Albany, New York, U.S.A., a neighborhood classified as a "food desert" by the federal government. On a personal level, this meant that despite our deep commitment to feeding our young children fresh food and despite our extensive farming skills, structural barriers to accessing good food stood in our way. The corner store sold only packaged chips and sugary beverages. We would have needed a car or taxi to get to the nearest grocery store, which served up artificially inflated prices and wrinkled vegetables. There were no available lots where we could garden. Desperate, we signed up for a farm subscription program, known as Community Supported Agriculture (CSA), and walked 2.2 miles to the pickup point with the newborn in the backpack and the toddler in the stroller. We paid more than we could afford for these vegetables and had literally to pile them on top of the resting toddler for the long walk back to our apartment.

About 24 million Americans live in food deserts, where it is difficult or impossible to access affordable, healthy food. This trend is not race-neutral. White neighbor-hoods have an average of four times as many supermarkets as predominantly black communities. This lack of access to life-giving food has dire consequences for our communities. The incidence of diabetes, obesity, and heart disease are on the rise in all populations, but the greatest increases have occurred among people of color, especially African-Americans and Native Americans. These diet-related illnesses are fueled by diets high in unhealthy fats, cholesterol, and refined sugars, and low in fresh fruits, vegetables, and legumes. In our communities, children are being raised on processed foods, and now over one-third of children are overweight or obese, a fourfold increase over the past 30 years. This puts the next generation at risk for lifelong chronic health conditions, including several types of cancer.

When our South End neighbors learned that my spouse and I both had many years of experience working on farms, from Many Hands Organic Farm in Barre, Massachusetts, to Live Power Farm in Covelo, California, they began to ask whether we planned to start a farm to feed this community. Firmly rooted in our love for our people and for the land, we accepted the challenge. Beyond working for "food justice," the right of peoples to healthy and culturally appropriate food produced through ecologically sound and sustainable methods, we thought about how to be in service to the more radical, international movement for food sovereignty. Food sovereignty puts the aspirations and needs of those who produce, distribute, and consume food at the heart of food systems and policies, rather than the demands of markets and corporations. It upholds the right of people to define their own food and agriculture systems.

In 2011, with the support of hundreds of supporters and volunteers, and after four years of building infrastructure, we opened Soul Fire Farm, a project committed to ending racism and injustice in the food system, providing life-giving food to people living in food deserts, and transferring skills and knowledge to the next generation of farmer-activists. We are part of a network of other land-based projects led by people of color and committed to reclaiming our rights to belong to land and have agency in the food system. This essay explores the rise, fall, and rebirth of radical black agrarianism and dives deep into the work of Soul Fire Farm. Our farm's five central objectives will frame the narrative: (1) to produce life-giving food for our people; (2) to uplift and implement the sustainable farming practices of our ancestors; (3) to train the next generation of activist-farmers; (4) to connect youth to the land; and (5) to build a broader movement for food sovereignty and racial justice.

Produce life-giving food for our people

If we want a society that values black lives, we cannot ignore the role of land and food. It is true that the U.S.A. has locked up 2.2 million people, 60 percent of them people of color. It is true that the police are killing black people in the streets at higher rates than other segments of the population. Soul Fire Farm is unwaveringly committed to the Movement for Black Lives and strives to end all forms of state-sponsored violence against black and brown people.

One of the most insidious and pervasive forms of state violence against our people is not gun violence, but the flooding of our communities with foods that kill us. From the corner store to the public school lunchroom to the prisons, our federal government is subsidizing the processed foods that undermine the health and future of our community. The United States Department of Agriculture (USDA) invests 130 billion dollars into industrial agriculture and commodity foods, such as wheat, soy, milk and dairy, and comparatively little into "specialty crops" like vegetables. Fast food chains and junk food corporations disproportionately target their advertising to children of color, resulting in an epidemic of childhood obesity and diabetes. One in three black children and one in four Latino children go to bed hungry at night. Clearly, the current food system does not have the best interests of our community in mind. We believe that the term "food desert" is too passive to describe the inequity in today's food system. Our mentor, black farmer-activist Karen Washington, taught us to recognize America for what it is: a deliberate "food apartheid," where certain populations live in food opulence and others cannot meet their basic survival needs.

As radical farmers, we began thinking about what role we must assume in dismantling racism in the food system. My partner's people are Jewish and there is a teaching in the Mishneh that says, "You are not obligated to complete the task, but neither are you free to desist from it." We are under no illusions that we have resolved the structural disaster that is our food system, but we do have a replicable model that provides food with dignity to our community.

About 25 miles outside of Albany, Soul Fire Farm intensively cultivates about two acres of rocky hillside in vegetables, fruits, and chickens for meat and eggs. Once per week we harvest this bounty and box it up into even shares that contain eight-to-twelve vegetables each, plus a dozen eggs, sprouts, and/or meat for the members of our farm share. The farm share is a subscription program, affectionately called "Netflix for vegetables" by our members, and known as "community-supported agriculture" in some circles. The farm share is based on the African-American Kwanzaa principle of Ujamaa, cooperative economics:

> In a world where greed, resource seizure, and plunder have been globalized with maximum technological and military power, we must uphold the principle and practice of Ujamaa (Cooperative Economics) or shared work and wealth. This principle reaffirms the right to control and benefit from the resources of one's own lands and to an equitable and just share of the goods of the world.
>
> (Karenga 2009)

Desiring to move beyond the casual and exploitative relationship between producer and consumer that capitalism celebrates, we develop long-term relationships of mutual commitment with our members. In early spring, members sign up for the program and commit to spend whatever they can afford on our farm's bounty. We use a "sliding scale" model where people contribute depending on their level of income and wealth. In turn, we commit to providing members with a weekly delivery of bountiful, high-quality food throughout the harvest season, which is 20–22 weeks in our climate. We deliver the boxes directly to the doorsteps of people living under food apartheid and accept government benefits as payment, such as the federal Supplemental Nutrition Assistance Program (SNAP). This reduces the two most pressing barriers to food access: transportation and cost. Using the farm share model, we can feed 65–85 families, many of whom would not otherwise have access to life-giving food. One member told us that "we would be eating only boiled pasta if it were not for this veggie box." We are working with other farmers in our network to adopt similar models and pressuring the government to fix the systems that make it challenging for farmers to accept SNAP.

To uplift and implement the sustainable farming practices of our ancestors

The history of black farming and food did not begin with enslavement, nor is it defined solely by interactions with Europeans. My African ancestors were instrumental in the domestication and refinement of food crops that have become global staples (albeit co-opted by industrial agriculture), including coffee, palm oil, melon, plantain, and rice. My ancestors honed the art of animal husbandry, especially the use of the donkey. They invented the long-handled hoe, the most commonly used farming implement in the world. My African ancestors developed thoughtful systems for mutual aid and wrote work songs to unite and motivate themselves during hard labor and long days.

So many of the farming technologies that white intellectuals appropriate and lump together under the umbrella of "permaculture" or "sustainable farming" were developed or refined by my ancestors over thousands of years. African people implemented farming technologies like adding manure and crop residue to enrich soil, planting beans and leguminous trees for nitrogen, leaving a fallow for soil regeneration, polyculture with canopy and ground cover, rotations between herding and crop cultivation, and reliance on tubers and plantains as climate-resilient stable food.

Contrary to U.S. mythology, European enslavers did not kidnap 10 million humans from the African continent from the 1600s–1800s to work their plantations in the Americas solely for their capacity as laborers. Enslavers targeted specific African communities known for expertise in necessary farming technologies, such as rice-growing and animal husbandry.

My ancestors knew the value and sanctity of their agricultural heritage, both the knowledge contained within them and the genetic history contained in the seeds they bred. Before boarding transatlantic slave ships, grandmothers and mothers would braid okra, rice, and other seeds into the hair of their children. Despite odds, they believed in a future on land where they could plant, harvest, and survive. As Amani Olugbala, black farmer and poet at Soul Fire Farm explains, "They can't squash our revolution if they can't find our seed."

Sadly, I was not raised on these stories. Farming skipped a generation in my family and I found my way back as a teenager. I attended sustainable farming conferences and worked on organic farms throughout the Northeast U.S. to build my skills. The books I read, the speeches I listened to, and the farmers I looked to for mentorship were all white. I thought that organic farming was invented by white people and struggled with a feeling that a life on land would be a betrayal to my people. I could not have been more wrong. At the 2005 annual gathering of the Northeast Organic Farmers Association, I decided to ask the handful of people of color at the event to gather for a conversation, known as a caucus. In that conversation, I learned that my struggles as a black farmer in a white-dominated agricultural community were not unique, and we decided to create another conference to bring together black and brown farmers and urban gardeners. In 2010 the National Black Farmers and Urban Gardeners Conference (BUGS) was born and continues to meet annually.

Through BUGS and my growing network of black farmers, I began to undo the false assumptions of my sustainable-agriculture education. I learned that "organic farming," as we understand it in the U.S.A., was invented by a black farmer, Dr. George Washington Carver of Tuskegee University, in the early 1900s. Carver conducted extensive research and codified the use of crop rotation in combination with the planting of nitrogen-fixing legumes, and detailed how to regenerate soil biology. His system was known as "regenerative agriculture" and helped move many southern farmers away from monoculture and toward diversified horticultural operations.

Carver's student, Dr. Booker T. Whatley, was the inventor of community-supported agriculture (CSA), which he called a "Clientele Membership Club." He advocated for diversified pick-your-own operations that produced an assortment of crops year-round. He developed a system that allowed consumer members to access produce at 40 percent of the supermarket pricing.

Further, I learned that land trusts were first started in 1969 by black farmers, with the New Communities movement leading the way in Georgia. Black farmers also demonstrated how cooperatives could provide for the material needs of their members, such as housing, farm equipment, student scholarships and loans, as well as organize for structural change. The 1886 Colored Farmers National Alliance and Cooperative Union and Fannie Lou Hamer's 1972 Freedom Farm were salient examples of black leadership in the cooperative farming movement.

When we as black people are bombarded by messages that our only place of belonging on land is as slaves, performing dangerous and backbreaking menial labor, to learn of our true and noble history as farmers and ecological stewards is deeply healing.

Industrial agriculture is trashing our planet. According to the World Resources Institute, agriculture is responsible for 24 percent of climate change, 70 percent of water use, and 37 percent of land use (2013). Our African ancestors and our indigenous brothers and sisters around the world have figured out farming systems that can feed the community without destroying our ecological foundations. Our commitment at Soul Fire Farm is to implement these regenerative practices and to name and honor the people who originated the practices.

As ancestor Carver taught us, we prioritize soil life above all else on the farm. We use a low-till system, with the long-handled hoe as our primary tool. The soil is covered with straw mulch or a living mulch understory of dwarf white clover at all times. As ancestor Whatley taught us, we maintain a high diversity of around 90 horticultural crops and rotate these crops to minimize pest buildup and maximize soil nutrients. We intercrop compatible plants, like tomatoes, with fava beans, and maize with pole beans and pumpkins. Each month, we hold a "konbit," a collective work party in the Haitian tradition where people come together to gift their labor to the land, share food, and sing work songs.

Just as my ancestors in the Dahomey region of West Africa build their homes of earth, so we have constructed our home and educational center from local clay, straw, sand, ground limestone, local wood, and recycled materials. The primary building is a timber-frame strawbale structure with passive solar design, interior thermal mass, earthen floor, and solar panels for heat and hot water. Choosing to build in harmony with nature is not the quick and easy path. We do not subscribe to the capitalist perspective that buildings should go up in a few months and be disposable after 30 years. It took us over three years to construct the durable primary building and we endured many challenges along the way. For example, when we had almost finished digging the foundation using our undersized tractor and hand shovels through the hard, rocky clay of the mountainside, we realized that solar and magnetic south are about 13 degrees different in our area. This "magnetic declination" matters because a solar home must face solar south. Needless to say, many tears of frustration were shed as we picked up the shovels to re-dig the foundation in the correct direction. We drew strength from the deep knowing that our ancestors faced greater challenges, and endured.

Train the next generation of activist-farmers

According to the U.S. census, farming is one of the whitest professions in the country today (2012). The federal government counts only "principal operators" as farmers, which excludes farmworkers, farmers who are not managers, and farmers who operate outside of the market system. The reality is that 76 percent of the nation's food is grown by Latinx and Hispanic people, while only about 2.5 percent of farmland is owned by this community (ibid.). African-American farmers once owned and operated 14 percent of the nation's farms, and now control around 1 percent (ibid.). This reality is the result of a deliberate, historical process designed to maintain the white owning class and keep food cheap through exploited labor. Let's review the history.

In 1865, two years after the Emancipation Proclamation was signed, General William T. Sherman's Field Order #15 deeded "40 acres and a mule" over to black families on the South Carolina and Florida coasts, so that they could begin to build economic independence. President Andrew Johnson reversed the policy and most never received their allotments. Black families were forced to remain on plantations as tenant farmers and sharecroppers, an economic situation akin to slavery. Despite this major setback, black farmers pooled resources and were able to purchase almost 15 million acres of farmland by 1910.

Threatened by black farm ownership, white supremacists worked hard to undermine black farmers by excluding them from the cooperative unions, targeting them with threats and physical violence, and denying agricultural assistance. For example, during the boll weevil epidemic and cotton price plummet of 1915–1923, white farmers would go to the National Farm Loan Association for assistance. Black farmers were systematically denied support. In 1964, decades of USDA discrimination against black farmers was exposed by the US Commission on Civil Rights, but black land ownership had already declined to six million acres. As historian Pete Daniel explained, "The situation for rural blacks was bad enough before the Brown decision, but [after Brown] USDA programs were sharpened into weapons to punish civil rights activity" (Daniel 2015). In an eleventh hour effort to save their way of life, 1000 black farmers filed a class action lawsuit against the USDA in 1996, which was settled out of court for a meager $50,000 per farmer: about enough to purchase a commercial tractor. By the time of this victory, only 1 percent of American farmer-operators were black.

Unwilling to pay people fairly for their labor, the U.S. capitalist system had to come up with a replacement for the sharecropping and tenant farming system. Our country began importing low wage workers from Mexico and other nearby countries through the Bracero program, now known as H2A. These workers are excluded from many of the protections afforded to other laborers, including overtime, days off, minimum wage, and the right to collectively bargain. As a result of our reliance on exploited labor, the U.S. spends less on food than any other country in the world as a percentage of household income.

At Soul Fire Farm, we are working to reclaim the collective right of black and brown people to have agency in the food system, to be farmers, and to participate in food production with dignity. In 2012, we started a beginner's apprenticeship program designed to address pervasive issues of cultural erasure and racial discrimination in the predominantly white sustainable farming network. We received calls from aspiring black farmers from several states who told us they were ready to quit after their experiences attempting to learn to farm. One young woman reported, "While I was picking beans with the farmer-owner at my World Wide Opportunities on Organic Farms (WWOOF) placement, he asked me to explain why 'black fathers abandon their children and wives' theorizing that this 'pattern' goes back to male hunting customs in Africa." While this statement is problematic and inaccurate from every angle, it is sadly not unique. People of color travel thousands of miles to train on our farm, so as to be free from the constant barrage of racial micro- and macro-aggressions.

Our farm is still experimenting with models for farmer training that are non-exploitative, dignified, and accessible for people with various levels of experience. At the time of this writing, we operate a weeklong Black and Latinx Farmers Immersion for novice growers with a "train the trainer" track for experienced growers. Additionally, we offer a seven-month farm-manager apprenticeship. Aside from people of color leadership, a unique and important feature of these programs is attention to cultural and emotional relevancy. We dive deep into crop planning, soil management, whole foods preparation, and farm strategic planning. At the same time, we are able to stand by the edge of the pond, breathe deeply, and offer one another trauma-releasing spiritual herbal baths in the tradition of our West African people. We are able to reenact our histories of land loss and resistance by firelight and then dance under the full moon. It is because we can show all of ourselves in the space—intellectual, spiritual, emotional, cultural—that participants testify at the end, "I have a love hangover. You believed in me. I am not going to settle for anything. Freedom is not a lofty goal. We are going to win."

For community members who might not be ready to commit to farmer training for a week, never mind an entire seven-month season, we have also designed week - end workshops on specific skills. For example, fall is an appropriate time to practice and teach food preservation in the Northeast, given the bounty of nutritious perishables like tomatoes, beets, and peppers. While it would be easy to follow online instructions for canning, we use the opportunity to give a black elder in the community voice, power, and belonging. Mother Isola grew up on a farm in Mississippi and her family produced all of the food they ate except for the sugar and flour purchased at the town store. Canning was integral to their way of life.

Now in a retirement home close by, Mother Isola comes to Soul Fire Farm to teach the community how to prepare for a bountiful winter. With her weathered cookbook and strict gaze, she lovingly admonishes us that our spouses will leave us behind if we didn't get our kitchen skills in shape. We get in line and produce dozens of quart jars full of colorful and tasty preserves.

Of course, training alone is not enough to correct the racial injustice in farming. The long history of land- and wealth-grabbing at the expense of people of color has resulted in the persistent 16:1 asset-gap ratio between white and black. *Yes! Magazine* calculated that these stolen resources amount to $64 trillion dollars in reparations due to Black America (Loeffelholz Dunn and Neumann 2015). For this reason, we work closely with the Movement for Black Lives, US Food Sovereignty Alliance, and Agricultural Justice Project to dismantle the structural barriers to land ownership, credit, fair working conditions, and government support for farmers of color.

Connect youth to the land

Kareem arrived on the farm last summer with 13 of his Albany peers, full of excitement and trepidation. We asked him to find an object from the natural environment that represented how he felt that day and bring it to a circle of sunny benches for an introductory conversation. Kareem hesitated for words during those initial minutes, explaining later that he does not usually talk in front of groups and was significantly outside of his comfort zone far from the pavement of Albany's South End. We toured the farm and the young people quickly saw that their gleaming sneakers would be ruined in short order and had the courageous idea to go barefoot instead. Amidst giggles, warm mud oozed between toes and worms found their way into hands. The spoken content of the tour was nearly drowned out in deference to the more compelling tactile experience of land connection. The rest of the day was filled with "hands on the land" practical farming experience, cooperative preparation of a vegetable rich meal, spontaneous group dance, and creative live commercials serving as an antidote to corporate media's promotion of food that kills.

At the day's end gratitude circle, Kareem found his voice. He shared an experience so profound that the truth of it alone justifies the immense grit required to maintain Soul Fire Farm. Kareem explained that when he was very young his grandmother had shown him how to garden and to gently hold insects. She died long ago and he had forgotten these lessons. When he removed his shoes on the tour and let the mud reach his feet, the memory of her and the memory of the land literally traveled from the earth, through his soles, and to his heart. He arrived "home." He went on to complete his summer film program, where he created a documentary on honoring the memories of our ancestors.

Sadly, young people are often disconnected from a relationship to land and to healthy food. Today's generation of children are spending less time outdoors in nature than previous generations. "Nature deficit disorder" leads to ADHD, anxiety, depression, poor eyesight, and lower achievement in school. At the same time, children are being targeted by fast food and junk food advertising at an unprecedented rate. Children trapped in food desert neighborhoods have little or no access to lean protein and fresh fruits and vegetables. This trend is resulting in diets higher in calories, saturated fats, cholesterol, sodium, and refined sugar, and lower in vitamins and minerals. As a result, childhood obesity has more than doubled in children and quadrupled in adolescents in the last 30 years, putting youth at higher risk for heart disease, diabetes, sleep apnea, psychological problems, and later in life, stroke and cancer.

Soul Fire Farm's Youth Food Justice Program attempts to address the dual challenges of increasing access to the outdoors and access to healthy food. With young people at the center, we tend the earth, cook for one another, explore the forest, tell stories, climb the trapeze, and sit with the novel discomfort of dirt in the creases of our hands. Perhaps more important than the tangible skills transfer is our effort to create an environment that challenges internal self-degradation. Of all the threats facing black and brown youth, we are most concerned about the pervasive perspective that "there is no future worth investing in—it does not make sense to care for our bodies or for the land because incarceration and violent death are our destiny." While there is no prescription for creating a healthy and healing space, some of the principles that guide our youth programming are listed below:

Youth programming principles at Soul Fire Farm

- You are part of our family and welcome in our home and at our meal table.
- We honor our Black, Latinx, and Native ancestors and heroes with storytelling.
- We incorporate art, music, rhythm, and creative expression to learning experiences.
- We form a circle often and everyone is given voice.
- We trust youth by telling the whole truth.
- We trust youth by sharing real "adult" skills.
- We honor the dignity of youth by shielding them from outside "observers" who want to document and consume their image.
- We design programs in collaboration with youth.
- We make space for identity caucus groups to meet and share experiences.
- We engage in thoughtful critique of media, capitalism, mass incarceration, white supremacy, and other institutions that oppress youth.
- We offer tangible "take-aways" that youth can apply back home.
- We strive to eliminate the oppressions facing youth and in doing so, ultimately rendering our organization obsolete. The mission is more important than institutional self-preservation.

One of the most powerful recent developments in our youth program is the collaboration we formed with Mission Accomplished Transition Services and the Albany

County District Attorney's Office to offer an alternative to the school-to-prison pipeline. A good friend and farm share member who worked as counsel for the DA approached us with concerns about the way the criminal punishment system traps black youth into a downward spiral of increasingly harsh sentencing. Boys in their early teens are being arrested for loitering and petty theft, and assigned a public defender who encourages them to "cop a plea" and settle for a lighter sentence, regardless of their guilt or innocence. Once they have a record, these children are more likely to be targeted by law enforcement and it becomes disconcertingly predictable to determine which middle-school students will be in prison by the time they turn 18. Together with our lawyer friend, we decided to introduce legislation for a restorative justice project that we termed "Project Growth." Instead of receiving punitive sentences, court-adjudicated youth would be able to complete a 50-hour training program at Soul Fire Farm and other community organizations and earn money for the time they invest. The youth were obligated to first use the funds to pay off any restitution owed to those impacted by their crimes and then use the remainder as discretionary income. Our proposal was approved for a three-year period and we mentored 15 young people through the program.

Very early on in the piloting phase, the DA threatened to cancel the program after an incident where one of the youth stole an iPhone from an adult working on our farm. While the phone was found and returned, the DA was trapped in a "no second chances" mentality and wanted all of the youth in the program to be dismissed and returned to the traditional punishment system. We convinced them to give us a few days to demonstrate our techniques for accountability and justice. They reluctantly agreed. Unfortunately for our tenuous bargain, Sam, the young person who stole the phone, did not show up to the program the next day. Our son Emet, then nine years old, had formed a close bond with Sam and was devastated at his absence. The two had planned to make bow and arrows and play a game in the forest. Emet contacted Sam in tears and convinced him to return the next day. To the surprise of the DA staff, Sam did return, apologized for his theft, signed a behavior contract, and completed the program with excellent focus and no further breaches of trust. One thing we must remember is that healing is an extended process during which patience is in order. Just as the Emancipation Proclamation did not erase the effects of 500 years of enslavement, so a few days of a restorative justice program cannot erase the emotional and spiritual impacts of inherited and lived trauma on youth. All of our young people deserve to enjoy a sense of purpose, the acquisition of real skills, and the opportunity to contribute to the betterment of the community.

Build a broader movement for food sovereignty and racial justice

At Soul Fire Farm, we are attempting to meet a challenge presented to us by Baba Curtis Hayes Muhammad, the veteran civil rights activist. "Recognize that land and food have been used as a weapon to keep black people oppressed," he said, while sitting at our dinner. "Recognize also that land and food are essential to liberation for black people."

Muhammad explained the central role that black farmers had played during the civil rights movement, coordinating campaigns for desegregation and voting rights as well as providing food, housing, and safe haven for other organizers. Independent black farmers were not sharecroppers or domestic workers, and as such could not be fired by retaliatory white bosses for their audacity to attend a meeting or register to vote. This modicum of independence catapulted black farmers into a leadership role in the civil rights movement. With his resolute and care-worn eyes, immense white Afro, and hands creased with the wisdom of years, Muhammad was a man who inspired us to listen attentively so that we might stand on the shoulders of activists who had gone before. "Without black farmers, there would have been no Freedom Summer—in fact, no civil rights movement," he said.

We are asking ourselves how we can stand on the shoulders of our elders and ancestors who selflessly gave their land, leadership, and resources to the broader movements for justice and dignity. One of the most tangible offerings that we make to the activist community is the farm itself—which we offer for meetings, training, retreat, meals, and safe haven. Dozens of groups including the New York State Prisoner Justice Coalition, Wildseed Community Farm and Healing Village, Natural Resources Defense Council, and the Liberty Partnership Program have their meetings and retreats at Soul Fire Farm. We offer facilitation and training services to these groups tailored to their needs. Admittedly narrow in my thinking about what constitutes "activism," I was surprised and hesitant when the Troy Little League organizing committee approached us about leading a strategic planning session for them. As I came to understand, the Little League was a central grassroots organizing body in economically impoverished North Troy. Concerned parents wanting to provide their children with a meaningful activity formed the league and use it as a springboard for addressing social and racial challenges in their community. While the children play, they organize. This powerful example is a reminder that grassroots activism naturally arises out of the felt and stated basic needs of the community and becomes more impactful when honored and supported.

In addition to providing space and training for activist groups, we organize ourselves on a local and international level. Our primary coalition is the Freedom Food Alliance, which black farmer and prison abolitionist Jalal Sabur helped to start in 2009. We are a collective of farmers, political prisoners, and organizers in upstate New York who are committed to incorporating food justice to address racism in the criminal punishment system.

One of the Freedom Food Alliance's central efforts is Victory Bus Project, a program that reunites incarcerated people with their loved ones while increasing access to farm-fresh food. The New York State Department of Corrections once operated free buses for visitors to all 54 facilities across the state, but shut the program down in 2011 for budgetary reasons, leaving many of its 2,120 monthly passengers with no way to see their family members.

Together with other local farmers, Soul Fire Farm contributes produce toward food packages, which families of prisoners can purchase using SNAP. Once they purchase the food, families get a free round trip to visit their loved ones at correctional facilities in upstate New York. Families may choose to give the food to prisoners as a care package, take it home, or do both. While on the bus, Jalal facilitates conversations about the prison-industrial complex and food justice, using texts such as Michelle Alexander's *The New Jim Crow*.

The Freedom Food Alliance coalition is also working to coordinate farmer training, land-based trauma healing, political campaigns to weaken the mass incarceration system, and support for formerly incarcerated people.

Committed to a food system that is globally just, not simply fair for people in our region, we seek to work in solidarity with other campesinos and peasant farmers beyond U.S. borders. In 2013, the Global Food Sovereignty Prize was awarded to the Dessalines Brigade in Haiti for their cooperation to save Creole seeds and support peasant agriculture. The group earned international attention when they set fire to hybrid seeds Monsanto donated after the 2010 earthquake. These seeds were dumped on the Haitian market at the time of the rice harvest, threatening to outcompete and undermine the local smallholder agricultural economy. Flavio Barbosa of Brazil, representing the Group of 4/Dessalines Brigade, explained, "Haiti is a country that everyone talks about helping because it has a lot of needs, but in the twenty-first century, Haiti has been recolonized." These modern-day colonizers include the Haitian government, NGOs and biotech companies like Monsanto; "helping" the Haitian people has resulted in monocropping, deforestation, the destruction of Haitian markets, hunger and poverty.

Inspired by the Haitian peasant movement and my own obligation to participate in the healing of my grandfather's homeland, I linked Soul Fire Farm with Ayiti Resurrect (AR):

> Ayiti Resurrect is a collaboration of visionary artists, community builders, holistic healers, and sustainable farmers from Komye (Leogane, Haiti) and the Haitian and African Diasporas. [They] came together in the spirit of friendship and people-to-people solidarity in the aftermath of the January 2010 earthquake to support the social, spiritual, emotional, physical, and environmental health of a rural community in Leogane. [Their] aim is to cultivate people-to-people solidarity among African heritage people while reinforcing the strength and autonomy of Haitian residents. [Their] initiatives focus on arts, education, health, the environment, and women's self-determination with the goal to transform trauma through collective healing, and contribute to building a more just and sustainable existence for the future generations of Komye residents.
>
> (Ayiti Resurrect 2016)

Soul Fire Farm's role in AR has been to collaborate with Komye farmers on a massive reforestation project that has nurtured thousands of mango and moringa trees, a composting initiative that has spread to almost all farmers in the town, a small-scale solar mango-drying operation, and most recently, the installation of a new water well. When we travel to Haiti for work projects and information exchange, each international facilitator is paired with a local facilitator for distributed leadership. We seek to dismantle the paternalistic NGO model that feeds on the misery of the poor and primarily benefits foreigners who receive salaries from the charitable organization. We are an all-volunteer solidarity delegation that prioritizes the projects agreed upon by members of the Komye community.

On both the domestic and international level, we work to increase communication and decrease competition within the food sovereignty community. Our work is not unique. We learn with and from Malik Yakini and Dr. Monica White of the Detroit Black Community Food Security Network, Dennis Derryk of Corbin Hill Food Project, Tasha Bowens of the Color of Food, Karen Washington of Rise and Root Farm, Diana Robinson of Food Chain Workers Alliance, Kolu Zigby of Noyes Foundation, Gail Meyers of Farms to Grow, Josefino Martinez of the Triqui Region, Oaxaca, Kiado Cruz of the Zapotec Region, Oaxaca and many others. Together we are organizing ourselves into the National Black Food and Justice Alliance and internationally we are organized as Via Campesina.

We are not obligated to complete the task, but we are required to act at the intersection of our capability and what the world needs. To maintain silence is to cast our vote for the status quo, to passively endorse a racist and exploitative food system, and to deny ourselves agency over the destiny of our community.

As one graduate of our program humbly reflected,

> I am going to look into what already exists in my own community, and if there is nothing, I will create it. I have the bad habit of forgetting that, once, none of these projects existed and people had to work to produce them. I think I am realizing the purpose of this planet, this universe, and this life. I am realizing the potential for real community, real solidarity. We are winning.

References

Arc of Justice: The Rise, Fall, and Rebirth of a Beloved Community. 2016. San Francisco, CA: Open Studio Productions, 2016. DVD.
Ayiti Resurrect. 2016. Available online at: www.ayitiresurrect.org (last accessed 5 May 2017).
Carney, Judith and Richard Nicholas Rosomoff. 2011. *In the Shadow of Slavery: Africa's Botanical Legacy in the New World.* Oakland, CA: University of California Press.
"Child Watch Column: 'Urban Food Deserts Threaten Children's Health.'" *Children's Defense Fund.* January 1, 2010. Available online at: www.childrensdefense.org/newsroom/child-watch-columns/child-watch-documents/urban-food-deserts.html?referrer=https://www.google.com/ (last accessed 5 May 2017).
"Childhood Obesity Facts." *Centers for Disease Control and Prevention.* August 27, 2015. Available online at: www.cdc.gov/healthyschools/obesity/facts.htm (last accessed 5 May 2017).
Daniel, Pete. 2015. *Dispossession: Discrimination against African American Farmers in the Age of Civil Rights.* Chapel Hill, NC: University of North Carolina Press.
"Declaration of Nyéléni." *Nyeleni 2007.* February 27, 2007. Available online at: https://nyeleni.org/spip.php?article290 (last accessed 5 May 2017).
"Farm Subsidy Primer." n.d. *EWG's Farm Subsidy Database.* Available online at: https://farm.ewg.org/subsidyprimer.php (last accessed 5 May 2017).
Ferdman, Roberto A. "The Disturbing Ways That Fast Food Chains Disproportionately Target Black Kids." *The Washington Post.* November 12, 2014. Available online at: www.washingtonpost.com/news/wonk/wp/2014/11/12/the-disturbing-ways-that-fast-food-chains-disproportionately-target-black-kids (last accessed 5 May 2017).

"Food Sovereignty Prize Honors Grassroots Initiatives in Haiti, Brazil, Basque Country, Mali and India. *Food Sovereignty Prize.* August 13, 2013. Available online at: http://foodsovereigntyprize.org/wp-content/uploads/2013/08/Food-Sov-Prize-Honorees-2013-Press-Release-8-13.pdf (last accessed 5 May 2017).

Gabrielson, Ryan. "Deadly Force, in Black and White." *Pro Publica.* 2014. Available online at: www.propublica.org/article/deadly-force-in-black-and-white (last accessed 5 May 2017).

Gilbert, Charlene and Eli Quinn. 2002. *Homecoming: The Story of African-American Farmers.* Boston, MA: Beacon Press.

Gugliotta, Guy. "Nation's Crop of Black Farmers Is Dying Out." *The Washington Post.* August 26, 1990. Available online at: www.washingtonpost.com/archive/politics/1990/08/26/nations-crop-of-black-farmers-is-dying-out/5040f1de-54ef-45bd-8e0a-b92c20beb485 (last accessed 5 May 2017).

"The Impact of Food Advertising on Childhood Obesity." *American Psychological Association.* 2016. Available online at: www.apa.org/topics/kids-media/food.aspx (last accessed 5 May 2017).

"Inventory of Farmworker Issues and Protections in the United States." *United Farm Workers.* March 2011. Available online at: www.ufw.org/pdf/farmworkerinventory_0401_2011.pdf (last accessed 5 May 2017).

Jordan, Jeffrey, L., Edward Pennick, Walter A. Hill and Robert Zabawa, eds. 2007. *Land and Power: Sustainable Agriculture and African Americans.* Waldorf, MD: Sustainable Agriculture Publications. Available online at: www.sare.org/content/download/50650/665630/file/landandpower.pdf (last accessed 5 May 2017).

Karenga, Maulana. "Principles and Practices of Kwanzaa: Repairing and Renewing the World." *Official Kwanzaa Website.* 2009. Available online at: www.official kwanzaawebsite.org/documents/PrinciplesandPracticesofKwanzaa.pdf (last accessed 5 May 2017).

Liu, Y.Y. "Good food and good jobs for all: Challenges and opportunities to advance racial and economic equity in the food system." 2012. Available online at: www.raceforward.org/research/reports/food-justice (last accessed 5 May 2017).

Loeffelholz Dunn, Tracy and Jeff Neumann. "40 Acres and a Mule Would Be at Least $6.4 Trillion Today—What the U.S. Really Owes Black America." *Yes! Magazine.* May 14, 2015. Available online at: www.yesmagazine.org/issues/make-it-right/infographic-40-acres-and-a-mule-would-be-at-least-64-trillion-today (last accessed 5 May 2017).

Louv, Richard. 2008. *Last Child in the Woods: Saving our Children from Nature-Deficit Disorder.* Chapel Hill, NC: Algonquin Books.

"Magnetic Field Calculators." *National Centres for Environmental Information.* Available online at: www.ngdc.noaa.gov/geomag-web (last accessed 5 May 2017).

Mahapatra, Lisa. "The US Spends Less on Food Than Any Other Country in the World." *International Business Times.* January 23, 2014. Available online at: www.ibtimes.com/us-spends-less-food-any-other-country-world-maps-1546945 (last accessed 5 May 2017).

Penniman, Leah. "Radical Farmers Use Fresh Food to Fight Racial Injustice and New Jim Crow." *Yes! Magazine.* September 5, 2015. Available online at: www.yes magazine.org/peace-justice/radical-farmers-use-fresh-food-fight-racial-injustice-black-lives-matter (last accessed 5 May 2017).

Plumer, Brad. "The $956 Billion Farm Bill, In One Graph." *The Washington Post.* January 28, 2014. Available online at: www.washingtonpost.com/news/wonk/wp/2014/01/28/the-950-billion-farm-bill-in-one-chart (last accessed 5 May 2017).

"Racial Disparity." *The Sentencing Project.* 2016. Available online at: www.sentencing-project.org/issues/racial-disparity (last accessed 5 May 2017).

"Selected Statistics on Farmworkers." *Farmworker Justice*. 2014. Available online at: www.farm workerjustice.org/sites/default/files/NAWS percent20data percent20factsht percent201-13-15FINAL.pdf (last accessed 5 May 2017).

Sullivan, Laura, Tatjana Meschede, Lars Dietrich, Thomas Shapiro, Amy Traub, Catherine Ruetschlin, and Tamara Draut. "The Racial Wealth Gap: Why Policy Matters." *Demos.org*. 2015. Available online at: www.demos.org/sites/default/files/publications/Racial-WealthGap_1.pdf (last accessed 5 May 2017).

Thompson, Derek. "The 33 Whitest Jobs in America." *The Atlantic*. November 6, 2013. Available online at: www.theatlantic.com/business/archive/2013/11/the-33-whitest-jobs-in-america/281180 (last accessed 5 May 2017).

United States Department of Agriculture. 2009. "Access to Affordable and Nutritious Food: Measuring and Understanding Food Deserts and Their Consequences." Accessed February 23, 2015. www.ers.usda.gov/webdocs/publications/ap036/12698_ap036fm_1_.pdf

United States Department of Agriculture. 2012. "2012 Census of Agriculture: Race/Ethnicity/Gender Profile." Available online at: www.agcensus.usda.gov/Publications/2012/Online_Resources/Race,_Ethnicity_and_Gender_Profiles/cpd99000.pdf (last acc - essed 5 May 2017).

Whatley, Booker T. 1987. *Booker T. Whatley's Handbook on How to Make $100,000 Farming 25 Acres*. Emmaus, PA: Rodale Press.

"World Resources Report 2013–2016: Creating a Sustainable Food Future." *World Resources Institute*. 2015. Available online at: www.wri.org/our-work/project/world-resources-report/world-resources-report-2013-2015-creating-sustainable-food (last accessed 5 May 2017).

12 Defining the process of re-indigenization through soil communities

Ruth Lapp and Robert Lovelace

The purpose of this chapter is to discuss an understanding of re-indigenizing agricultural communities through a fusion of analysis and practice. The method of presentation is largely based on an experimental discussion between student and instructor that took place during some experimentation with soil communities. We began the experiment asking the question: can soil communities provide a starting point for a larger analysis of human communities striving for self-sufficiency and balance with natural ecosystems? Soil has a life completely independent of humanity, yet it is the sustainer of all human life. As such, soil and humans have forged complex relationships that range from Indigenous to colonial. Within these paradigms, the meaning of human sustainability is experienced, and the codes for diverse co-dependencies are written. As technological advancements and social/cultural amalgamation continue to take place incrementally in the twenty-first century, understanding how this coding can be translated into emerging indigenous cultural systems will be essential for marginalized and displaced populations. In the end, we didn't find a definitive answer to our question. What we did discover was that the conversation evolved as the kind of indigenous science in which knowledge begins to take root. We have decided simply to present a discussion, hoping to invite others to get involved.

Bob

A year later Ruth and I are walking out on the Fundy salt marshes behind her farm in Nova Scotia reviewing the progress with her PhD work and reflecting on the final course work/experiment we had conducted the previous summer. It is hard to take my attention from the expansive scope of the tidal marshes and the river as it sweeps away toward the Bay. I am a stranger here. Ruth is telling me about the Mi'kmaq, Acadian and Englishmen who worked this ecosystem and their various intentions of how to know it. The vast aura of green marsh hay with a touch of dew is deepened by the grey sky overhead. The red-brown riverbank glistens as it drains and deepens, exposed but never dry, not as long as there is an ocean to fill it back up. The salt marshes are all but forgotten now. Some have been diked to create fields for conventional crops but many are left, as they were, indigenous zones, where progress has stored them away until they can be "reclaimed." The Mi'kmaq are reserved, the Acadians dispersed and the Englishmen have retreated to oil and gas, mega-crops and tourist haunts. For all of them, communities have come and gone. There is a kind of reel, danced through the time of a space, a flirtation and sometimes a marriage, with the indigenous place and human cultures that mark it. I think this is what we were trying to understand with our course/experiment at my own place in Ontario last summer. Using a "restoration" project to bridge the metaphorical connection between soil communities and human communities, we wanted to learn something. We didn't have a hypothesis to test, which would have been the conventional way to do things. Perhaps we were doing our best simply to discover creative interplay, which is often how ecological realities and human societies' interactions intersect.

Ruth

In the spring of 2015, I came to the land at Bob's farm with a purpose. What I had in mind was to restore a small patch of land that had been disturbed through "anthropogenic perturbation." My objective to restore the land was to fix the perceived problem of degraded and compacted soil that had resulted from an agricultural project—the dredging of an irrigation pond. It was evident to the naked eye that this land was compacted by the machinery used to dredge the pond; but more than compacted, the soil horizons had been completely altered, and the flora and fauna communities that had existed prior to the excavation were no longer represented. What was now at the soil surface was what had once been buried, deep beneath the surface of a fen or bog. We now stood on silt and clay, rather than the accumulated organic matter typical of a fen ecosystem, and the disturbed surface soil had little in the way of organic matter or humus. As agriculturalists, we surmised that there was little in the way of fertility and tilth that we knew was required for growing crops. Our plan was to apply several different agricultural techniques to facilitate a transition of the land into another state of being—what we referred to as 'healing' the land. Methodologically, the end state we sought was one of enhanced agricultural productivity. Ultimately, our plan was to expand the garden space Bob had previously established when he cleared a small section of the forest immediately surrounding his house.

In addition to the disturbed soil structure, the patch of land we were about to work with had been altered in another significant way. There was no longer a forest canopy to filter solar radiation or moderate rates of evaporation. The space was now fully exposed to sunlight, which meant it had full access to processes of photosynthesis. Structurally and systemically, this patch of land had been flipped into an altered ecological state.

It is now a year later, and, as I consider this patch of land and the objectives I brought to it, I realize that my intention to restore the land was never about returning or reconfiguring the space to some imagined prior state of nature. The fact was, we couldn't; the land had been completely altered. But even more importantly, it had never been our intention to return the land to a previous state. We were not planning on recreating a fen; we were not intending to reassemble the forest with its complex of trees, plants, and fauna that had previously occupied this space. So why was I thinking in terms of restoration? Where did that notion come from and how did it determine my relationship to the soil?

The concept of restoration is a seductive one, embodying an ethical imperative that is perfectly aligned with Western scientific reductionist thinking that conceives of the whole as the sum of discrete parts. Restoration is an ideologically constructed stage upon which human beings enact morally determined gestures to reconfigure an imagined past. As Eric Higgs tells us, restoration "connotes a fixed, historic, and static notion of ecosystems (although this is what few proponents, especially ecologists, want)" (Higgs 1997, 347).

The notion of restoration is socially, culturally, and economically appealing to a wide array of folks. This is significant. We can trace this appeal to the cognitively latent but culturally powerful narrative of Romanticism—the notion of pristine wilderness and the sublime state of nature. In this way, the work of restoration ecologists reflects a moral as well as an aesthetic positionality. At a glance, what is valued and deemed purposeful about restoration appears to be the antithesis of processes of resource extraction and productionism. Restoration projects appear to give back the land, rescuing it from the effects of economic productionism and exploitation—the cultural (im)pulse of capitalism and our dominating social narrative. But like the economics of productionism and capital accumulation, environmental restoration is also a cultural construct rife with expectations that are informed by a conceit of nature that allows for the imagined meaning of wildness as purposeful and subject to measures of value through relationships of exchange. The restoration impulse is emergent from and is, therefore, contingent on a narrative predicated on anthropogenic perturbations being an accepted or, at the very least, inevitable component of human and more-than-human relationships. In this light, ecological restoration is not a departure from, but rather reaffirms, a particular story. As Eric Higgs pointed out nearly two decades ago, driven by an imaginary of "ecological fidelity," ecological restoration projects tend to emphasize "structural replication, functional success and durability"(1997, 339). Product-oriented in their design, efforts to restore degraded ecosystems are rife with a compensatory objective (Hiers 1995) that tends to 'fix' the natural world into static and manageable states of being. In my own backyard, the compensatory objective is evidenced by the government of Nova Scotia's policy on salt-marsh restoration ("Nova Scotia Wetland Conservation Policy" 2011) that sanctions the industrialized despoliation of one wetland by restoring another wetland in a different part of the Province ("Nova Scotia Prepares" 2016). Such slight-of-hand manoeuvring belies a mechanistic view of planet earth. In contrast, the imperative of re-indigenization—"to continuously sustain a unity of existence through societal knowledge and reverent individual practice of respect toward all life forms" (Armstrong 2009)—compels us to engage with the dynamic processes and evolutionary creativity of a living earth.

Evaluating ecological systems through relationships of exchange is manifest in the identification and assessment of ecological goods and services. Ecological exchange valuation has provided and continues to provide the thematic basis and metaphorical palate for ecological restoration. Within a narrative structure that is directed towards enacting solutions for existing problems, the possibility or at least the necessity for righting past wrongs is the central trope. Technological interventions including research design and equipment are the tools for both enacting and measuring meaningfulness. It was to that narrative and those technological tools that I turned as I stood on the patch of disturbed and agriculturally unproductive land: a problem that required a solution.

As a farmer, I have equipped myself with certain tools to be used for certain tasks. Most of these tools, by contemporary agri-industry standards, would be deemed rudimentary or crude and most certainly not considered efficient from a production standpoint. In part I have selected these tools precisely because using them limits the extent of my ability to destroy certain natural qualities that I understand to be needed for optimal crop production. I also choose to use these tools because they appeal to me aesthetically, and that is far more difficult to define or quantify. My tool set is comprised of more than just the objects or material culture that reproduces the meaning of my engagement with the natural world; meaning, itself, is a tool, in the sense that it is the cultural lens or filter, through which I engage perception and take action. The order and magnitude of the choices or actions I make to impact the land are shaped through a cultural inheritance in much the same way I might inherit, from a grandparent, a simply designed and well-worn hoe.

Bob

The elements of design were drawn from Ruth's experience as a farmer and my experience as a horticulturist. Ruth is from Pennsylvania Dutch heritage and I am from a mix of Cherokee, Algonquin, French and English. What we had in common was our interest in soil, the idea of re-indigenization, and a Lutheran upbringing that we had both discarded, as much as one can, at the end of childhood. The design of our course of study and what products would emerge was facetiously considered a kind of theological insurrection (intellectual rebels). More seriously, it was an attempt to get to some fundamentals of how soil works indigenously, how human inter-ventions affect soil communities and how modern human communities might mimic or follow basic patterns, which are observed in the evolution of some soil communities. In addition to a standard selection of the site and choosing three different soil interventions, I had asked Ruth to create weekly video essays with which to solicit community input and comment through a serialized Facebook page. Albeit a virtual community, it would become a focus of information and discussion representing community development that could be observed over the duration of the course. I suppose this requirement initiated the conventional division understood as the teacher/student relationship; however, I know I learned as much from Ruth as she may have learned from me.

So we went to work. While Ruth was thinking restoration, I was thinking process. Anishnàbèmòwin and many other Indigenous languages are verb-based; that is, they reflect the process of, and between, things, rather than static descriptions. For me, Indigenous knowledge is rooted in understanding behaviour and not so much in material description. But as an academic I have also become inclined toward accepting the quantitative/qualitative nature of things. We did agree on three distinct interventions. Plot #1 was Hugelkultur, or what is commonly anglicized as 'hoogle mound.' Plot #2 was to use standard cover-crop strategies to encourage nitrogen, phosphate, and potassium production and loosen the tilth of the compacted clay. Plot #3 was to be left to its own devices; that is, no intervention on our part was to take place, only observation of what might be considered "natural" processes.

Ruth

From my kitchen door, it's a five minute walk to the Cogmagun River. I walk there every day with my dog Charlie. My home in Hants County West, Nova Scotia, is in Sipekne'katik, one of the seven territorial districts of Mi'kma'ki. As a settler, I occupy land where the Mi'kmaq or L'nu have dwelt for thousands of years. The arrival of European imperialists and migrant diaspora, some four hundred years ago, set into motion the colonization of Indigenous people and the dispossession of their homeland. But the L'nu have never gone away.

I never tire of my daily pilgrimage to the river: walking the winding trail that threads through my back fields, which are being reclaimed by alder, poplar, ash and oak, down the forested ravine of yellow birch, Eastern hemlock, and stripped maple, to the open prairie expanse of salt marsh grasses and other halophytic flora, demarcating the zone between land and sea. The sharp brine of river mud and sweetness of salt marsh reach me through my sense of smell long before ocular perception confirms my situation.

The Cogmagun River, with its diurnal tide cycle, is a story of replenishment. Twice daily the river is inundated with the sea. Salt water fills the deep, winding channel, at times spilling over the banks to flood the flat marsh land that fringes the banks of the river. With this flood comes a gift: the deposition of silt and mud which, over an impossible-to-imagine span of geological temporality, has built up the land. But as the river gives, so does the river take. This is part of its story. In the winter, huge icebergs scour the marsh, ice-rafting and gouging, in places razing the marsh grasses down to muddy stubble; the ebb tide carries detritus and nutrients out to sea. This interface of land and sea is biologically rich and trophically dynamic.

The known benefit of salt marshes to human social well-being is extensive (Turner, van den Bergh, and Brouwer 2003; Daiber 1986). Western science tells this story through quantifying the goods and services salt marshes provide, and by ascribing keystone status to this briny ecosystem. The list of ecological goods and services of salt marshes include carbon sequestration, fish nursery habitat, macro and micro-climate stabilization, the absorption of heavy metals, and storm-surge protection (Chmura, Anisfed, Cahoon, and Lynch 2003; Turner, van den Bergh, and Brouwer 2003). I have come to understand that Western science tells only a partial and therefore limited story of the interconnectedness of human and more-than-human relationships that are bound to the limitless unfolding of salt-marsh ecosystems.

To live with the land, it occurs to me that you must become known by it. This is a relationship built on faithfulness. It cannot be sustained through instant gratification—although there is always love at first sight! It's been almost twenty years since I first came to my small parcel of farmland in Nova Scotia. At first sight I loved the land—the old house and barns, the rich garden soil and remnant orchard, the quiet spaces, and the creative possibilities this place offered. For two decades, I have added my labour to the soil. In turn the soil has fed me, along with many others—building bone and muscle, making possible laughter and tears. Faithfully, I have fed the soil the compost from kitchen and animal bedding, seaweed I've gathered from local beaches, and leaves I've carted home from the city in the back of my car. And while labour-intense and fundamental to my very way of being, I am aware how these gestures of reciprocity are but a glimmer of the deep and abiding relationship the L'nu have with this land. It is a depth of love, commitment and belonging that I can only try to imagine. My own intimacies with the land and soil are not even a lifetime old. And these are restrained by the common-law parameters of hedgerows, the vagaries of neighbourliness, and the necessity of having to make the land financially viable. I am a traveler—a "come from away"—as much as I desire and strive to be kin.

In an even more pronounced way, I am a traveler in Eastern Ontario, the Algonquin's homelands, and the location of the hardpan clay flat perturbation—the site of our course experiment. I am only beginning to become acquainted with this place, having spent a mere season's internship while studying in Bob's garden, walking the fen and forest, and fishing Eel Lake. So, when it came to considering how best to remediate the perturbation caused by pond dredging and soil compaction, I did not start from an indigenous thought process or relationship to the land. Rather my ideas came bidden from a cultural legacy that allows me to think in terms of "best practices," "productivity," and other universalizing ways of relating to the land. The applications I elected for our restoration experiment reflect the mindset of a traveler or foreigner.

Bob

I had never used a cover crop, so when I went to the local Farm Supply I was somewhat timid in asking for what Ruth had prescribed for Plot #2. The salesman knew exactly what I wanted and already had it bagged: triticale, barley and peas. The next step was easy: put the rototiller on the tractor and scuff the clay until the seed could find enough cover to germinate. Yes, it was that bad. Had it not been for the blessing of a wet year the hardpan may have been completely impermeable. We planted the cover crop by hand, broadcasting and then raking over the clods that had been tilled several times. Germination was slow. When plants began to develop, it was apparent that the soil was not breathing well, a combination of the compaction and a regularly wet surface with little percolation. However, by August, we could agree that the first cover crop was a mild success. Nodes on the pea roots indicated that nitrogen fixing was occurring. By introducing specific species, we had focused (in anthropocentric terms) soil behaviour to produce anticipated results.

The work with Plot #2 was not yet complete. I went back to the Farm Supply with another prescription from Ruth—tillage radish. It wasn't in stock but the salesman would order it. "Not too many people around here need that anymore," the salesman informed me with a kind of quizzical and accusing tone. Tillage radish is a vigorous white radicle capable of drilling down through almost any soil condition. Fast-growing and hardy, this would be our second cover crop. This strategy represented the natural process of succession in which some species prepare the environment for the in-migration of other species, which in turn make further modifications that enhance diversity and adaptation. Our objective with the tillage radish was to improve the tilth of the soil in the hope that eventually we could use this plot for a "cash" crop. The first cover was rototilled and tillage radish was planted in mid-August by students visiting the farm. By September the seeds were showing a good germination and with some luck would have a two month growing season until late October frosts would catch up to them.

Plot #1, the hoogle mound, does not depend on tillage. Basically, the hoogle mound is a selective mimicking of forest humus build-up, but positioned in full sunlight conditions. It is constructed of plant debris, leaves, branches and even stumps that decompose and compost over months and years. Soils are added to create planting pockets and to inoculate the natural composting processes. Our hoogle mound was a fresh construction using mainly waste from my previous winter's logging operation, spring leaf raking and some garden soil. As hoogle mounds go, it was a rather large structure that Ruth built singlehandedly as I used the tractor bucket to bring and drop material. The structure was finished with a liberal covering of semi-rotted straw. I was excited to put in "sunshine" squash and watch them take off by early summer. Our expectations were running high. The hoogle mound, although technically constructed, seemed to us to be the most natural. After all, isn't this how soil development happens in the "real world"?

Plot #3 was simply ignored, like many roadside ditches and Eastern Ontario's lower fields that have been abandoned because today's larger ag-equipment can't negotiate wet spring conditions that were once worked by real horsepower. It was hard to pay attention to the emergence of pioneer plants and the refugees that had been either mulched or tilled in the other two plots. There was also a tendency to focus our attention on the other plots because we, as John Locke would agree, were building a sense of ownership through our "work" with #1 and #2. This would come to haunt my thinking about Plot #3. Nevertheless, a green mass of diverse Indigenous and colonial shoots began to emerge chaotically in the hardpan and uneven orphaned soil. Old friends like English daisy and plantain, sedges, pine spouts, milkweed, cattails and an assortment of pioneering strangers emerged.

Ruth

Indigenous places and people are well-acquainted with travelers like me. For a long time now, it has been the prerogative of such travelers, who carry a passport of colonialism—whether traveling first class or economy—to make themselves unreservedly apparent to Indigenous peoples and places. But it has not, for the most part, been the way of colonialist travelers to be observant, let alone understanding and honouring of indigeneity. Lately, however, it appears the unilateral nature of this relationship is taking a turn. This is signaled by the piqued attention a particular guild of colonialist travelers—a host of Western science practitioners—have directed towards traditional ecological knowledge (TEK), sometimes also known as Indigenous knowledge (IK). There has been a propensity, however, for these learned and lettered travelers to fix their gaze on a flattened horizon of possibility, perpetuating the notion that only the quantifiable, extractable and commodifiable signposts and markers can guide and keep us from falling off the edge of the world. It's almost as if we colonialist travelers can't help ourselves. We are, it must seem to anyone observing us, imprinted at a cellular level with the propensity to see the smaller picture. Of course, I don't have any scientific proof of this—only metaphor.

Somehow, without Bob and me even articulating, let alone agreeing upon, the methods of our experiment to restore the hardpan soil perturbation, I found myself directing the first steps in the experimental design process. Of course, this is the heady time of any experiment or dialectical engagement—getting to draw from the reservoir of what one already knows, and then seeing whether there is anything more to be learned. So that is how we ended up planting the cover crop of triticale, barley and field peas. I already knew a lot about cover crops. I had studied and practiced this agricultural method of enhancing soil fertility and stabilizing tilth for several decades. Cover crops make a lot of sense. They are an old agricultural tool— a crop grown with the expressed purpose of facilitating indigenous processes of restoring the land. Paradoxically, cover crops are utilized most intensively on land that has been disturbed or degraded through agricultural processes of planting and harvesting crops. Cover crops are widely used by organic and conventional or non-organic farmers, which is the reason why the cover-crop mix Bob purchased at his local feed store was in stock.

Triticale, barley and field peas. Not the exact cover-crop mix I was hoping for, but it will have to do. I had wanted oats and peas. Why? For no other reason than this is what I am most accustomed to using. It's relatively cheap to buy; multi-functional from an agro-ecological standpoint; compositionally complementary— the grasses offering structure for the climbing peas—and it's easy to plant by merely broadcasting the relatively large seeds onto freshly tilled or scuffed earth and then lightly raking to ensure the seed has made contact with the soil. The mix Bob purchased was comprised of two grasses—barley and triticale and a legume. The grasses would quickly cover the soil that if left bare would continue to erode from rain and wind. Triticale and barley, both grain crops, grow lushly in their short vegetative growth stage. They are shallow-rooted annuals, and expeditious in stabilizing soil particles and cooling the soil surface, providing an enhanced environment for the field-pea seed to germinate. In their decomposition, or digested state, the triticale and barley would also build the humus of the soil. We can sort of think of grasses as the carbs of soil nutrition.

It is more than coincidence that the bulk of the weeds we encounter in our gardens, especially those garden spaces where we turn or till the soil, are annuals. Annuals thrive in freshly disturbed soil. On the heels of a perturbation, they come quickly, restoratively, to cloak and assuage the earth. That is their nature. Annual weeds provide many of the same services to their soil community that we were counting on our commercially obtained grain-grasses to do.

It is difficult to re-situate myself into the mindset of my early expectations for outcomes for this restoration project. What I can recall is that the land, while clearly disturbed and somewhat degraded from the pond dredging was also just as clearly in a state of self-repair. There were many weedy plant species already present early in the spring that indicated earth healing was well under way. Deep-rooted dandelions and tenacious broadleaf plantain—or white man's foot print—both pioneer plant species, as well as perennials, were well represented in the degraded soil zone. Their presence signaled processes of ecological transformation and an advanced state of regeneration. Left uninterrupted, these common weeds were already playing their part in transitioning the land back into an ecological complex of plants that would, over time, appear, at a glance, to be an undisturbed biologically diverse forest. What is of interest to me now is that we only considered the presence of these indigenizing plants and processes as relevant to one of the three restoration practices we planned to utilize—the section we set aside for fallow regeneration. With the other two sections—hugelkulture and cover crop—we were intent on imposing human-engineered remedies to combat compaction and loss of fertility. Although it is true that letting land lie fallow is an ancient agricultural technique employed by farmers worldwide to let the land rest and replenish, our current industrialized agricultural agenda cannot accommodate the wait. The sabbatical, instituted by an agrarian culture to assure of ecological sustainability, social justice and civility, is contemporarily understood to mean a break or rest for a mostly elite group of workers, the essence of vineyards and grain fields having long been driven to the margins of relevancy and meaning in this cyclical practice of seasonal replenishment.

My expectations were to see whether human ingenuity combined with manual labour could induce a state of soil repair, while simultaneously providing a decent crop of winter-storage squash and potatoes. I had little in the way of expectations for the fallow section, because I had not seen much evidence that the surrounding landscape of forest and fen was naturally abundant in provisioning what I recognized as food.

Bob

In keeping with my role of "instructor," I needed to justify some kind of accomplishment. After all, I was going to give Ruth a grade on this course of study. I also needed to grade myself: was this a useful endeavour or just something to do? Human community is often left out of academic production. Too often papers get read once and then filed. There is no interaction other than a calibrated mark for effort and expertise and the student moves on to the next hurdle. Beyond the metamorphosis of soil communities, I also want to know how human communities develop and whether there are axiomatic principles at work. So I asked Ruth to produce video essays of the stages of our experiment and use social media (Facebook) to engage people with these essays. Ruth had never worked with video recording and she had been an avowed Facebook-atheist. The first frame of the first video was of a shovel blade turning the nearly impenetrable hardpan. I was hooked and so were other people invited to the Facebook page. Ruth's competence as a writer had translated almost seamlessly to this new medium. The Facebook community grew. At the end of the project Ruth was invited to install the videos in an exhibition at Harbour Front in Toronto.

Human community development, like soil communities, has at its roots organic codes. Like soil, this imperative with humans can be harnessed and, when regulated by ideology, can even be mistaken as natural. The fault with "sustainability" practice may be that we too often attempt to preserve our ideology and fail to understand the breadth of our epistemological scope. But more importantly, when we hit upon a good notion we tend to want it to last forever, rather than understand the subjectivity of replenishment cycles. The axiomatic principles of indigeneity, that is, evolutionary changes, tend to hold us to task: whether a field of corn, an orchard, fish farm, commune or city, development and adaptation is governed by original instructions beyond our own doing. While Ruth's videos are still available on Facebook, the community has taken what it needed and moved on.

At the end of an academic term we give the grade and move on. Seldom do we reflect on where the imparted knowledge will take the student or how the student will synthesize the knowledge gained through the classroom experience with other acquired knowledge. Plot #3 was like that really from the start. We both had high hopes for #1 because we both inherently favoured the "beauty" of the permaculture approach. We also came to #2 and #3 with some prejudice. Since we didn't have to do anything to #3, we felt it didn't owe us anything, so starting out we not only didn't have expectations, we wouldn't have known how to frame them even if we had had any. It was only through retrospection and a sense that we had missed something that #3 began to have meaning. #3 could not be understood as agricultural or horticultural. It could not be decoded as something that had been produced. Clearly something had happened. Of the three plots, it was the only one that maintained some surface water throughout the summer. It was also overgrown with a diversity of annuals, perennials, hardwood shrubs and tree saplings, grasses, sedges, prairie and bog wildflowers. From an agricultural point of view, it was a consummate "wasteland." It was not until one morning in the fall that I began to do an informal inventory and asked the question that we had forgotten to ask: "What happens if I apply Anishnàbèmòwin to what I see here?" Right away I was identifying edible plants, browse and bedding for deer and rabbits, loads of sources for pollinators and honey producers, berries, grapes, medicine plants! Without a knowledge system that identifies the Indigenous codes, we are ignorant. The values, which we have accepted as modern and progressive, are in fact a self-imposed ignorance. Call it agriculture, horticulture, organic farming, permaculture, whatever, we will always run the risk of failing to know our real dependency on indigenous relationships if we make ideology that prioritizes production our goal. Soil or human, communities in synthesis are the rule of the real world.

There was a discussion about those squash in the hoogle mound. At first, I thought it was lack of water so I gave them some. It didn't help. I felt responsible, as Ruth had been away for a week or so. Upon closer examination, I found grubs in the stems. Fruit had been produced, mature enough to secure viable seed for another year, and, if harvested, it could still be winter-stored. But that wasn't the end of it. Upon her return, Ruth was mad at the squash beetle that had laid its eggs on our beautiful lush plants in the hoogle mound on which she had dedicated so much labour. We went about meticulously crushing them to make sure that they (at least these) would not return next year. My take on it was that we had moved the forest soil environment into the sun for monocultural production, so we should have expected unexpected predation. It was only natural. After all there was a kind of balance: the squash had matured, the beetle got what it wanted (or at least tried to before we came along), and then the plant was terminated before it could extract more nutrients from the soil. Everyone should have been happy. In retrospect, I am not sure if this was all about natural balance, but I would like to think so. Like my ancestors' science, it would take years, if not generations of observation to understand how this process works. I'll let Ruth give you her take on the squash.

Ruth

Initially I was disappointed; more than disappointed. I experienced that sinking feeling any farmer experiences who labours a whole growing season—shepherding a food crop from seed to seed—in the hopes of having food to eat for the coming winter and regenerating the seeds needed to start the growing cycle up again the following spring. I have spent many years working in many different gardens, learning about "pests," those pesky relations that come to your garden uninvited, stay way too long, disrupt the flow of your day-to-day, and only leave once your sacred dwelling and your mental health has been trashed. The vine bore is not only a pesky relation, it is an unattractive one—taking the form of a white, glistening grub that, as its name implies, bores into the base stalk of your perfectly healthy squash plant, and proceeds to consume it from the inside out. I don't know how to stop a vine bore infestation once it is underway. I am sure there are chemicals that you can purchase to poison the vine bore right out of existence, and in the process, poison the rest of your soil community. But there wasn't really even any point of considering pesticides. By the time I had returned from my vacation, the squash plants in the hoogle mound were little more than disintegrating heaps of yellowing leaves and mushy stalks—the vine bore was well-underway in fulfilling its own original instruction. Oh yes, as Bob pointed out, there were a few sunshine squash fruit scattered here and there that we could still harvest, but not the crop I had envisioned at all.

I like sunshine squash. They are sweet and their flesh is dense and dry in texture—exactly the kind of squash I crave if I imagine the joy of preparing and eating a winter-storage squash. The hybrid and open-pollinated varieties of squash I favour the most, buttercup, red kuri, and sunshine, are also highly favoured by pretty well every pest a squash grower dreads encountering. It turns out we are not all that dissimilar, the pests and I. Our tastes are the same; our needs are the same, and when we are sated we tend to get on with life in a not dissimilar fashion, searching for the companionship of kith and kin, and our next meal.

If I were to try to situate myself back in time, to that late summer day when Bob and I walked out to the garden to view the progress of our experiment, I would have to say that my first take on the hoogle mound was that it was a sound failure. As an ecologically minded farmer I immediately went to work on problem-solving. The most significant problem, in my estimation, was that we had planted a monocrop, thus inviting, if not through probability alone, the onslaught tribulation of pests that would result in failed crop production.

Western scientific research on traditional ecological knowledge practices of multi or polyculture agro-ecological systems indicates that "multiple species management approaches result in soil fertility improvement and crop protection through the integration of trees, animals, and crops" (Berkes, Colding, and Folkes 2000, 1255), increasing the variability and social purposefulness of crops grown in a single locale—food, fibre, medicine, fodder—and the reduction of the risks and societal impact associated with single crop failure. For millennia, Indigenous agriculturalists have known that squash thrives when inter-planted with corn and beans (Postma and Lynch 2012)—the corn providing the structural apparatus for the tendrilling squash vines; the beans supplying the nitrogen or nutrients required by the heavy feeding corn and squash; and the squash providing the protective cover for the soil—moderating soil surface evaporation and creating a naturally emergent barrier against marauding raccoons and other varmints that have an appetite for corn. Poly-cropping replicates the ecological competency of nature. "Three sisters" honours the meaning and celebration—the cultural script (Berkes 2008, 191)—of communal interdependency. Poly-cropping is both beautiful and intelligent in its composition and design.

But if hindsight is 20/20 vision, merely confirming what Bob and I should have already known about planting a single variety of ultra-sweet squash in one location, I still needed to reconcile myself to having faith in the soil-building processes the hugelkulture mound would continue to generate for years to come.

Modern, industrial agricultural cropping systems are not designed to accommo-date failure. That is why industrialized agriculturalists pay for crop insurance. Within the industrialized paradigm, a growing season is understood as a discrete, commodified unit of production. In this paradigm, there is no need for foresight or engaging with one's own indigenous intelligence and creativity; no need to observe seasonal rhythms or attend to the intricacies of renewal cycles. The vernacular quality of hugelkulture is replaced by universal protocols and practices with the objective of maximizing production. In industrial agriculture, soil is merely a substrate; its primary function is to anchor a stock of corn or soybean plant to the ground. In contrast, the hugelkulture mound, designed to mimic the processes of a healthy forest ecosystem, embodies the inherent intelligence of renewal and, if planted in a polyculture (as a viable forest would be), an assurance that if one community member becomes ill or even dies, the rest of the community, while impacted by the loss, will likely continue to thrive. In the forest, death (and decomposition) is not an endgame, it is integral to regeneration. This is my takeaway. This is why I continue to play with, learn from, and encourage the people I love who grow food to build hugelkulture mounds and plant for biological diversity.

Bob

As technological advancements and social/cultural amalgamation continue to take place incrementally in the twenty-first century, understanding how Indigenous coding can be translated into emerging cultural systems will be essential for margin-alized and displaced populations. After all, the study of re-indigenization—a quality of community life having adapted a knowledgeable culture in a specific place where human and ecosystem activity support and enhance one another—is all about contextualizing the future in useful ways. Those of us who are privileged can afford to transition toward more sustainable food and energy production. Others, partic-ularly those of recent displacement from indigenous means, will find it more difficult.

However, those folks are the reservoir of Indigenous knowledge and processes and deserve both justice and the rights to reclaim their belonging to the land. We all do. At present, indigenization is marginalized and opposed by modernization. Where it does exist, the power imbalance controlled by Nation States undermines its viability with only lip-service to protection when it serves the interest of the state as high-minded morality or for political reputation. The movement to re-indigenize will emerge and is emerging from collective efforts among ordinary people. The human genetic coding, in which every infant in the womb is born with the expectation that they will emerge into an indigenous world, pulls toward symbiosis with ecological realities and is manifest in urban, rural and what are recognized as natural environ - ments, and can be observed gaining momentum. Re-indigenization research is reflective of an organic academy, in which Indigenous knowledge can never be captured, but rather must be shared and taught at a cultural level among people who have an interest in living well.

Drawing conclusions can be tricky when examining the results of one season. But it was not the objective of this course/experiment to produce better crops. The fact that I now have extended garden space is a bonus. My goals emerged from a set of questions stimulated by the process. The very form this essay has taken is a direct result of that process. The roles of student and teacher became interchangeable and therefore required authorship that reflected a fusion of individuality and community. The goals developed within their own replenishment cycles, emerging, rooting, branching, fruiting, and decaying in blended successions with each other.

People come to visit my farm mostly to sit and talk about ideas. The shade of the flower gardens and the evening fire pit are scenes of intense discussions about politics, history, religion, insurgency and of course, re-indigenization. When the conversation dulls or becomes convoluted, I often say, "come on over here and let me show you what Ruth and I are up too," or, "I'll show you something that Ruth and I did last summer." The space has now become a narrative. The lessons learned from each plot, and together, are described to anyone who will listen to the story. But it is not a story of how to grow better plants or even which method is best. The story is about how to be surprised.

I have often asked the question of whether there are underlying and universal principles inherent in Indigenous cultures. The question can also be extended to include non-human communities as well. Describing indigeneity by comparisons with what it is not is not really an honest inquiry, because such imposed conditions are at best transitory. Along with experimentation must come experience, and experience must then become something else. Experience must be expressed in the way that we dance, the poetry and tone of stories and songs, the ways we touch the earth and each other; in unexpected questions from children, and in the ways we choose to defend our spaces and place. Perhaps those universal principles are only visceral. Perhaps theory cannot explain what we can only know.

References

Armstrong, J.C. 2009. "Constructing Indigeneity: Syilx Okanagan Oraliture and *tmixʷcentrism*." PhD thesis, Arndt Universität Greifswald, Germany.

Berkes, Fikret. 2008. *Sacred Ecology*. 2nd ed. New York: Routledge, Taylor & Francis.

Berkes, F., J. Colding and C. Folkes. "Rediscovery of Traditional Ecological Knowledge as Adaptive Management." *Ecological Applications* 10, no. 5 (2000): 1251–1262.

Churma, G.L., S.C. Anisfed, D.R. Cahoon, and J.C. Lynch. "Global Carbon Sequestration in Tidal, Saline Wetland Soils." *Global Biogeochemical Cycles* 17, no. 4 (2003): 22(1)–22(12).

Daiber, F.C. 1986. *Conservation of Tidal Marshes*. New York: Van Nostrand Reinhold Company.

"Nova Scotia Wetland Conservation Policy." Government of Nova Scotia. September 2011. Accessed November 5, 2016. Available online at: https://novascotia.ca/nse/wetland/docs/Nova.Scotia.Wetland.Conservation.Policy.pdf (last accessed 5 May 2017).

Hiers, Kevin. "Nature Invented: An Ethical Critique of Preservation and Restoration Ecology." *Trumpeter* 12, no. 2 (1995): 84–87.

Higgs, Eric S. "What Good is Ecological Restoration?" *Conservation Biology* 11, no. 2 (1997): 338–348.

"Nova Scotia Prepares for Road Building Boom." *The Chronicle Herald*. Accessed November 5, 2016. Available online at: http://thechronicleherald.ca/novascotia/1373743-nova-scotia-prepares-for-road-building-boom (last accessed 5 May 2017).

Postma, J.A. and J. Lynch. "Complementarity in Root Architecture for Nutrient Uptake in Ancient Maize/Bean and Maize/Bean/Squash Polycultures." *Annals of Botany* 110, no. 2 (2012): 521–534.

Turner, R. Kerry, Jeroen C.J.M. van den Bergh, and Roy Brouwer. 2003. "Introduction." In R. Kerry Turner, Jeroen C.J.M. van den Bergh, and Roy Brouwer (eds) *Managing Wetlands: An Ecological Economics Approach*. Cheltenham, UK: Edward Elgar Publishing.

13 Sharing food, sharing knowledge

Food and agriculture in contemporary art practices

Amanda White

> Of course art cannot change the world alone, but it is a worthy ally to those challenging power with unconventional solutions.
>
> Lucy Lippard, *Undermining*

Lippard's statement, quoted above, emerges from a distinct moment in the history of art, one in which classic avant-garde pursuits are increasingly being abandoned while contemporary practices are concerned more and more with current pressing issues existing outside of the art world. Artists today are often immersed in issues of political significance, and here I will examine those interrogating the global food system, using their work to redefine ideas about land, community and agriculture, and by extension human relationships to nonhuman species. Though Lippard is surely right that these are not problems that can be solved entirely through artistic endeavors, as she notes, contemporary art may participate in these projects by providing alternative models. Because art challenges us to think differently and to question social norms, it presents ways of thinking that are integral to developing unconventional solutions to problems.

Agriculture is established through human intervention with other species, and therefore food and agriculture represent the spaces where the social and cultural aspects of our relationship to the natural world are apparent and our interdependency undeniable; it is through the act of eating that we come face to face with the species that are selected and cultivated by our human needs, and who in turn nourish us. In his book *Eating Anxiety*, Chad Lavin writes that the mouth is the border between nature and culture, between human and nonhuman; it is through eating that we cross that border (Lavin 2013). Michael Pollan echoes this sentiment in his popular book *The Omnivore's Dilemma,* in which he writes that "the act of eating in fact represents our most profound engagement with the natural world. Daily, our eating turns nature into culture, transforming the body of the world into our bodies and minds" (Pollan 2006, 10). These authors are both simply putting into words what we experience physically through our embodied sensory relationship with all that we eat.

Rapid changes in the technologies of agriculture that have taken place within the last century, in particular the 'green revolution' technologies of the 1950s, have caused great shifts in the ways in which food systems function globally and locally. More recent trends—including a substantial decrease in agro-ecological species that are farmed for food (Khoury 2014); an aging and declining farming population, particularly in the global north (Boyce 2006); and an increasing urbanization of human populations – together represent an interconnected web of effects brought by changes to modes of agriculture. While we are only beginning to understand the impacts that some of these shifts will have in the long-term on the planet, both ecologically and culturally, they have undeniably affected both personal relationships with the land and the way in which social interactions occur with and around food. While new technologies in food production on the farm and in the kitchen respectively have allowed for greater freedom in some aspects of contemporary life for many, the costs of these changes have included a homogenization of crop species, a loss of cultural knowledge around food, and a substantial loss of small-scale farmers and knowledge of related farming practices (ibid.).

A growing skepticism concerning the sustainability of our increasingly precarious globalized food system has been a catalyst toward developing alternative farming practices such as community-shared agriculture and permaculture farms. Popular interest in practices which emphasize sustainability and self-sufficiency, such as foraging, urban community gardens, fermenting, and canning, has also grown. These cultural shifts all indicate a grassroots approach to creating community around agricultural issues on a micro-scale (as a counter to globalized monocultures), and these have been accompanied by efforts to share knowledge through hands-on, embodied experiences in order to keep these cultural practices from being lost. Sharing knowledge and exchanging ideas about the facts of food production is therefore a political act, motivated by an underlying resistance to a global food industry, whether it materializes as a grassroots initiative or an artist's project.

For artists, these locally scaled exchanges can also represent a utopian possibility, suggesting alternative forms of being together and within ecological relationships. After all, as art historian Grant Kester writes, the constitution of modern art in general is "the ability of aesthetic experience to transform our perceptions of difference and to open space for forms of knowledge that challenge cognitive, social or political conventions" (2011, 11). In their text "Becoming Ecological Citizens: Connecting People Through Performance Art, Food Matter and Practices," Emma Roe and Michael Buser point to the current understanding of artistic practice as a mode of research inquiry and suggest that sharing food can represent particular forms of knowledge wherein "knowledge is derived from doing, and from the senses" (2016, 5). Food-based artistic practices may use materials such as ingredients and kitchen tools, which are objects of everyday use, but can transform them into something new, with the understanding that "by interacting with them intensively and creatively, possibilities for new ways of knowing emerge" (ibid.).

The simple act of sharing a meal alone can create conversation, community, and connect us to the land through the food it produces. Contemporary artists, who are making, growing, or sharing food, embed themselves into food systems, whether at the level of the farmer or the cook, and, through their work, present observations about industrial foods systems and suggestions for reconceptualizing the ways in which communities form and interact around food and farming. This work can be read as both an artistic practice and a political act, where agriculture is the subject of the work, as well as the material. Beyond simple hospitable moments of breaking bread, these projects present community-building gestures that stand against the globalization of food cultures and look to imagine new possible futures.

Situating present innovations in the contexts both of their art-historical precedents and of current social and political movements, this chapter examines aspects of this intersection between food politics and the arts by turning to a selection of artists who engage with the land and its cultivation, and for whom the processing and sharing of food is a central feature of their work. The works described here do not represent an exhaustive survey, but rather a cross section of well-known examples. I describe these projects here in the interest of bringing this work to a wider audience of potentially interested scholars, artists, and activists, who might share the political and ecological aims of this work but not be familiar with the particularities of this kind of artistic practice. Ultimately, the works of art presented here challenge us to think differently about both art and the politics of food. Since their practices are in many ways similar to those of community and food justice activists, these artists seem to suggest not only that staging equitable and sustainable food systems might be an appropriate role for art, but also that living such systems is itself an artistic practice.

Using food's symbolic powers—and in particular conceptualizing the making and sharing of food as works of art—has emerged occasionally in various forms over the past century. For example, the Italian futurists understood that food held great cultural power, and even believed that what people eat had enormous effects on what they do—how they think, act and even dream. They wrote about this in their *Manifesto of Futurist Cooking* published in 1930, which included their views about Italian food and nationalism, as well as recipes for outrageous conceptual meals that they believed could be a tool towards political action. Decades later in 1971, a group of New York artists associated with the Fluxus art movement, who were similarly interested in the political potential of food, started an artists-run restaurant experiment and urban intervention called *FOOD*. In this instance, the artists were interested in merging art into life, rejecting the values of the commercial high-art world and instead making art out of everyday objects and experiences. The familiar and ephemeral quality of food made it an ideal substance for this kind of anti-materialistic art movement. The restaurant experiment *FOOD* was open from 1971–74; run and staffed by artists, it is often described as something between a meeting place and a restaurant, featuring artist-designed meals that were often conceptual as well as edible.

More recently food has played a central role in the development of the 'social turn' in contemporary art, the tendency (since the 1990s) towards participatory, collaborative, and community-based practices. Through the orchestration or mediation of social situations, artists have been turning their focus towards creating relationships, and these practices often feature shared meals. While theories and discussions around socially engaged art have proliferated in recent years and there have been many changing terms and philosophies to describe its various elements, this movement is most simply described as a recent abundance of works that are "characterized by their project of challenging art's symbolic capital towards constructive social change" (Bishop 2012, 13). As critics and scholars on the topic (including Claire Bishop, Nato Thompson, Grant Kester and Pablo Helguerra) have argued, these works expose both the potentials and the limits for art's effecting of actual change. An often cited example is a well-known work from 1990 by the artist Rirkrit Tiravanija. Simply titled *Pad Thai,* this project featured the artist cooking and serving the dish at a New York gallery to those in attendance. *Pad Thai* created a social interaction, which was a novel purpose for an artwork at the time; however, works such as this one, wherein the social interaction takes place in a pre-existing community of friends and gallery attendees, have since been criticized for a lack of critical rigor in their design (Bishop 2004, 65). More recent socially engaged works are often concerned with the orchestration of a unique social interaction. For example, consider a social sculpture work by Chicago-based artist Michael Rakowitz titled *Enemy Kitchen,* in which Rakowitz serves food and provides culinary workshops based on Iraqi cuisine to an American public. Begun in 2004, the *Enemy Kitchen* project has developed over the course of the Iraqi-American conflict. During a group exhibition in 2012 hosted by the Smart Museum of Art in Chicago, titled *FEAST: Radical Hospitality in Contemporary Art,* Rakowitz's project was performed in public as a street-vendor food truck. In this instance, dishes were prepared by Iraqi refugee chefs and served by American veterans of the Iraq war. Like *Pad Thai, Enemy Kitchen* similarly involves sharing food with the public in order to create a social exchange, but *Enemy Kitchen* also takes this further, illustrating a method by which artists may use the social realm to broach more difficult political topics and create community, either where none existed previously, or with more risk involved. This work exemplifies the power of food to go beyond a simple gesture of breaking bread between like-minded individuals—in this instance, sharing food is an act of peacemaking by creating dialogue between people from two countries in conflict, even those from either side of a military conflict. Many socially engaged projects involve food as a mechanism for bringing people together in such a manner; they also often take place in the world outside of institutions, involving participation and collaborations with communities and publics outside of the realms of art. Due to the form and site of such works, incorporating such activities as growing, making and sharing food, they could easily be read as community work or grassroots activism rather than art depending on the audience. In his book *The One and the Many: Contemporary Collaborative Art in a Global Context,* Grant Kester describes this as part of a changing attitude towards the definitions of art itself. As Kester notes, while collaborative and socially engaged art practices are gaining increased legitimacy in the mainstream art world today, they would have been dismissed as 'community arts' in the recent past (2011, 9).

In all of the above examples—*The Manifesto of Futurist Cooking, FOOD,* and social engagements such as *Pad Thai,* and *Enemy Kitchen*—it is notable that while food is the medium, it is not the subject of the works. However, there are many recent projects in which food sharing is not just a mechanism to engage communities, but also the central focus of the resulting dialogues. Lucy and Jorge Ortas's *70 × 7 The Meal,* for example, is a series of urban interventions in which community-based meals, typically realized as enormous productions with hundreds of guests, are situated in public areas such as a town center. Through a unique network of invitations, based on the premise that if you invite seven people they will bring seven more and so on, a large community is gathered, sometimes citywide in scale, and participants may create new connections in the process. The focus of the work is on mobilizing local issues, particularly around food and agriculture, while the table is set with project-specific dinnerware or other table elements designed by the artists. The Ortas believe that there is political power in such gatherings, stating in a recent interview that "nobody can change the world with a meal, but each meal, in its infinite accumulations, has the potential to change the world, even if in a small way" (Seymour 2016).

While sharing and eating food may offer an entry point to agricultural issues, many artists have also been engaging with growing food, addressing its production as well as consumption, in order to examine a deeper relationship with agricultural issues, creating gardens or agricultural interventions. The work of Canadian artist and activist Ron Benner, for example, has often involved garden installations and is centered on the social impacts of global food systems, particularly as these relate to indigenous agricultural species and farming practices. His projects can be decades long and involve researching, mapping, and tracing trade routes and agricultural species through the Americas, often looking at the relationship between food plants and colonialism. Some of these works exist in gallery spaces, while some are garden-based or both. Additionally, each year Benner holds public corn roasts with his sculptural corn roasting *Maize Barbacoa*, usually at the site of one of his exhibitions. For example, 2016 marked the tenth annual roast at a permanent garden and photo-based installation titled *As the Crow Flies* at Museum London (London, Ontario, Canada) where Benner is based. The work was part of a larger research project, tracing the plant species, historical trade routes, and bodies of water from north to south along a particular latitudinal line through the Americas. During the *Maize Barbacoa* roasts, the politics of agriculture can be discussed while eating corn—one of the ongoing subjects of these works—and the history of corn in the Americas becomes the topic of conversation or meditation while it is being consumed, implicating the eaters in this relationship. These politics are thus explored through the sensory experiences of taste, smell and touch, rather than being conceptualized through ideas alone. Writing about artists who share food with their audiences, curator Stephanie Smith discusses how this kind of work functions in the art world, proposing that it is the embodied, sensorial experience of eating present in these projects which makes them unique. Yet she also expresses concern that as social, performative, and participatory works become more commonplace, there is a "risk" of this kind of practice trumping the contemplative experience of more traditional object based artwork (Smith 2013, 17). This concern is indicative of the way in which the art world favors more cerebral, contemplative and passive engagements. Eating is an everyday activity and food an everyday object; therefore, while eating is viscerally powerful, it is the kind of experience that has historically been devalued by the art world. Arguably, though, participating in a powerful sensory experience can indeed be contemplative, if it relates to the concept of the work, and eating may even introduce new forms of understanding and knowledge not possible through strictly visual mode of comprehension.

Such acts of engaging with the politics of food by sharing it can open new dialogues, and the specificity of the places in which these dialogues take place has proven to be an important element in the potential for political power in this work.

Figure 13.1 Ron Benner, Maize Barbacoa, installation and performance (corn roast). Justina M. Barnicke Gallery, University of Toronto, 2015.
Image courtesy of Jessie Lau

Figure 13.2 Ron Benner, Maize Barbacoa, installation and performance (corn roast). Justina M. Barnicke Gallery, University of Toronto, 2016.
Image courtesy of Jessie Lau

As Smith argues, presenting some of these works in a traditional gallery space can risk stripping them of any meaning or power (Smith 2013, 17), and as discussed earlier with projects such as Tirivinija's *Pad Thai,* such venues risk creating a social engagement lacking any political potential. In Benner's work, for example, by mapping, cultivating, and serving the corn that is also the subject of his work, his practice illustrates that the places where food plants are grown are very much tied to their identity as food, reminding us that, just as we should recognize the link between the number of species that are farmed and the number of farmers, we cannot disregard the link between the products of farming and their cultivation processes. Human relationships with the land and ideas about the natural world have always been reflected by artists in their work, whether it be a celebration of the domination of nature as depicted in early pastoral landscape paintings, or the awe-inspiring images of remote wilderness favored in the Romantic period, or as a form of material to be manipulated in the monumental earthworks of the 1960s and '70s. Indeed, current practices like Benner's might be read as responses to the "land art" movement. The most iconic works of that earlier genre were realized on a massive, monumental scale with pieces such as Robert Smithson's *Spiral Jetty* or Michael Heizer's *Double Negative,* both from 1970, which involved moving large amounts of earth or reconfiguring a landscape towards aesthetic ends. At the time, these artists (like the Fluxus artists discussed earlier), were turning their backs to the commercialized art centres, pushing the limits of art by working outside of its designated spaces and materials, and conceptualizing the land—or nature itself—as a material for site-specific works. While these artists may indeed have been influenced or informed by certain concurrent environmental ideas, by today's standards many of their methods seem antithetical to ideas of conservation and preservation. More recently, the ethics of early earthworks have been questioned for both this reduction of the earth to aesthetic material and for the way in which the emphasis on *site*-specificity in such practices often lacked any attention to *place*-specificity (Lippard 2014, 82). As Lippard notes, in many cases the "local geology, identity, history and residents are secondary, if acknowledged at all" (ibid.). As a result, rather than creating work informed by both the aesthetics of a place and its existing social realities, this mode often reduced places to sites for artworks, bringing the art world and its concerns to these spaces, and thus ultimately remaining tied to conventional art discourses.

These criticisms and observations are, of course, generalizations; 'land art' was not an organized movement or group per se, but rather a tendency among certain artists to work in a more expanded field of sculpture. Indeed, some projects that have been categorized in this tradition represent more direct antecedents in a lineage that includes the more recent work that engages with food, the social, and addresses agriculture in more embedded forms. For example, both Bonnie Ora Sherk's project *Crossroads Community /The Farm* and Agnes Denes's work *Wheatfield; a Confrontation,* relate to some of the land art concerns through their form and scale; however, they also speak directly to local and social issues, bringing the politics of food and the land directly into the city, rather than addressing the landscape as distant from the urban environment. In 1974, Bonnie Ora Sherk created *The Farm,* on 2.2 hectares of land beneath an overpass in San Francisco, envisioning the work as a "multicultural, agricultural, collaborative artwork" (Sherk 2012, 165). *The Farm* included gardens, farm animals, performances and programming for local children. Similarly positioning agricultural space in an urban centre, over the course of four months in 1982, artist Agnes Denes planted and farmed 2 acres of wheat on a plot of land in Manhattan. The work, aptly titled *Wheatfield; a Confrontation*, was two blocks from Wall Street, with a view of the Statue of Liberty. In both instances, the artists created an engagement with the community by farming the land in urban space. These works represent ties between land, people and food, raising questions about the price of real estate in major cities, as well as about agriculture, sustainability and local access. By connecting the land to its inhabitants, these works shift the artists from a position of observation and response to a more active role of engagement and intervention.

In a 2005 roundtable amongst artists and theorists published in *Artforum*, titled "Land Art's Changing Terrain," the discussants agreed that while the land artists of the '60s and '70s were engaged with the expanded field of sculpture and its possibilities, "today's artists are working within an expanded cross-disciplinary field more likely to involve research as a geographer, social worker, anthropologist, activist, or experimental architect" (Griffin et al. 2005, 288). As a result, the new direction of art that engages with the land more clearly incorporates elements of the social. While Sherk and Denis relied on the symbolic gesture of importing a farm or juxtaposing the rural landscape with the urban space to make a statement, contemporary artists are working within the existing city infrastructure and networks in

Figure 13.3 Fallen Fruit (David Burns, Matias Viegener, Austin Young), *Public Fruit Jam*, Event Documentation, 2005–ongoing.

Image courtesy of Fallen Fruit (David Burns and Austin Young)

Figure 13.4 Fallen Fruit (David Burns, Matias Viegener, Austin Young), *Public Fruit Jam*, Event Documentation, 2005–ongoing.

Image courtesy of Fallen Fruit (David Burns and Austin Young)

order to create new systems that incorporate the social from start to finish. Creating a sustainable, functional farming system in the urban environment—in accordance with the goal of social practice arts toward instigating real social change—requires working more closely with and within communities. The ongoing *Fallen Fruit* project for example, developed in collaborations between David Burns, Matias Viegener and Austin Young in Los Angeles in 2004, focuses on pre-existing agricultural possibilities in urban spaces. In this work, the artists began by collecting fruit and mapping local urban "public fruit" trees: trees that currently either grow on or overhang public spaces. These maps were followed by participatory events called *'Fallen Fruit Jams'* in which local community members were invited to bring in found fruit and collaborate in groups to develop recipes and make jam together (Thompson 2012, 150). This work focuses on food production, but looking specifically at the existing intersection of human culture and foraging possibilities in the urban environment. Like *Wheatfield* and *The Farm*, the artists behind *Fallen Fruit* intend to raise questions about land use and real estate in urban space, about public and private land, and how the food that sustains us is often excluded from that framework. Unlike the aforementioned works, however, the *Fallen Fruit* project incorporates a social engagement with the public that can exist outside of the artists' purview and outlast their engagement, inventing new possibilities in the real lived experiences of city dwellers. By asking community members to participate in the harvest and find new uses for local and overlooked food by sharing and eating it, participants who engage with the project may begin to ask themselves about their own relationship to related issues, perhaps changing they way they move through their communities or think about local public fruit trees. Similar impulses characterize the work of Leila Nadir and Cary Peppermint of the collective *EcoArtTech*. Diagnosing an "industrial amnesia" and "a cultural memory disorder" (Nadir and Peppermint 2005) in the trends of agricultural industrialization and societal urbanization, they create small gatherings that include workshops on fermentation processes and tasting, reading groups focused on food politics, and art production, during which the participants engage in all of these intellectual and sensorial activities.

Of course these ideas are not unique to the arts. There are many initiatives that are equally intent on reinvesting in farming practices and related politics, that similarly function on a smaller scale or local level to allow for the transmission of farming knowledge through generations and across communities. Small farmers are integral to maintaining a diversity of agricultural practices and species, but are now themselves an "endangered species" in agricultural ecosystems (Boyce 2006, 10). In her essay "Microutopias: Public Practice in the Public Sphere," Carol Becker asserts that while these projects and artistic gestures may seem small in light of the massive issues they address, these "microutopian" efforts are an essential approach to facing the biggest problems in the world (2012, 68). Even small home or community gardens are spaces in which investment in knowledge can occur and be maintained at a local level. In an article titled "Home Gardens: Neglected Hotspots of Agro-Biodiversity and Cultural Diversity," the authors assess home gardens as spaces where this kind of knowledge transmission is actively taking place, describing them as "important social and cultural spaces where knowledge related to agricultural practices is transmitted" (Galluzzi et al. 2010, 3635). Further, because home gardens are usually integrated within a larger ecosystem, they also function as complex micro-environments consisting of domesticated, semi-domesticated and wild species cohabiting. While small, these kinds of spaces can still represent important agro-ecosystems, and like these artistic gestures, they may be sites of continued transfer of information and knowledge, in which farming or food cultivation practices exist in novel forms—reaching a different audience of interested neighbors, rather than art aficionados. Indeed, these lay microutopian practices may now look so similar to those practiced by artists that the distinction between gardening and making art is increasingly blurred.

There is a cultural memory and practical knowledge that is embedded in everything that we eat. As Bob Stirling writes in his essay, "Work, Knowledge and the Direction of Farm Life," "Rural and urban people must recognize that the important issue is not only the quality of food they eat, but also the social relations under which it is produced" (2001, 259). This ethos is reflected in the work of *Kultivator*, a project which is simultaneously a working farm, a space for experimental artwork, and a community. Situated on an existing functional farm near Oslo, Norway, and developed in collaboration between several farmers and artists, *Kultivator* is not one particular project, but an alternative farming community hosting resident artists and developing interventions on and around the farm. Here, social interactions and projects are developed, often between the species that live there. The work *Dinner With Cows*, for example, features sharing food, but as a cross-species social event in which outdoor tables are set for people on one side and for cows on the other; a meal is served for both to enjoy (Howells 2014, 153). Through the aesthetic and sensory experience of eating a meal together, cows and humans experience a levelling of the hierarchies generally embedded in this relationship, presenting an alternative and utopian proposition.

In recent years, a pattern has emerged of artists' collectives and socially engaged art practices such as this one, all of which embody what Richard Noble describes as a "utopian impulse" in contemporary art (2009, 12). This impulse is often realized by using innovative design and DIY technologies, in order to produce social interventions that imagine a better world through alternative ways of living and engaging with each other and the environment, or, here, with agricultural species. Noble writes that "all utopian art is political. It proceeds from an awareness of the imperfections of our social and political conditions towards some sort of under-standing of, and possible solutions to, what the artist perceives these to be" (2009, 14). Once again, the social comes into play, here by way of imagining possible futures that include the invention of communities as a necessary element, where collectives and groups re-imagine ways of being, living, and engaging with each other and the land. Artists' projects and collectives such as the *Fallen Fruit* project, *Kultivator*, *EcoArtTech*, the Ortas' *70 × 7 The Meal*, and the others discussed here, represent only a small number of many socially engaged arts projects that draw on the lineage of environmental art, while being preoccupied with re-imagining communities around food. Becker speaks to the way in which these artists have "taken on the task of creating micro-utopian interventions that allow us to dream back the communities that we fear we have lost" (2012, 71). In his introduction to the book *Nature* – a survey of

Figure 13.5 Kultivator, *Dinner With Cows 2*, 2015.
Image courtesy of Kultivator – Malin Lindmark Vrijman

artists working with ecology and nature as a subject – art historian Jeffrey Kastner indicates that while art that focuses on ecology is not a new phenomenon, new approaches to the topic have more recently shifted, and the strict boundaries of modernism had until recently maintained certain limitations on the scope of concepts, materials and audiences that mainstream art would provoke or engage, a status quo which has been slowly unraveling. Today, more recent contemporary art's rejection of disciplinary specificity has allowed artists to engage with nature as a subject in a way that was never before possible; many practices are now converging with growing environmental movements, using scientific methodologies, or creating social situations. While artists have always engaged the political, this more recent rejection of the separation of nature and human culture, coupled with this shift in methodologies and emphasis in contemporary art on communities and the social, have led overall to a deeper and combined engagement with ecological and social issues. Food-based practices are unique in that the materials are already tied to both the natural world and the social; there is cultural memory, practical knowledge and therefore a social aspect embedded in everything that we eat, and everything we eat connects us to the land. In this way, the act of sharing food possesses an innate political power; it engages community and ties us to the land through the inevitable, necessary, and common act of eating. Here, the distinctions between art and life blur, allowing for microutopian interventions that point us toward a more sustainable relationship with the species we eat and the practices we use to cultivate them.

References

Becker, Carol. 2012. "Microutopias: Public Practice in the Public Sphere." *Living as Form: Socially Engaged Art from 1991–2011.* 66–71. New York: Creative Time.

Buckley, Annie. "Fallen Fruit." *Art in America.* October 22, 2009. Available online at: www.artinamericamagazine.com/reviews/fallen-fruit (last accessed 5 May 2017).

Bishop, Claire. "Antagonism and Relational Aesthetics." *October*, 110 (2004): 51–79.

Bishop, Claire. 2012. *Artificial Hells: Participatory Art and the Politics of Spectatorship.* London: Verso.

Bourriaud, Nicolas. 2002. *Relational Aesthetics.* Dijon: Les Presses du réel.

Boyce, James K. 2006. "A future for small farms? Biodiversity and sustainable agriculture." In Keith B. Griffin, Stephen Cullenberg, Prasanta K. Pattanaik (eds) *Human Development in the Era of Globalization: Essays in Honor of Keith B. Griffin.* Northampton: Edward Elgar Publishing.

Denes, Agnes. "Wheatfield/Tree Mountain." *Art Journal* 51, no. 2 (1992): 22.

Drobnick, Jim. Review of *Gardens of a Colonial Present,* by Ron Benner. *public* 41 (2010): 198–199.

Galluzzi, Gea, Pablo Eyzaguirre and Valeria Negri. "Home Gardens: Neglected Hotspots of Agro-Biodiversity and Cultural Diversity." *Biodiversity and Conservation* 19, no. 13 (2010): 3635–3654.

Griffin, Tim, C. Bishop, P. M. Lee, L. Cooke, P. Huyghe, A. Zittel, and R. Tiravanija. "Remote Possibilities: A Roundtable Discussion on Land Art's Changing Terrain." *Artforum International* (2005): 288–366.

Helguera, Pablo. 2011. *Education for Socially Engaged Art.* New York: Jorge Pinto Books.

Howells, Thomas and Leanne Hayman. 2014. *Experimental Eating.* London: Black Dog Publishing.

194 *Amanda White*

Kastner, Jeffrey. 2012. *Nature*. London: Whitechapel Gallery.

Kastner, Jeffrey and Brian Wallis. 2011. *Land and Environmental Art*. London: Phaidon.

Kester, Grant H. 2011. *The One and the Many: Contemporary Collaborative Art in a Global Context*. Durham, NC: Duke UP.

Khoury, Colin K.; Bjorkman, Annie D.; Dempewolf, Hannes; Ramierez-Villegas, Julian; Guarino, Luigi; Jarvis, Andy; Riseberg, Loren H.; Struik, Paul C. "Increasing Homogeneity in Global Food Supplies and the Implications for Food Security." *Proceedings of the National Academy of Sciences of the United States of America* 111, no. 11 (2014): 4001.

Lavin, Chad. 2013. *Eating Anxiety: The Perils of Food Politics*. Minneapolis, MN: University of Minnesota Press.

Lippard, Lucy R. 2014. *Undermining: A Wild Ride Through Land Use, Politics, and Art in the Changing West*. New York: The New Press.

Nadir, Leila and Cary Peppermint, "Os Fermentation." *Ecoarttech*. 2015. Available online at: www.ecoarttech.net/project/fermentation (last accessed 5 May 2017).

Noble, Richard. 2009. *Utopias*. London: Whitechapel Gallery.

Pollan, Michael. 2006. *The Omnivore's Dilemma: A Natural History of Four Meals*. New York: Penguin Press.

Roe, Emma and Michael Buser. "Becoming Ecological Citizens: Connecting People Through Performance Art, Food Matter and Practices." *Cultural Geographies* 23, no. 4 (2016): 581–598.

Seymour, Harry. "Lucy Orta On the Politics and Power of Food as Art." *AnOther*. July 14, 2016. Available online at: www.anothermag.com/design-living/8851/lucy-orta-on-the-politics-and-power-of-food-as-art (last accessed 5 May 2017).

Sherk, Bonnie. 2012. "Crossroads Community: The Farm 1977." In Jeffrey Kastner (ed.) *Nature*. London: Whitechapel Gallery, pp. 165–166.

Smith, Stephanie. 2013. *Feast: Radical Hospitality in Contemporary Art*. Chicago, IL: Smart Museum of Art, University of Chicago.

Stirling, Bob. 2001. "Work, Knowledge and the Direction of Farm Life." In Roger Epp and Dave Whitson (eds) *Writing Off the Rural West: Globalization, Governments, and the Transformation of Rural Communities*. Edmonton: University of Alberta Press, pp. 247–262.

Thompson, Nato. 2012. *Living as Form: Socially Engaged Art from 1991–2011*. New York, NY: Creative Time.

Thrupp, Lori Ann. "Linking Agricultural Biodiversity and Food Security: The Valuable Role of Agrobiodiversity for Sustainable Agriculture." *International Affairs* 76, no. 2 (2000): 283–97.

14 The end(s) of freeganism and the cultural production of food waste

Leda Cooks

In Jonathan Miles's 2013 novel *Want Not*, Crabtree, an older ex-inmate out on parole, whose income comes from collecting cans from dumpsters/bins, confronts Talmadge, a young freegan picking out his next meal from a nearby dumpster. Maddened by the ridiculous scene of a seemingly well-off, able-bodied white man picking produce out of the trash, Crabtree asks: "The fuck you *doing*?...You eating from the trash?" (emphasis original) (2013, 9). Talmadge says that yes, yes he is, and that the excesses of capital are ruining society: people are starving while supermarkets dump perfectly good food. Crabtree responds that Talmadge is crazy if he thinks anything is changed by going through the garbage. Crabtree was with Bobby Seals and the Panthers, really making a difference, "but this shit... this shit is worthless man. You ain't even got a right" (10). Talmadge offers to share his finds, but the frustrated Crabtree refuses him, preferring to collect cans for cash and to buy a meal where civilized people eat. Although the argument is framed in rather comical fashion, with Crabtree finding a used condom amidst Talmadge's "dinner," the underlying values (of autonomy, justice, choice, and capitalism) belie the tensions between symbolism and materialism of food and waste.

Although the movement has been around in various forms for many decades, freeganism and the freegan lifestyle gained in notoriety in the US, UK, and Australia in the mid-2000s (Corliss 2014). Freegans (a term that combines "free" and "vegan") are dedicated to participating as little as possible in a capitalist economy, choosing instead to forage and salvage unused or wasted consumer goods as a means of sustenance. According to Nguyen, Chen and Mukhergee, "Freeganism is a nexus of anti-consumerist and sustainability discourses" (2013, 1). In the mid-2000s freegans brought visibility to the issue of food waste, revealing the diseases of capitalism through exposing its excesses at sites of disposal. While several ethnographic (e.g. Barnard 2016; Gross 2009; Corliss 2014), legal (Thomas 2010), medical (Tibetts 2013) and journalistic accounts (Friedman 2012) have worked to explain the movement's history, principles, members and practices, none have explored how freegan discourses and practices function in relation to newer movements for food waste and recovery. Such a comparison is useful, in order to examine both the sustainability of radical food movements and the ways such movements contribute to and are coopted by more popular movements for reducing and recovering food waste. This chapter looks at the discursive construction of freeganism in academic and popular media coverage, and in light of the more recent and widespread food waste and recovery movement. Building on the work of critical geographers, sociologists and other cultural studies scholars, the chapter explores the ways that spaces and places for food, waste and bodies intersect in these movements' discourses, performances, and the media coverage thereof.

Freeganism highlights ethical conundrums of participation in capitalist systems and social justice issues of autonomy over food choice. Freegans worry over a sustainable food system while utilizing the "spoils" of currently wasteful practices. Most freegans are white, in their 20s to early 30s, well-educated, and middle and upper class (Barnard 2016), although certainly this profile does not represent all who choose to be part of the movement (Corliss 2014). By the end of the first decade of the 21st century, freeganism gained a foothold in the US, UK, Canada and Australia, and in smaller numbers in Scandinavia, other parts of the EU, Brazil, Argentina, South Korea (Dettwyler 2011) and Japan ("Japan Inc"). Despite such recent growth, there is little evidence online or in news coverage that the groups still exist in all but the US, UK and Australia, and in these countries numbers have dwindled along with coverage of the movement (Barnard 2016). There are many reasons why freeganism is losing members and popular support, not least of which are: the difficulties of adhering to freegan principles in a sustainable manner; the transient and transitional status of many members; and, as this paper documents, the rise of the food waste and recovery movement and subsequent increased regulation of informal waste economies (Gille 2012; O'Brien 2012).

Revisiting the social history of trash (Strasser 1999), in this chapter I am interested in how, in media and scholarly reports, freegans and their dumpsters have become spaces for an (anti?) capitalist politics of visibility and choice (resisting corporate waste) while the invisibility of hunger and lack of choice that often necessitates trash picking have been downplayed. The chapter then explores the ways the alternative food movement led to more effort toward food justice, opening avenues for large-scale efforts to bring attention to food waste and recovery in the 2010s (Bloom 2010; Stuart 2009). As news stories about freegans waned, coverage of food waste grew exponentially (Cooks 2016). In such coverage, gone was the mention of corporate greed and its excesses, and of dumpster diving as (disgusting) spectacle; in its place were stories of hunger amidst a land of excess, where our oversupply of unused food should not be decreased, but might be redistributed to feed those in need.

The food-recovery movement has focused on making the recovery of waste both part of the green economy and a solution for hunger. Rather than presuming ready-made connections between food-waste reduction and social justice, or between environmental and food insecurity movements, this chapter asks how the environmental and social justice goals and means to those goals have been constructed both in the freegan movement and the later food-recovery movement. To do so, I look to the ways the movements have been described in scholarly and popular texts and performances. Although space limitations preclude an in-depth textual analysis, several paradoxes and tensions readily emerge in this analysis of the politics of in/visibility of waste and the food movement in the early part of the twenty-first century. To conclude, the chapter asks what is lost and what is gained when a more radical movement, its spaces and ideologies, is replaced by an ethics of moral responsibility in a neoliberal society?

Food = waste

This simple fact—that food and waste necessarily coexist—has been obscured in modern society for seemingly logical, but mostly political, economic, and social reasons. As food became part of a market economy, new means of valuation meant the separation of food from that which was less desired or could not be eaten. The positive valuing of matter constituted as food coincided with the negative valuing of waste as civilized societies developed (Mennell 1997; Strasser 1999). Correspondingly, those higher in status in society were identified as such through the distance they could maintain between an aesthetics of consumption and the excess waste (viscera, labor etc.) that made such consumption possible. This meant, too, that the separation of food from waste was always symbolic as well as material: everyone needed to eat to survive, and so lesser gradations of food value aligned with lesser status groups. Although increasingly hidden from larger society, waste remained necessary to social production and indeed to survival. Food waste was accorded different values in this hidden economy (Gille 2012), depending on access and choice over what was left over.

Martin O'Brien observes that "waste exhibits fundamental social political and economic vitality: any and all waste is a fundamental component of social organization that references political and economic interests, establishes (and disrupts) social relations and inspires technological development and bureaucratic regulation" (2012, 195). As societies developed and differentiated economies for food and for waste, so too valuations were made about spaces for consumption of food and for its disposal. That which was left over, no longer or never part of the labor of producing food, was designated for other spaces, to be picked up and reevaluated and designated once again. The regulation of spaces for disposal, alluded to by O'Brien, also speaks to the regulation of spaces for those less valued in society. Throughout the development of "civilized" society, association with and proximity to sites of disposal, whether through employment (sorting and hauling waste), occupation (scavenging for food), or residence, has meant social invisibility, or visibility as an abject/object in need of charity. Nonetheless, such spatial and social designations can be politically and economically useful, both for their "hiddenness" (e.g., alternative il/legal economies) and for their potential for disruption, as first the homesteaders and later the freegan movement amply demonstrated with varying degrees of success (Gross 2009).

Freeganism: an anti/social movement?

Freegans assert one main principle that guided their practices: the belief that capitalism is ruining society, and that the planet and its people are suffering. Freegans have vowed to fight back, but how they do so has been left fairly open-ended, and varies individually and among groups. For these reasons, freeganism's status as a social movement is also debatable, with some scholars (Barnard 2011; 2016) calling it a New Social Movement, others calling it an anti-consumerist or sustainability movement (Corliss 2014; Nguyen, Chen and Mukherjee 2013; Thomson 2016) and many others simply calling it a lifestyle, philosophy or set of practices (*Oprah Winfrey*

Show 2008). While citing humankind's history of hunting, gathering, and scavenging, many scholarly accounts of freeganism trace the movement's beginnings to "the Freegan Manifesto," a pamphlet and call to action originally written by Against Me! drummer Warren Oakes in 1999. The Manifesto emerged in the contexts of the 1999 WTO Seattle protests over globalization, multinationals, and free trade agreements, and it built on the momentum among younger people to take collective action against inequities perpetuated through these policies and institutions. In 2005, the Manifesto was posted on the home page of freegan.info (the primary source for information about the freegan movement). It is divided into sections explaining why freeganism is an important activist movement against consumerism, its relationship to veganism, and how to participate in freegan activities (Oakes). As a call to action, it is mostly focused on interventions at the individual level, though it (and presumably freegans) espouses community, humanitarian and environmental ethics. The Manifesto proposes a series of principles and actions that demonstrate a commitment to sustainability, interrupting capitalism and consumerism through il/legal activities, and discovering a life worth living apart from dehumanizing systems. Most suggestions deal with food and its waste. While promoting activities such as dumpster diving and living off-the-grid, the Manifesto encourages people to quit their jobs, and to stop wasting energy and commodities. Smaller steps and interruptions of business-as-usual are also encouraged, such as shoplifting, employee theft, foraging/gardening, home canning and brewing, and the reuse of discarded goods. Although freegans are often also vegans, the section on veganism clearly differentiates the two. Vegans are concerned first and foremost with boycotting and/or not eating animals or any animal products, while freegans, the Manifesto states, boycott all products that are ruining people and the environment.

Freegan ideals embody many anti-capitalist philosophers' critiques of waste as both expenditure of labor in the service of (privileged) others and as the excess necessary to the production of surplus commodities that drives those who have and divides them from those who have not. Thorstein Veblen discussed the dualities of waste in capitalist society: positive waste is conspicuous and conspicuously consumed in the form of leisure, while negative waste is associated with matter not useful to capital (1899). Ironically, even as freegans try to intervene in these dualities of waste in a consumer-driven society, they do so from a position of choice and racial ("Freegans of Color?" 2008) and economic privilege, often while holding steady jobs and owning property of the sort to which many hungry people have no access. Some freegans acknowledge this contradiction (Barnard 2016) but argue strongly that any action to disrupt capitalism-as-usual benefits hungry people and the environment. Freeganism also has defined itself in relation to other radical and countercultural movements, namely anarchism: a rejection of governmental authority. Anarchist freegans that "homestead" on abandoned property, do not have paying jobs or receive money, and scavenge or steal for all their personal needs may be seen as more ethically in line with freegan philosophy, but tend to live on the margins socially and legally and thus are less likely to be a visible part of the movement.

Other influences on the Manifesto were the counter-cuisine and punk move - ments of the 60s and 70s that fought the commodification and industrialization of food through growing, canning, and foraging, and buying healthier but marginalized foods (Gross 2009; Corliss 2014). The fight against hegemony, for these movements, was enacted through diet. Mass production and consumption was making our bodies docile and accepting of the processed and fast food increasingly fed to them symbolically through the media and materially available in every expanding market. These movements celebrated the body as a site of (healthy) resistance through choosing to eat home-grown and unprocessed food made with healthy ingredients. Most freegans, however, prioritize anti-capitalism: thus, procurement of (any) wasted food was prized over any inherent nutritional or environmental value. Corliss observes that, "no matter what the food is and what it is made of, for a freegan it holds value because it has been recovered, saved from the ideological grasp of 'waste'" (2014, 13). Likewise, Barnard notes that freegans aren't just concerned with where food comes from but where it's going (2016). Although sometimes associated with alternative food and food-justice movements, such as organic, local and GMO-free food, etc., this lack of criteria regarding "taste," nutrition or quality food is one of several practices that place freeganism at the fringe of the alternative food movements.

These radical beliefs and practices contributed to freegan notoriety by making food waste visible (although often as spectacle) for the mainstream US media audience. In the mid- to late-2000s, at its peak, news and academic coverage of the groups mirrored each other in registering freeganism as spectacle, as a fringe movement focused on food waste whose dumpster diving practices were reported for entertainment value. In a feature called "Living Off Trash" on the Toronto news program *16:9*, freeganism is described as a remnant of the 1960s anti-globalization movements that advocates not "free love" but "free trash." The reporter observed that, "Freeganism exists not in spite of consumerism but because of it." Such news accounts often focused on "trash tours" (done precisely to attract media and public attention) that invite groups of reporters, newly minted and veteran freegans to go through curbside trash bags or dumpsters behind high-end supermarkets and restaurants. While this vision of freeganism often promoted the freshness and (healthy) quality of the food in these high-end disposal sites (*New York Post* 2007; *CBS Early Show* 2007), off-camera, freegans generally targeted sites with less public visibility and greatest ease of access. Other media accounts (e.g. *Oprah* 2008; *CBS Early Show* 2007) focused on freegan anti-consumerist practices even as they noted (without irony) the high educational and financial status of many members. Given the movement's radical goal, to live their lives outside of capitalism, academic analyses of freegans (Barnard 2011; Corliss 2014; Gross 2009) discuss the inevitable contradictions between living off of capitalism and its excesses while critiquing it: the range of employment, property ownership and income of many freegans, as well as their primary means of coordinating and publicizing their movement (cell phones and the Internet). Nonetheless, Barnard argues that the movement exploded in the media (citing 600 stories about freegan.info by 2009) with groups starting up around the world (2016). While this paper does not dispute the attention garnered by the movement by 2009, it does argue that the coverage was more for the freegan spectacle of dumpster diving (Lindeman 2012) than the movement's substantive critique of food waste and capitalism.

Freeganism's displacement of bodies and spaces for discard and consumption raises questions about who belongs where and under what conditions. The potential to interrupt capitalism-as-usual through choosing to consume discarded items is inseparable from the inscriptions of poverty tied to some bodies and not others, with implications for the cleanliness and dirtiness of those bodies as well as their un/authorized presence in those spaces. Critical geographers of food (Alkon and Agyeman 2011; Guthman 2008; 2011; Ramirez 2015; Slocum 2011) have focused scholarly attention on the means through which race, ethnicity, gender and class are implicated in alternative and mainstream food spaces. Rather than the straight-forward designation of urban, suburban and rural spaces as food deserts/oases or obesogenic/leptogenic environments, these scholars are interested in the various ways social identities are (re) constituted and represented in these domains. Less studied are the spaces of and for food waste and intersecting dynamics of need, economy, charity and taste.

The Manifesto includes a section on privilege, which states:

> We, in America, have so much and so many people all over the world have so little. Why do we have more? Because we're number one! Other folks are literally starving so that we can have fully stocked shelves at our supermarkets and health food stores. If this concerns you (as it should) you can protest the unbalanced distribution in America and the world by sacrificing some of your privilege and feeding yourself off of the ridiculous excess of food instead of consuming products from that supermarket shelves we are so unjustly privileged to have access to.
>
> (freegan.info)

Whether living off trash is a sacrifice of privilege or a demonstration of it is the tension in the argument between Talmadge and Crabtree that opens this paper and underlies definitions of freedom of (individual) choice and autonomy over diet that are basic to neoliberal society. The real problem for freegans seems to be that the excessive and unlimited choices among commodities benefit an unjust and unsustainable system, and therefore they can reduce their own choices by living off of what is left over. Yet, the tension over the privilege to consume is not just over choice and sacrifice, but that we all don't have the same or even nearly similar choices. Still, the movement's overt message, the need to reduce reliance on capital, places it as the more "alternative" of the multitude of alternative food movements to gain national and international attention in recent decades (e.g. "local," "organic," and "slow food" movements).

Alternative food movements and food recovery

As alternative food movements have become increasingly central to food politics, less attention has been paid to the discursive problems upon which these movements are constructed and the various solutions proposed. Critics of the term "alternative" in the alternative food movement have long pointed to the coop-tation of (local, organic, artisanal) movement ideals by large corporate entities in order to reach better educated and higher economic niches while continuing to produce lesser "quality" industrialized food for the masses (Guthman 2008; 2011; Slocum 2011). This marketing of differentiated tastes and quality also corresponds to social-marketing campaigns around issues designed to appeal to different demographics: local and organic foods are often understood as a priority for well-educated, high-earning families, while access to any food, and preferably with a wide selection and cheap prices is (often, though not always) the priority for families with less income. The overlap of movement and (social and commodity) marketing "alternatives" have led to often confusing goals and means to those goals. What seems to be common across all goals is that we all need to eat healthier, yet the means to getting there are often hypocritical and contradictory. Food education and justice movements (and corporate versions of charity events) often emphasize "healthism" (Guthman 2008) and preach the benefits of healthy food and diet to presumably less educated, poorer populations, or those immigrant populations assumed to have an unhealthy diet because "they" don't eat what "we" do. Food-sovereignty movements, which emerged precisely over the issue of colonial control over the (national) food chain, have increasing presence in the US at the community level (Broad 2015). Such movements often embrace nutritious food while trying to combat "healthism" and build collectively a sustainable food system that meets community standards for quality and taste. Yet, as Broad observes, community-based food movements for sovereignty are often reliant on large corporate grants for their programs (2015). The ethical assumptions that underlie discourses of food justice and sustainability enhance the image of large corporations through their involvement in local efforts for healthy diets. Community contributions and events by corporations also enhance the image of (their) "good" food while distracting us from the means through which such food is produced and marketed. The intertwining of social and corporate marketing, while beneficial to movements and the corporations that support them, often results in attention to food commodities (whether designated local, artisanal, organic, etc.) and obscures the unjust and unhealthy working conditions and wages across the food chain (Alkon and Agyeman 2011).

Within this suturing of food justice and food marketing, in the last five years attention to food waste has grown to the point of an almost daily news story of excess (Cooks, in press 2016). We are told we eat too much, waste too much, but remarkably don't consume too much. Instead, one simple and markedly ethical solution is to transfer our waste into the mouths of the hungry. In a December 1, 2014 article in the *Guardian*, Clare Druce argued that food insecurity has become the rallying cry of the food-loss movement. As more people have less access to healthy food, tax incentives and policy efforts are aimed at large corporations, not to get them to reduce production of surplus commodities, but to incentivize redistribution to food banks and shelters. Thus, corporate production and consumerism become part of the solution to both food waste and food security. Another, more recent and increasingly promoted solution is to repurpose food waste into new consumer products. Stories in popular news outlets such as the *New York Times, NPR, Huffington Post* and the *Washington Post* discuss new technologies that repurpose food waste into everything from plant and animal food to artisanal beers to paper plates.

These start-up businesses often get their funding and endorsements from food- and popular celebrities such as Beyoncé, Michael Pollan, Michael Simon and Mario Batali, to name a few (Strom 2016). Tristram Stuart, longtime activist in the global food-waste movement, helped to found an artisanal ale company (Hester 2016). The startups are a win–win for celebrities who can associate their brand with an important social and environmental issue, increase their virtuosity in the public eye, and thus enhance their primary product: their image. Association with the repurposed food products and celebrities that make and use them also increases the social capital of the consumer. The aspects of food waste that capital tries to erase: its imperfections, its decomposing nature, remain invisible. All that remains is the "trace"—the virtual food waste product—and the good feeling that results from purchasing and eating ethical and tasty food. Hester cites food-systems researcher Neff who observes, "When you're eating a food that would have been wasted, and tastes perfectly fine, there's no inconvenience to you" (2016).

As the stature of food waste as a social and environmental justice issue has grown, so too has its social-marketing potential. Much like the local, organic and artisanal movements discussed above, the focus of policy and popular efforts to reduce waste is on food commodities, rather than the processes through which they are produced. The drivers of over production of food include: (1) consumer demand for overstocked displays of perishable, perfect foods, resulting in an over-abundance of perfect looking food that gets thrown out at the end of the day; (2) packaging of multiple fruits and vegetables, rather than selling in bulk; (3) misleading labeling ("sell by," "best by" and "use by" dates) (Milne 2012); and (4) cultural beliefs that discourage eating otherwise edible food. Also in the shadow of the products sold under the "repurposed" food-waste halo is the labor that goes into producing food, whether from food or from its "scraps" or waste. We are told to feel guilty about our excessive eating and our excessive wasting, but not told nearly as much or at all to demand less, rather than more, from the producers of much of our food.

Food waste, ethics and affect

The separation of food and/from waste may be social, historical and political, as this chapter has argued, but the matter of waste is not merely theoretical. The meanings and consequences of waste's construction may be more or less immediate depending on social position, but they are clearly experienced, and so appeals to reduce waste are situated among ethical positions that implicate religious discourses of charity and gluttony and capitalist discourses of individualism and consumerism. These reasons for the waste problem largely propel the solutions on offer by food-recovery efforts and policies, and so beg further attention. O'Brien notes that the moral dilemma of waste presents the world as it is and the world as it should be, and this dilemma blames individuals for the present circumstances without examining social structures and political economies (2012). Building from O'Brien's argument, I would argue that, on a discursive level, the constant presentation of this ideal posits a world without waste; where in actuality this world without waste is no world at all. Waste is necessary to society and survival. Excessive waste is destructive to people and our environment. Somewhere between these sentences there are important questions to ask about the goals of activist efforts and how those goals are communicated, as environmental and social sustainability, and as solutions to hunger and waste reduction.

Without dismissing all ethical appeals to reduce waste where they tap into values for sustainability of people and the planet, critical scholars might ask how the framing of the waste problem and its solution re/create binaries and assign status to those who have taste—who have choice over deciding what is quality food and what to throw away—and those who do not. Where, not too long ago in media and academic discourse, dumpster diving was almost exclusively associated with hunger, and dumpster divers were objects of pity and/or disgust (Eikenberry and Smith 2005), now food insecurity is tied to food recovery, and reuse can provide an unlimited supply of food aid. Is this the same articulation (Hall 1996) or power dynamics among bodies, identities and food dressed in new discourse? While it may be argued that the visibility of hunger and the poor's alienation from capital has remained unchanged, or increased, the options for resolving hunger have become more politically and socially regulated via a capitalist system. In this manner, the guilt of wasting may be absolved through (regulated) acts of redistribution and charity, but not through reducing waste at the source: supposedly the primary goal of environmental policy efforts (EPA Food Waste Hierarchy). Other binaries separate (good) food from (bad) waste in popular media, and in scientific and social scientific research on the topic. These bipolarities signal that food must look perfect while waste is flawed, however these flaws are defined: food is clean, while waste is dirty; food is safe, waste is risky and potentially dangerous; food represents taste and quality, while waste is indicated by quantity and potential to satisfy hunger (Cooks, in press 2016). While waste has the potential to become food, its value is predetermined by the commodity status of the food. The Ugly Produce movement (Figuerido 2016), while noble in its intent to market flawed fruits and vegetables, relies on a niche marketing strategy that seems intended to exoticize carrots with two legs, and will continue as long as such items are novelties that boost the progressive consumer's social status. For these reasons, too, the edibility of the food/waste is a concern, not only because non-food-like (decomposing) waste is a cultural object of disgust and a potential health danger but also because decomposing food contains little (capital) value.

Uncertainty and risk are an inherent quality of food/waste, and thus raise the questions both of the visibility and inevitable materiality of food and bodies. Thus, even as this chapter analyzes the social construction of food and waste, it does not deny its material de/composition nor its necessity for social life. Waste is visceral, embodied and primal, and for these reasons those with privilege and capital have developed classifications, institutions, and commodities to distance themselves from it. Yet we exist in, through, and because of waste, and its classification as unnecessary and without value also shapes current efforts to revalue it to existing systems of production and consumption. These divisions and classifications, created in the separation and positive valuing of food apart from negative valuation of waste, perpetuate social inequities, and do further damage to the environment. Such revaluation already exists, and is more present in societies considered underdeveloped: where food status is less dependent on market valuation, where hunger is a visible part of everyday life, and inequities harder to ignore. But these spaces too are changing, as markets, media and technology connect us all. While I'm wary of romanticizing poverty and waste, I'm curious about the mediating power of capital and its impact on bodies in relation to one another when it comes to a need as basic and universal as food.

We are at a significant juncture in the movement to reduce food waste: between the environmental crisis and concerns for the sustainability of our food system, and our social crisis of hunger and malnutrition. To value one over the other is taken to be unethical, yet we might ask how these two came to be connected in the first place? Freegans seemed to have asked these questions and their prioritizing of waste as the byproduct of capitalist excess(iveness) speaks to the commoditization of food and resulting inequities between haves and have-nots. Disregarding the paradox of living off the very system you critique, freegans rarely acknowledge that they have the privilege to disavow a system that others might dream of participating in, in order to live a good life. Freegans are a metonymic device for both the commodity culture and the privilege attached to acts of resistance to the commoditization of food. If food is a commodity, then hunger too is tied to that commoditization. In the scene that opens this chapter, Crabtree might prefer cash to trash, if someone took the time to ask him. As long as food (and hunger) is commodified, freeganism is unsustainable as a collective movement for change, and will likely remain at the fringes, as spectacle.

Sharp et al. observe that the word "alternative" itself raises the possibility of different ways of acting, although as many have pointed out, always in reaction to current institutions and their practices (2015). Critical food scholars have acknowledged the ways "quality," "good taste" and health, all accessible through certain forms of material, social and cultural capital, are promulgated and proselytized through the alternative food movement (Guthman 2008; Slocum 2011). Few scholars, if any, have looked at the ways such judgments are attributed (or not) to food waste and, correspondingly, those who reuse it, or for whom (e.g. aid recipients) it is recovered. Although advocacy for eating any food (waste) seems dubious at best, this non-judgmental aspect of freeganism provides an opening for an alternative food system that refuses to link judgments of taste and quality to social and cultural capital. It is this aspect of freeganism that has all but disappeared in current efforts to reduce and recover food waste. What if we all (not just those forced to do so) widened the possibilities for our diet to include food that appears to be, and is, imperfect? What if we were able to divorce, or at least temporarily uncouple, such food from an aesthetics of (capital) consumption and instead placed value on production or even, in the case of foraging, for its unplanned or accidental creation. What would such valued food look like? What qualities become important?

Also, and acknowledging that we all are embodied in different ways in relation to social and cultural capital, what if we openly practiced thrift in buying and preserving food? Thrift is not unproblematic in its differential attribution to the bodies that perform it (Watson and Meah 2012) but, practiced collectively, might seek reduction and reuse, rather than simply cheaper commodities. Thrift is not a rejection of capital, but exists in tenuous relation to it. Thrift is (sometimes) attributed to those bodies who have social capital and poverty to those who do not, but as conspicuous consumption (Verblen 1899) has increased and become normalized, conspicuous thrift is to be hidden or disavowed if social status is to be maintained. If we can begin to view food waste as embodied and affective rather than simply disembodied quantities to be donated or commoditized (though I do not dismiss these among a range of options) we can open new and more sustainable possibilities for our food system, one in which food and waste are both inseparable and a necessity for life.

References

16:9. "Freeganism: Living off trash." YouTube video. 15:06. Posted August 2012. Available online at: www.youtube.com/watch?v=yCyPv0j4bPw (last accessed 5 May 2017).

Alkon, Alison Hope and Julian Agyeman. 2011. *Cultivating Food Justice: Race, Class, and Sustainability*. Cambridge, MA: MIT Press.

Barnard, Alex V. 2016. *Freegans: Diving into the Wealth of Food Waste in America*. Minneapolis, MN: University of Minnesota Press.

Barnard, Alex V. "'Waving the banana' at Capitalism: Political Theater and Social Movement Strategy Among New York's 'Freegan' Dumpster Divers." *Ethnography* 12, no. 4 (2011): 419–44.

Bloom, Jonathan. 2010. *American Wasteland: How America Throws Away Nearly Half of Its Food (And What We Can Do About It)*. Boulder, CO: Da Capo Press.

CBS News Early Show. "Freegan way of life." YouTube video. 3:32. Posted October 8, 2007. Available online at: www.youtube.com/watch?v=KB56aGTgfVE (last accessed 5 May 2017).

Cooks, Leda. 2016. "What Is (Not) Waste and How to Consume It? Constructing Food Waste as a Social Problem." In Peter Naccarato and Katie LeBesco (eds) *Handbook of Food and Popular Culture*. London: Bloomsbury Press.

Dettwyler, K. 2011. *Cultural Anthropology and Human Experience*. Long Grove, IL: Waveland Press.

Druce, Clare. "Politics of Food Waste and Poverty." *The Guardian*. December 1, 2014. Available online at: www.theguardian.com/society/2014/dec/01/politics-of-food-waste-and-poverty (last accessed 5 May 2017).

Eikenberry, Nicole and Chery Smith. "Attitudes, Beliefs, and Prevalence of Dumpster Diving As A Means to Obtain Food by Midwestern, Low-Income, Urban Dwellers." *Agriculture and Human Values: Journal of the Agriculture, Food, and Human Values Society* 22, no. 2 (2005): 187–202.

"Food Recovery Hierarchy." n.d. EPA: US Environmental Protection Agency. Available online at: www.epa.gov/sustainable-management-food/food-recovery-hierarchy (last accessed 5 May 2017).

Evans, David. "Blaming the Consumer—Once Again: The Social and Material Contexts of Everyday Food Waste Practices in Some English Households." *Critical Public Health* 21 no. 4 (2011): 429–40.

"Freegans of Color?" *Vegans of Color* (blog). June 2, 2008. Available online at: https://vegansofcolor.wordpress.com/2008/06/02/freegans-of-color (last accessed 5 May 2017).

Friedman, Kelly Ernst. "Trash Tours: Untying What Freegans Get Out of the Garbage." *Anthropology Now* 4, no. 3 (2012): 33–42.

Gille, Zsuzsa. "From Risk to Waste: Global Food Waste Regimes." *The Sociological Review* 60, no. S2 (2012): 27–46.

Gross, Joan. "Capitalism and its Discontents: Back-to-the-Lander and Freegan Foodways in Rural Oregon". *Food and Foodways* 17, no. 2 (2009): 57–79.

Guthman, Julie. "Bringing Good Food to Others: Investigating the Subjects of Alternative Food Practice." *Cultural Geographies* 15, no. 4 (2008): 431–447.

Hall, Stuart. 1996. "The Problem of Ideology: Marxism Without Guarantees." In D. Morely and K.H. Chen (eds) *Stuart Hall: Critical Dialogues in Cultural Studies.* London: Routledge, pp. 25–36.

Hester, Jessica Leigh. "Artisanal Food Waste: Can You Turn Scraps into Premium Products?" *NPR: The Salt.* August 19, 2016. Available online at: www.npr.org/sections/thesalt/2016/08/19/490499715/artisanal-food-waste-can-you-turn-scraps-into-premium-products (last accessed 5 May 2017).

"Japan Inc." *Japan Inc.: Business, People, Technology.* Available online at: www.japaninc.com (last accessed 5 May 2017).

Lindeman, Scarlett. "Trash eaters." *Gastronomica: The Journal of Food and Culture* 12, no. 1 (2012): 75–82.

Mennell, Stephen. 1997. "On the Civilizing of Appetite." In Carole Counihan and Penny Van Esterik (eds) *Food and Culture: A Reader.* New York: Routledge, pp. 315–337.

Miles, Jonathan. 2013. *Want Not.* Boston, MA: Houghton Mifflin Harcourt.

Milne, Richard. "Arbiters of Waste: Date Labels, the Consumer and Knowing Good, Safe Food." *The Sociological Review* 60 (2012): 84–101.

New York Post. "Freegans Take Green to the Extreme" YouTube video. 3:05. Uploaded August 18, 2008. Available online at: www.youtube.com/watch?v=VOEF75VwAtY (last accessed 5 May 2017).

Nguyen, Hieu P., Steven Chen and Sayantani Mukherjee. "Reverse Stigma in the Freegan Community." *Journal of Business Research* 67, no. 9 (2014): 1877–84.

Oakes, Warren. "Why Freegan? An Attack on Consumption—In Defense of Donuts." *Freegan.info.* Available online at: http://freegan.info/what-is-a-freegan/freegan-philosophy/why-freegan-an-attack-on-consumption-in-defense-of-donuts (last accessed 5 May 2017).

O'Brien, Martin,. "A 'lasting transformation' of Capitalist Surplus: From Food Stocks to Feedstocks." *SORE the Sociological Review* 60 (2012): 192–211.

Oprah Winfrey Show, 2-27-2008 Oprah Winfrey Network (OWN).

Ramirez, Margaret Marietta. "The Elusive Inclusive: Black Food Geographies and Racialized Food Spaces." *Antipode* 47, no. 3 (2015): 748–769.

Sharp, Emma, Wardlow Friesen and Nicolas Lewis. "Alternative Framings of Alternative Food, A Topology of Practice." *New Zealand Geographer* (2015): 6–17.

Slocum, Rachel. "Race in the Study of Food." *Progress in Human Geography* 35, no. 3 (2011): 303–327.

Strasser, Susan. 1999. *Waste and Want: A social history of Trash.* New York: Metropolitan Books.

Stuart, Tristram. 2009. *Uncovering the Global Food Scandal.* London: Penguin Books Ltd.

Thomas, Sean. "Do Freegans Commit Theft?" *Legal Studies*, 30 no. 1 ((2010), 98–125.

Thomson, Karl. "Freeganism: A Definition and Overview of the Movement." *Realsociology.* February 16, 2016. Available online at: http://realsociology.edublogs.org/2016/02/16/freeganism-a-definition-and-overview-of-the-movement

Tibbetts, Janice. 2013. "Freegans Risk the Hazards of Dumpster Diving." *Canadian Medical Association Journal* 185 (7): E281–E282.

Veblen, Thorsten. 1899. *The Theory of the Leisure Class.* Project Gutenberg. Available online at: www.gutenberg.org/ebooks/833 (last accessed 5 May 2017).

Watson, Matt and Angela Meah. "Food Waste and Safety: Negotiating Conflicting Social Anxieties into the Domestic Practice of Provisioning." *The Sociological Review* 60, no. S2 (2012): 102–120.

Poem

the Gleaner difference

Natalie Joelle

propel the grain through
air created by the transverse

you want to reduce grain loss
you want slope sensitivity
you want to reduce field compaction

a combine processor likes to be fed with a flat and
                                consistent crop mat
straight into the combine, straight into   and
                                straight out the back

the Gleaner Natural Flow System
360 degree threshing system allows grain to pass
                                through the cage

Afterword

Gleanings

Molly Wallace

Natalie Joelle's found poem shares its title with the subtitle in the advertising brochure from which the poem itself was gleaned: "the Gleaner difference."[1] In its original context, this phrase operates as an eye-catching slogan, highlighting what sets this new series of the combine harvester advertised apart from its predecessors and its competition, or "how we are completely better and completely different from everyone else" (Gleaner brochure, 6). Highlighted there are the efficiencies of the machine, its multifaceted capacities and agility, its comfort for the operator. But clearly what is not "different" about the Gleaner combine is its facilitation of the kind of farming that has become dominant—monocrop agribusiness, with its attendant chemical arsenal. The combine gets its name from the fact that it "combines" what used to be separate tasks—reaping, threshing, and winnowing—in a single operation. But in the case of the Gleaner, the combine takes on a fourth role. If, historically, gleaning was the practice by which those less fortunate might gather what the reapers left behind in the field—the rights to which were once open to all—the Gleaner combine seems to lay claim to that process too, ensuring that every grain enters into the industrial food chain on its way to market, with nothing left behind to chance.

The Gleaner combine, then, would seem to be the ultimate capitalist machine—the emblem of the kind of large-scale, environmentally destructive agricultural practices that care neither for the earth, nor the people, nor for any form of "fair sharing." Gleaning material from this brochure, however, Natalie Joelle indeed makes a "difference." As though gathering some of that grain that has passed "through the cage," as her last line tantalizingly suggests, she forages in the ad copy, reading in effect "against the grain" and remaking it anew in poetic form. As poet and essayist Annie Dillard notes in her description of her own found work, this kind of poem, foraged out of other texts, provides a doubling of contexts, as the "original meaning remains intact, but now it swings between two poles," as the signifiers become unmoored from their signifieds, and signs from referents (1995, ix). Now the "you" and the "combine processor" become characters in a new drama, no longer aligned but at odds. The addressee in the anaphoric "you want" is ambiguous, but arguably could be the reader, not of a brochure, but of a poem, who may indeed want to "reduce grain loss," practice "slope sensitivity," and "reduce field compaction," but might now ask what "grain loss" might mean, how a giant machine might be "sensitive," and whether some other form of agriculture might better reduce soil compaction. The desires of the combine now take on a more sinister cast as the machine itself becomes a giant maw that "likes to be fed"—"straight into the combine, straight into   and/straight out the back." The gap in the line leaves a space for the reader to insert a destination—straight into what?—but the "straight out the back" makes clear the consumptive and excretory function of this machine, excretions that are likely far from the nourishing stuff of manure.

Joelle's poem, which thus gleans something more productive from the mono-cultures of the present, offers a model for what our contributors do in the essays in this volume. As critics have suggested, we all live in the Anthropocene. There is no easy way out of the large-scale "machine" that the Earth has become. Some commentators advise us to accept this responsibility and "steer," promoting large-scale geoengineering as the only way forward; others might suggest that it is only by overthrowing the machine wholesale—the collapse of capitalism, say—that we can proceed. The essays in *Perma/Culture* offer a different approach. Proposing neither to accept the present course nor to await the new post-capitalist utopia to come, our contributors glean from the present alternatives that can be lived in the present. Whether in re-readings of old texts—*Middlemarch, Ecotopia*—or of contemporary landscapes—Montreal, Transition Towns, Balcombe's anti-fracking protest—in experiments in agroecological practices and food reclamation; or in alternative economic practices of barter and gift, the essays offer ways of gleaning difference from what often looks like a depressing landscape of sameness—and of making a difference in a context in which change seems perpetually out of reach. And, rare in work in the environmental humanities, many of these essays also detail the material practices in which these contributors are engaged, on farms and gardens, running Community Supported Agriculture (CSA), in activist communities, and on the road.

And this brings me to the heart of what I would like to call "permacultural studies," a critical practice that I believe is nascent in the varied essays in this volume. In drawing out the critical import of Joelle's poem and in making the practices of gleaning that she highlights central to reading the work of *Perma/Culture* more generally, I am using "gleaning" in its metaphorical register. That is, to glean is to understand, to gather together information or experiences that produce new knowledge; in this vein, gleaning is akin to what we, in literary studies, call "reading," in the strong sense of producing, say, a reading of a poem or a novel, a critical approach that draws together details to produce a new narrative. But as Leda Cooks (in this volume) reminds us, gleaning is also quite literal, a practice by which wastes can be reclaimed as nourishment, not just for our thoughts and ideas, but for our bodies directly. And it is this bridge between the metaphorical and discursive and the literal and material that permacultural studies would aim to create.

In coining this term, I am alluding, of course, to the academic field of cultural studies, an interdisciplinary critical practice that takes culture as its object. Though cultural studies has, arguably, long treated issues of nature and ecology (see the work of Raymond Williams, for example), its focus on discourse, image, and text has, perhaps, mitigated against a full engagement with ecological practices. "Nature," in cultural studies, is often subsumed by "Culture," as critics remind us of the "cultural construction" of the term. Such work has been essential to the new and varied understandings of the non-human world that have shaped the contemporary environmental humanities, a set of fields to which any "permacultural studies" would absolutely be indebted. But as Jennifer Daryl Slack (2008) notes in a retrospective on the term "ecocultural studies," cultural studies has still, arguably, not fully embraced the "eco"—in part, she argues, because of this focus on discourse. The "culture" in "permaculture" has quite a different pedigree, originating in agriculture or horticulture, and therefore the term retains some of the residue of that more practical, earthy work, which "permacultural studies" aims now to bring into conversation with cultural studies more broadly. And, as the work of the graduate students in the field of cultural studies published in this volume—Ruth Lapp and Amanda White—suggests, cultural studies may indeed be in the process of shifting in permacultural directions.

But the supplement that permacultural studies might provide to cultural studies is not only to offer a material and ecological component, to insist upon the dual process of analyzing text and engaging in material ecological practices. As David Carruthers and I suggest in the introduction to this volume, permaculture also insists on an affirmative engagement with the present—offering not only a critique, say, of the Anthropocenic machine, but also a set of practices designed to mitigate it. Given cultural studies' Marxist roots, critique is very much built in to the fabric of the practice, and critique is a vital tool for attacking the unjust and ecocidal Machines that confront us. Many cultural studies practitioners are also activists, participating not just in the classroom but in the streets or at the pipelines. Such work is absolutely compatible with our project here. But the change that such protest brings can be transitory and therefore unsatisfying; a permacultural studies would aim not just to illuminate a more "permanent" way forward for human societies on earth (not permanent growth, but permanence), but also to make our own work in the academy more "sustainable"—and I mean this in multiple senses: teaching or writing about sustainability, enacting sustainable practices (in our lives and in our courses), and sustaining our efforts and interests, our dedication, even in the face of what may seem like perpetual defeat. Permacultural studies aims to get our hands dirtier, literally, such that our own metaphorical "dirtiness," our complicity with a system that inevitably contains and overreaches us, is acknowledged and, to some extent, countered.

As a way to flesh out the complexities (and potential pitfalls) of the "perma" supplement to cultural studies that I am suggesting, I will pursue "gleaning" in its more literal register as well, for contemporary discourse on gleaning offers something like an ecotopian narrative of everyday abundance, drawing attention, in the face of talk of food shortages and austerity, to the bounty that is presently wasted. Regardless of whether such ecotopian aims will actually come to fruition, many of those concerned with environmental crisis and food insecurity (myself among them) have turned to gleaning as a way to contribute in a tangible and material way to movements for food justice and sustainability. My own experience with gleaning came first in the fall of 2014 when a local food security organization with which I had been volunteering began a gleaning program in my community. Motivated in part just by a desire to get out of town with my then four-year-old daughter, I answered the call, and we met on a rainy September morning in the tomato fields of a local organic farm. There, my daughter and I and a few other volunteers gathered tomatoes and squash that the farmer had determined not fit for market. It was an idyllic experience of fresh air and exercise, interesting people for my highly gregarious four-year-old to talk to, all with that added peace of mind that comes from knowing that the crops haven't been sprayed (or have been minimally sprayed, and not recently). We gleaned a number of things that day beyond the vegetables— memories, experiences, photographs—and we went on in subsequent gleans to gather grapes, apples, and pears from urban backyards, and beans, corn, and carrots from other local farms. All of the produce went either directly to soup kitchens or to the organization's so-called "preserve reserves," another team of volunteers who processed, canned, and froze perishable produce for distribution in the winter months. Which, of course, meant that we also gleaned a sense of satisfaction for being part of getting local, organic food to a food-insecure population in our community.[2] This experience, not necessarily typical of all gleaning programs, had something highly utopian about it, as though we all lived in a world in which small-scale organic producers within a few kilometers of our homes actually produce our food.

This experience was quite satisfying in and of itself, of course. And it was hardly unique. Many academics volunteer in the communities in which they live and work. Indeed, gleaning itself has become for some urbanites a "secular Sabbath," as Susan Harding describes it, an opportunity for environmentalists to "worship" the world as we believe it can be—bountiful for all.[3] But the experience prompted for me a set of research questions, and, as I began to investigate them, I learned that I was hardly the first to have them (as my reference to Harding suggests). From Benjamin's "rag picker"[4] to Donna Haraway's "bag lady practice of storytelling"[5] (2007, 160), critics have long mobilized gathering, trash picking, and gleaning as metaphors for critical or artistic practices, variously highlighting or eliding the class politics thereby mobilized. Gleaning's ambivalent transfer—literal, metaphorical—makes the term especially fruitful for thinking through a permacritical practice that might also retain, as it were, some of the soil clinging to its permacultural roots.

In this context, I turn to French filmmaker Agnès Varda's film *The Gleaners and I* (2000) as itself a kind of critical intervention in the practices and discourses of gleaning. Varda's documentary tracks different forms of gleaning, both the gathering of surplus produce in rural areas, and something closer to trash picking and dumpster diving in the urban context, repurposing food waste and garbage either for practical or artistic ends. The gleaners in the film are highly various, including homeless people living in urban or rural areas who are reliant upon gleaning for livelihood, as well as artists, like the filmmaker herself, who glean for other purposes. Varda's own practice represents a kind of meta-gleaning, in that the film itself is a collection of sequences with different gleaners that she represents without much commentary. There is little distinction made among the sorts of gleaners or what they glean. Indeed, at one point, she includes random footage of her own lens cap, which she took by accident in the course of filming, and she seems to have found in going back through the footage to assemble the film. This is presented alongside footage of a grape glean, both "found" objects; that these would have different material effects or consequences is left to the viewer to consider.

There is thus a seemingly neutral political affect to the film. Varda doesn't exactly condemn the wastage of food that she documents, nor is she careful to distinguish her own gleaning from that of the homeless men and women who rely upon the food they gather for basic sustenance. The viewer is thus tasked with the job of deciding whether the differences among these gleans make a difference and, if so, what kind? This task is made especially complicated in the scenes depicting the most egregious example of food waste that Varda documents. In this sequence, Varda journeys to a place where potato growers dump large mountains of potatoes that do not fit the standards for size and shape. Left out in the sun, these potatoes quickly turn green and sprout, rendering them inedible. Varda films a series of gleaners who seem to have an inside scoop on where this dumping will occur, though it is not publicized and the place changes periodically. Gleaners of the potatoes range from a couple of kids to an organized group of gleaners, gleaning for themselves and for others in the community, and some fairly desperate members of a homeless community nearby. Among these gleaners is Varda herself who takes a liking to the heart-shaped potatoes she finds, filming them together and separately for the film. Varda interviews a number of these gleaners, offering the viewer valuable insight into the varied lives involved. When she leaves, she brings a few of the heart-shaped potatoes as a souvenir. She lays them lovingly down as a display in her home, and later documents them as they sprout into inedibility.

Varda's sprouted potatoes appear later in the film, documenting the passage of time. One of the themes in the film *is* temporality, including the aging of Varda herself, so here the potatoes re-enter the narrative as the "rot, leftovers, waste" (Varda 2000) that she chronicles in this frame. Realistically, many edible potatoes sprouted in the pile left in the field, even after the gleaners took what they could. Varda's small cache of wasted potatoes are hardly remarkable in that context, except perhaps as a sign pointing to that larger, off-screen waste. But the artistic rendering of the potato as aesthetic object also calls attention to the larger project of the film itself— and by extension any representation of these material conditions. The potatoes become a new aesthetic object, representing waste, but unless they are planted, they are also actual waste. One certainly hopes that Varda's spotlight on waste might have some utopian political outcome. As Tina Kendall argues, "trash can document the world as it is, but it can also open up a space for thinking in unabashedly utopian terms about the world as it might be" (2010). But there is also something at least incongruous, if not counter-utopian when the aestheticization of food seems to rob it of the potential for bodily sustenance. Here, questions of socioeconomic class come to the fore, as the artist/filmmaker's aesthetic relationship to the potatoes implies the fact of her own actual food security. In an interview, Varda acknowledges the ways in which gleaning can operate as a metaphor for other sorts of practices, including filmmaking. "It is true," she notes, "that filming, especially a documentary, is gleaning. Because you pick what you find; you bend; you go around; you are curious." But, she cautions, "you cannot push the analogy further … it's too heavy an analogy" (Indiewire 2001). There is something here, in the weight of the material, that refuses metaphoric transfer. Sprouted potatoes resist being metaphors for waste; artistic or critical gleaning cannot be collapsed with gleaning for sustenance.

Two problems thus arise for the permacritic/gleaner: the first, most immediate, is the question of whether literal gleaning in the field is just a form of charity that gives those of us who are food-secure a sense of being part of the solution—and maybe offers an opportunity for agricultural tourism—while doing little to address the problems of large-scale agribusiness, economic disparity, and food insecurity; the second, linked to it, is what the politics, then, of our own representations might be, as we "glean" material for our own critical or aesthetic work. Of course, politically, one of the appeals of gleaning is precisely that it is not utopian at all, but rather a highly pragmatic stopgap measure. The revolution is not necessary; we need not switch wholesale to organic, small-scale agriculture; we need not change much the supply lines or who controls them. Though my own experience was somewhat ad hoc and small in scale, the gleaning program that inspires Harding's "secular Sabbath" operates in that ground zero of unsustainable agriculture, California. Practices like gleaning arguably hold us accountable for something we *can* do, which, in a context in which problems seem so large and intractable, is a welcome change. And we need these kinds of practices while we buy ourselves some time. Gleaning has the merit of taking gleaners and those who write and think about gleaning to the fields, tracking back along the commodity chain between producer and consumer that is usually eclipsed in our present system. Our critical practices, then, might make these more visible, for our colleagues, our students, and ourselves. And if we use these experiences to "open up a space for thinking in unabashedly utopian terms," perhaps we may be a part of the "gleaner difference" that makes a difference.

But these questions about the limitations of small-scale affirmative practices and our participation in and representation of them remain thorny. Part of what is useful about gleaning is that the tensions between the literal and the metaphorical cannot be resolved in any easy rhetorical flourish. And this applies as well to permaculture more generally. Indeed, if permaculture can be described as "revolution disguised as gardening," it is just as possible that it yields "gardening disguised as revolution." In an essay on the politics of urban agriculture, Rebecca Solnit warns of the dangers of complacency and retreat that can accompany gardening:

> planting heirloom seeds is great, but someone has to try to stop Monsanto, and that involves political organizing, sticking your neck out, and confrontation. …The biggest problem of our time requires big cooperative international transformations that cannot be reached one rutabaga patch at a time.
>
> (2012)

In other words, local-scale investments in positive practices like urban farming, gleaning, or bicycling, those "microutopian" practices that Zavetoski and Weigert describe in their essay in this volume, may give practitioners the illusion of revolutionary action, when in fact they are mere lifestyle choices, unlikely to produce the large-scale effects necessary to counter the machine of late capitalism—the "Gleaner" of "the gleaner difference." Indeed, in some cases, permaculture manifests as 'capitalism disguised as gardening,' as permaculture-design courses (PDCs) become elaborate multi-week retreats, offering yoga, spiritual enlightenment, and other new-age practices—all for a hefty price tag sure to limit enrollment to the elite few. There is indeed no guarantee, despite the "earth care, people care, fair share" ethos of permaculture, that it is anti-capitalist at all.

Despite these twin dangers of quietism and complicity—indeed, in some ways, because of them—permaculture and the practices often associated with it offer something of value, both for survival in the Anthropocene, and for the more limited practices in which we Anthropocene academics might engage, mindful of the pitfalls. Concluding her piece, Solnit acknowledges:

> gardening and all its subsidiary tasks are sturdy metaphors. You can imagine the whole world as a garden, in which case you might want to weed out corporations, compost old divides, and plant hope, subversion, and fierce commitments among the heirloom tomatoes and the chard. The main questions will always be: What are your principal crops? And who do they feed?
>
> (2012)

Solnit seems to see the more revolutionary potential in the metaphoric extension, but, as a literary critic, I would emphasize also the limitations of metaphor. Grand tropes, too, can seduce into grand illusions; a turn in language rarely tropes the world. Gleaning art and discourse cannot substitute for gleaning sustenance; gardening "the whole world" will only represent a truly sustainable practice when it is accompanied by actual composting. In the hybrid world of permacultural studies, metaphor, heirloom tomatoes, and chard would not be separate, the plants mere vehicles for the more serious political work. Weekend gleaners, partaking of the secular Sabbath, may seem comically ineffectual against the Gleaner combine with its monocultural might. But the goal of permaculture is to scale up—not in a totalizing imposition of a new meta-system, but in a fractal proliferation of practices, including gardening, gleaning, alternative energies, bicycle commuting, intentional communities, all of which might, cumulatively, like the "experiments," the sturdy "weeds" that Callenbach and Carpenter describe (in Zavetoski and Weigert in this volume), eventually do the work of changing the whole. A perma-cultural studies would glean texts from these practices—and practices from these texts. By all means, let's uproot Monsanto, but let's be sure we have some sturdy practices to plant in its place.

Notes

1   See the brochure from AGCO, available at www.gleanercombines.com/content/dam/Brands/Gleaner/US/pdf/literature-brochures/gleaner-s7-series-combines-and-headers-%20GL13B001ST.pdf/_jcr_content/renditions/original.

2   For more information on the organization, Loving Spoonful, see their website: www.lovingspoonful.org.

3   See Susan Harding, "Portraits of Gleaners: Susan Finds Connections." Posted on the Gleaning Stories website: http://humweb.ucsc.edu/gleaningstories/html/gleaners/harding.html.

4   For a reading of Benjamin in the context of "gleaning," see Catriona Sandilands's "Green Things in the Garbage" (2011).

5   Haraway is not just one among many here, for she has recently been involved in what is called the Gleaning Stories Project, which gathers oral narratives from contemporary gleaners in California. See http://humweb.ucsc.edu/gleaningstories.

References

Dillard, Annie. 1995. *Mornings Like This*. New York: HarperCollins.

Haraway, Donna. 2007. "Otherworldly Conversations: Terran Topics, Local Terms." In Stacy Alaimo and Susan Heckman (eds) *Material Feminisms*. Bloomington, IN: Indiana University Press, pp. 157–187.

Indiewire. 2001. "Interview: 'Gleaning' the Passion of Agnès Varda." Available online at: www.indiewire.com/2001/03/interview-gleaning-the-passion-of-agnes-varda-agnes-varda-81092 (last accessed 5 May 2017).

Kendall, Tina. 2010. "Utopia Gleaners." *Alphabet City*. Available online at: http://alphabet-city.org/issues/trash/articles/utopia-gleaners (last accessed 5 May 2017).

Sandilands, Catriona. 2011. "Green Things in the Garbage: Ecocritical Gleaning in Walter Benjamin's Arcades." In Axel Goodbody and Kate Rigby (eds) *Ecocritical Theory: New European Approaches*. Charlottesville, IN: University of Indiana Press, pp. 30–42.

Slack, Jennifer Daryl. 2008. "Resisting Ecocultural Studies." *Cultural Studies* 22.3–4. 477–497.

Solnit, Rebecca. 2012. "Revolutionary Plots." *Orion Magazine*. Available online at: https://orionmagazine.org/article/revolutionary-plots (last accessed 5 May 2017).

Varda, Agnès. 2000. *The Gleaners and I*. Zeitgeist Films.

Index

For further Patrick Clemens and Lisart and further information, contact Lisa ...
... publisher ... Taylor for his commission with Taylor & Francis ...
... GmbH, Kaufmannstr. 31 30174 Vorsorge Germany.